The *Parents*™ Magazine Baby and Childcare Series combines the most up-to-date medical findings, the advice of doctors and child psychologists, and the actual day-to-day experiences of parents like you. Covering a wide variety of subjects, these books answer all your questions, step-by-important-step, and provide the confidence of knowing you're doing the best for your child—with help from *Parents*™ Magazine.

Parents™
Book for
The Toddler Years

ADRIENNE POPPER

BALLANTINE BOOKS • NEW YORK

PHOTO CREDITS

Kathryn Abbe, pp. 68, 72, 128
Barbara Campbell, pp. 20, 33, 76, 82, 100, 102, 157, 222
Ruth Kelly, pp. 54, 92, 120, 161, 190, 250, 252, 254
Barbara Kirk, pp. 168, 173
Barbara Kreye, p. 87
Ed Lettau, pp. 1, 8, 15, 36, 42, 45, 63, 105, 109, 114, 124, 143, 147, 163, 182, 194, 205, 209, 214, 220, 229, 236, 242, 246
Tina Mucci, cover
Marina Raith, pp. 29, 154, 201
Erika Stone, pp. 23, 136, 271

Library of Congress Catalog Card Number: 86-90928

ISBN 0-345-31429-8

Manufactured in the United States of America

First Edition: October 1986
Seventh Printing: May 1989

Contents

Expanded Contents

1. What Is a Toddler?

"What is a toddler?" asks one young mother. "It's a delightful creature that doubles as a human dynamo." Another calls her toddler a "one-woman demolition crew." Says a third, "A toddler resembles a visitor to Earth from outer space: not quite civilized, unfamiliar with society's customs, but having the intelligence to familiarize himself very quickly with the habits, rules, and language of this alien planet."

Experts, of course, define toddlerhood more scientifically. Perhaps the most common definition depends upon age span: A toddler is a child between one and three years old.

But age span alone doesn't tell the whole story, for the child who precociously walks or talks prior to his first birthday is a toddler too, even though technically he isn't old enough to be one. These two developmental milestones signal the end of infancy, and now the Age of Exploration begins in earnest.

When a child abandons crawling and masters the art of

balancing himself upright, his entire perspective of the world changes. From this marvelous new vantage point, the young explorer tries to chart what he views as fascinating, virgin territory. Though your child's behavior may seem puzzling or pointless to you at times, it is purposeful to him. He is educating himself about his environment.

Because there is so much to learn, his exploration takes the form of constant activity, which sometimes borders on the frenetic, especially during the early stages of toddlerhood. Racing around his room, he pulls supplies off the changing table, examines them, and tosses them aside. He grabs toys from the toy chest and tears books from their shelves. From time to time he may stop long enough to taste the toy or book in his grasp. Then he continues merrily along his destructive way, looking for other items of interest he can reach, examine, and discard. In the words of one exhausted mother, "A toddler is a tornado disguised as a child."

Keeping pace with this tornado can exhaust even the most energetic of parents. Trying to prevent the entire house from being swirled into its path often seems an exercise in futility.

There is a bright side to the situation: This activity is the sign of a normal, healthy mind seeking information. The object of his behavior—knowledge—justifies the means. How else to learn other than by touching, tasting, rolling, throwing, or otherwise mauling an item? Few adults utilize their five senses as completely as toddlers do, though vestiges of this kind of information-gathering activity linger throughout life—why else the "Don't Touch" signs in museums? Certainly not for toddlers who can't read!

Exasperating as all this exploration may be at times (when the hour is late and your patience is short, for example), you really wouldn't want your toddler any other way. He is simply behaving appropriately for his age and storing up valuable information, much of it for his own protection: Softness feels good; hard surfaces hurt if you bump into them; books do not make a gourmet meal, and so on.

This whirlwind activity that heralds the end of infancy doesn't mean that babyhood is over, though some parents misinterpret a child's increased proficiency in both communication and locomotion to signify just that. Even though he's no longer an infant, a toddler is still a baby who requires enormous amounts of time and attention. Not until he reaches the far side of toddlerhood—the preschool years—can he truly be considered anything but a baby. And before he relinquishes babyhood, he has some very important business to accomplish.

In infancy physical growth indicated maturation. You were able to observe your child growing bigger and rounder with each passing day. During toddlerhood physical changes will, of course, continue to occur. They just won't seem as acute as they did during your child's infancy because a normal toddler's weight gain and growth advance much more slowly than an infant's. Now intellectual and emotional maturation will take center stage, and physical coordination will improve dramatically.

During this stage of babyhood your toddler confronts two major tasks in his emotional development. Technically these two tasks are called separation and individuation. In plain English, these terms simply mean that your child will realize that he is a separate person from you and will discover his own individuality. In the emotional sense as well as the physical one, toddlerhood is the time when a child learns to stand on his own two feet. Wobbly beginnings characterize both undertakings.

One necessary adjustment your toddler makes requires allowing you to be out of his sight for periods of time. Since you represent security, comfort, love, and numerous square meals a day besides, his ability to let go of you is quite an accomplishment. The urge to hold fast is strong; the desire to declare independence is also intense. You will witness your child's steps toward accomplishing a balance between the two.

But your toddler isn't the only one fighting the battle of independence versus dependence. You will be waging the same war within yourself, trying to judge how much freedom, how much self-determination, to allow him in his everyday activities. How you resolve this problem will set the tone of your relationship together. Do not underestimate the import of this particular question. Newly settled territories soon begin to chafe under the restrictions of the mother country. Few explorers ever realize the ramifications of exploration; wars have been fought to resolve the same sovereignty problem you now face. So, a toddler is also a person whose maturation forces his parents to make some very difficult decisions about a most critical, basic issue for all the years of child-rearing to follow.

Having reasonable expectations for the two years of toddlerhood can increase the harmony in the relationship you share with your child. Recognizing typical toddler behavior will help you avoid setting unrealistic standards of obedience and discipline, a common problem confronting a toddler's parents. Understanding breeds tolerance, and tolerance provides the optimum environment for your child to establish his identity.

The stages of growth and development that are described in the chapters that follow show the typical toddler moving toward maturity. All behavior and accomplishments are age-approximate; each child has his own internal clock. The stages are followed in sequence by all toddlers, but each child moves through them at his own pace, racing through some, tarrying in others.

How quickly or slowly your child moves through any particular stage or gains competence at any particular task depends upon a variety of factors. These include sex (girls generally are more advanced than boys in many skills from the moment of birth until maturity), heredity, and environment. The speed with which your child manages his first step or utters his first word is insignificant when viewed from the prospective of his whole life. A first step at eight months doesn't presage a brilliant career in astrophysics.

You need this information, for in addition to the other traits that define this age, a toddler is a person who brings his parents' feelings of insecurity to full bloom. Perhaps due to the explosion of emotional and intellectual growth that occurs during toddlerhood, parents often feel inadequate to the task at hand. In many cases this attitude arises because parents presume that they alone hold the key to their child's future success. It would be hard to find any assumption more nerve-wracking than the belief that everything that befalls a child for good or ill is the direct result of actions you did or did not take.

Parents who succumb to this reasoning convince themselves that if they provide enough advantages (in the form of time and attention and the right combination of educational experiences and toys), they will at least be shaping a young achiever, the front-runner who outdistances the competition by a mile.

While parents do, of course, play a very important role in their child's development, this attitude is bound to create problems for both children and parents because it ignores the child's temperament, talents, and inner timetable. And it places an unsupportable burden on the toddler's parents, especially if, despite their efforts, their child turns out to be the one who tarries at every stage while others walk or talk or discard their diapers sooner.

"If I could raise my daughter all over again," says one mother, "I think this time I'd let her do the leading and I'd do the following. I regret that I didn't just relax and enjoy her more." Many parents echo her sentiments.

This advice doesn't mean to suggest that parents should make no effort at all to help their child achieve full potential. But it does mean that an overzealous attitude can cause parents as much regret in the future as an irresponsible one.

You cannot hasten the maturational process. The best parents can do is contribute to the ease with which their child adjusts to the difficulties inherent in growing up.

Many of us fantasize that the blueprint for raising perfect kids exists and that we can find a way to resolve the difficulties of guiding our children to maturity if we could just locate the right diagram. Unfortunately, this universal blueprint hasn't been discovered and never will be because children aren't programmable robots. Mother Nature doesn't provide an owner's manual telling how to get trouble-free, efficient service from the model that she designed just for us.

All any guide can do is offer suggestions that both experience and scientific investigation have shown to work well in general. To paraphrase Abe Lincoln, no technique works well for all of the parents all of the time. That reassuring maxim rings especially true of the toddler years. To think that you can do a perfect job of parenting guarantees a guilt trip. Free yourself of the belief that *everything* depends on you. You're important, all right, but not *that* important.

You might be surprised to learn that the greatest head start toward achievement you can give your toddler has nothing to do with the kinds of educational tasks many parents believe to be essential, such as teaching your child the alphabet or buying him educational toys. Recently a magazine writer set out to learn from successful adults if they could pinpoint the qualities in their upbringing that contributed to their achievements as adults.

Among the individuals she interviewed were a woman who is a university physics professor, another who serves as the secretary of economic affairs in a state cabinet, a musician and conductor, an athlete, and a novelist. Though their occupations varied widely, they did agree unanimously on the kinds of contributions parents can make in helping a child become a successful, happy individual.

All felt their parents had managed to be encouraging without being pushy. All felt their parents had set good examples in terms of their own achievements and giving their children fine role models to emulate. The parents also took their children's interests and talents seriously. Perhaps most important of all, each individual felt free to take risks and to fail at tasks.

What is more important than any lesson in letters or numbers or shapes or colors that you can teach your child is the lesson you can teach yourself: Let your child be his own person. Let him make his own mold instead of squeezing him into one of your choosing. Find ways when possible to accommodate his methods of doing the daily routines—feeding and dressing, for example.

Undoubtedly, your choices will have to prevail when time

is short and many chores need doing. Undoubtedly, doing everything your way all the time would be quicker and simpler. But just as undoubtedly, finding the time and patience to encourage your child's individuality and to enjoy this unique person you've created will foster the kind of relationship that grows richer year by year.

Obviously, the answer to the question "What is a toddler?" is quite complicated. Certainly, any real answer requires more than a one-sentence summation. That's a good point to remember whenever you feel overwhelmed by the enormous job you've undertaken. Complicated individuals defy easy solutions. In fact, most parents find that when one problem is worked out, there's always another to take its place. This is a truth of parenthood that doesn't change with time. One point can be made with certainty: A toddler is not simply a series of problems to be solved. You can't "solve" a toddler. But enjoying him is definitely within your grasp.

2. Twelve to Eighteen Months

How They Have Grown

Do you remember how your baby looked when you got your first glimpse of her? Perhaps you thought she was absolutely the most gorgeous baby ever born. Or perhaps you hoped her appearance would improve, since her head seemed somewhat pointy from her journey out of the womb.

That pointy head may have been bald, or it may have sported a shock of hair that stuck out in all directions. Your baby probably had numerous red marks on her face, and her nose may have looked a mite squashed or her eyelids swollen.

And when you examined her to reassure yourself that she possessed the requisite number of fingers and toes, you probably were surprised to discover body proportions that seemed almost distorted. Her head seemed huge in relation to the rest of her body, the trunk wide, and the arms and legs short and stubby.

Now, just one year later, your child's appearance has changed considerably. Even if you thought your baby the most beautiful ever, the chances are she has grown even better-looking since her birth.

Her head, which accounted for 25 percent of her total body size at birth, no longer looks quite so out of proportion to the rest of her. What you are witnessing is normal cephalo-caudal, or head to tail, development.

The growth pattern prior to birth accelerated the development of the head over the rest of the body. Subsequent growth reverses this trend so that the torso, arms, and legs now grow more quickly. These uneven rates of growth allow the body eventually to assume what we think of as normal proportions.

Between birth and maturity head size will double, but body size will increase five times over. By the time your child is fully grown, her head will account for only 10 percent of her total body length.

At this stage in her life, your child's torso is growing more quickly than the rest of her body. As she begins to stand upright more often, you will notice a "beer belly" physique with a bulging abdomen and an exaggerated spinal curve. Though her legs are obviously lengthening as well, their biggest growth spurt won't occur until adolescence. Internal organs, too, grow at varying rates until maturity.

As your child learns to stand and to walk, your attention often focuses on her legs and feet. You needn't be concerned if you notice bowlegs, a pigeon-toed stance, and flat feet. The chances are good that you *will* spot these conditions, since they are actually the norm for year-old children. They are not caused by anything you've done or haven't done. Some parents worry that helping a child balance while she practices walking, for example, puts too much pressure on the legs and causes this "deformity." This is nonsense. Most often the bowing results from the position she maintained during her months in the womb.

Bowlegs usually straighten gradually as the child grows. Sometimes children go from being bowlegged one year to knock-kneed the following one; this curvature, too, will ordinarily straighten itself out without any interference on your part.

Though your physician will note skeletal development during your child's checkups, he will probably not recommend special treatment unless your baby's legs turn in or out beyond the normal tendency to do so, remain curved beyond the age when they normally would straighten, or unless the curvature appears in only one leg. If the condition affects other family members and appears to be hereditary, he may also treat the condition rather than wait for Mother Nature to do so.

Unassisted, Mother Nature usually corrects the flat feet as well. Flat feet offer beginning walkers a larger area to use for balance during their first unsteady steps. The feet appear flat due to fat pads situated where the arch should be. Usually you can see some semblance of an arch when your child is sitting and not exerting any of the pressure which flattens the foot when she stands. Sometime around the second birthday, fat pads on both the feet and hands will disappear, and an arch will become visible. However, one child in seven will remain flat-footed.

Along with these other physical signs of growth and maturity, the hair your baby was born with has probably been replaced by now, though a few babies may still resemble actor Telly Savalas in an aerial view. These children may continue to look relatively bald for another year, or even two. The hair that has grown in is baby fine, silkier in texture, and lighter in color than it will eventually become.

If your baby's hair is quite thin, you may still be able to see the fontanel, or soft spot, atop her head. Sometime between twelve and eighteen months, the bones of the skull under this spot will fuse completely. In some children this fusion may not occur until twenty-four months of age.

At one year the average baby has six teeth, four on the upper gum and two on the lower. Usually the lower central incisors, or cutting teeth, make their appearance first, with the four upper incisors following a few months later. Several months may pass before the next six teeth appear: the two remaining lower incisors and the four first molars.

How early or late your child teethes is generally determined by heredity. Though parents tend to view the appearance of baby teeth as a "braggable milestone," no relationship has ever been noted between superior intelligence and the early emergence of a set of choppers.

All it does indicate is that your child is likely to chew on everything in sight while she teethes and to drool copiously in the process. In fact, some dentists feel that late teething may prove beneficial in the long run, helping an individual retain her permanent teeth longer in old age.

Parents sometimes worry about the spacing of the baby teeth as they cut through the gums. These teeth may look quite spread out, separated by large spaces, or jammed together with no room in between. The position of the baby teeth, however, does not necessarily indicate how the permanent teeth will align themselves, so don't worry about irregular spacing.

You may be surprised to learn that your child's permanent teeth, which won't emerge for approximately another five years, are already forming, even though only a few baby teeth have surfaced. Good nutrition now will play an important part in your child's attractive appearance in several years.

During her first year your baby steadily gained weight while all the changes in her body occurred. If your child resembled a plucked chicken at birth, she's more turkey-size now. On average, babies triple their birth weight at the end of the first year. Smaller babies may gain less weight, larger birth-weight babies more. Each will continue to grow and gain at her own speed, influenced by heredity, environment, and even gender.

From their very first day of life, male and female babies exhibit different growth patterns and proportions. Girls take an early lead in the race toward maturity. From two months old until school age, for example, they have longer legs than boys, and from infancy they are proportionally closer to their adult height. The female advantage in advanced physical maturity over males can range from one month in early infancy to twelve months at age six to two years at adolescence. As we shall see later, differences in developmental rates create personality differences between male and female toddlers.

What They Can Do

Developing Motor Skills

The toddler's body is growing, changing, and adapting itself for the skills it is developing. As we have seen, the body matures from the head downward. Muscular control proceeds in similar fashion. Your baby first demonstrated real muscular control by holding his head up unassisted. Day by day you noticed this skill improve until he became quite adept at peering over the crib bumpers to investigate his world.

Control of the upper arms followed this ability in an early, somewhat uncoordinated attempt to crawl. In fact, you may have been surprised to find how much territory an infant could cover in a crib between the time you put him in for a nap and the time you returned to check on him. Frequently babies "crawl" in the crib until their head touches the bumpers.

The kind of motor control you will witness over the coming months follows a pattern of mastery which begins at the center of the body and moves outward, toward its periphery. Large-muscle control develops first; small-muscle control follows.

Initially only the large muscles in the upper arm obeyed an order to reach and grab, so your baby could move his arm toward the desired object but had trouble executing the rest of his plan. By the age of one year, your baby has mastered the use of his upper arm, lower arm, and whole hand to assist him in crawling, reaching, and grasping. He has refined the use of the small muscles in his hand so that it can more accurately obey his wishes. The first finger and the thumb cooperate in a pincer-type grip to accomplish more delicate tasks.

He has probably already begun to play "Drop It"; if not, he will begin in earnest now and perfect his technique. These are the rules: Baby sits in his highchair or stands in his play yard or crib, surrounded by toys. One by one he grasps each toy and holds it over the railing. Delighting in his newfound skill, he then releases his grip, and the toy falls to the floor. The more noise the toy makes as it crashes, the better the game. As the months pass and his control increases, he will throw his toys instead of merely dropping them.

Your first impulse will be to join the game by tossing the items back into the crib or play yard, only to find them being jettisoned again and again with increasing agility and speed. Eventually you will tire of the game, but your toddler will continue to find it fascinating. The scene then changes to reveal a frustrated child whose toys are out of reach and an exhausted parent who is no longer a willing participant in this activity.

Do not attempt to solve the problem by tying the toys to strings attached to the side of the crib or play yard. Your child could inadvertently become entangled in the cords and strangle. In addition, he doesn't have the coordination to hoist the dangling object back inside with him anyway.

The only good solution to this situation is to tolerate the game for as long as your patience holds and to find alternate amusements, such as walks in the stroller, when tolerance wears thin.

"I really believe that Jordan keeps tossing his toys overboard just to drive me crazy," says one weary mother. Contrary to appearances, your toddler has no such diabolical plan in mind. He is *not* being perverse, though his incredible persistence in this activity makes him seem so. He is simply doing what a normal child of his age needs to do to acquire a necessary, new skill. (You probably won't recall this silly game years from now when your child enters school and learns to write his name, but without this early step toward manual dexterity he couldn't manage his signature.) Be-

sides, your repeated response demonstrates to him his ability to interact with others and to exercise some control over his environment. "Drop It" serves both physical and emotional needs well.

Other finger skills mastered in the next few months include the ability to remove items from a container and to build a block tower of two blocks at first and of three or four later. Even at eighteen months, the toddler excels at dumping items from a container but lacks the concern and coordination for putting them back in.

You can foster your child's new finger skills in a positive manner by giving him finger foods now and encouraging him to feed himself. Not only will he be able to practice his thrilling new ability, but you will be encouraging his independence from you, another skill that is learned in small but important steps.

Since he can also hold a cup, try letting him drink by himself as well. Because much of the liquid will land in places other than his mouth, offering only a small amount of milk, juice, or water at one time is a wise idea. "I gave all of my kids yogurt to drink when they were learning to manipulate a cup," says the mother of three sons, "and I found that this was a good first step, since it's thick and doesn't slosh all over them when their coordination is still unsteady."

If you can force yourself to tolerate additional mess, leaving a spoon on the highchair tray at mealtime also aids your toddler's developing coordination. Your child won't be able to manipulate it properly for some time yet, but he will enjoy practicing with it. Buy a junior-size spoon with a large, round bowl and a short, flat stem for easier manipulation by toddler fingers. A good time for this practice occurs near the end of a meal, when only a small amount of food remains in his dish. Avoid accidents by insisting that your toddler remain seated while he uses the spoon, and, of course, never leave your toddler unsupervised during the meal.

Be prepared for the dropping game to continue at mealtime. You might try thinking of your child at this stage of his life as a happy savage. He has no manners at all and is too young to learn any. He is as likely to drop the cup as drink from it; ditto for his food, which makes an intriguing new sound as it hits the floor. He seeks information, not social grace.

Being a good parent means developing the ability to tolerate some untidiness now for your child's future benefit. You could control mealtime mess by continuing to feed your child yourself. Don't succumb to the temptation to do this. The end result is an overly dependent child and a resentful parent.

In addition, some parents who continued to feed their toddlers, rather than let their children learn to feed themselves, feel that this situation explains why their children, now much older, never learned to eat neatly at all. "I should have realized that a messy one-year-old is preferable to a messy eleven-year-old," says one father.

Righty or Southpaw?

Once a child begins to use his hands for specific tasks, parents become curious about right- or left-handedness. Some children develop a preference for one hand as early as seven months; others not until two years. Some seem to prefer one hand to the exclusion of the other, only to reverse the preference several months later.

Investigations into the significance of dominance present a muddled picture. Past studies of handedness indicated that consistency of handedness (for either right or left) demonstrated advanced intellectual development. However, a recent study reveals that consistent hand choice indicates advanced intellectual development in infant and preschool girls but not in boys. No explanation has yet been offered that accounts for this curious discovery.

Most experts agree that changing a child's handedness is unwise. Though parents may worry about the inconvenience of being left-handed in a right-handed world, attempting to force a child to abandon his natural dominance may cause other difficulties, such as learning problems or stuttering, later on.

Sometimes parents can divine which hand a child will permanently prefer by noting either the child's dominant leg or eye. The dominant leg usually leads in such activities as climbing stairs or kicking a ball, and a child will depend upon his dominant eye in peering into an object that can't accommodate both eyes simultaneously, such as a camera viewfinder or toy telescope.

Learning to Walk

Learning to walk comes as naturally to babies as cutting teeth. Just as you can't cause your child's teeth to appear any earlier than nature has programmed them, you cannot successfully encourage your child to walk any earlier than his inner clock permits.

Before a child can walk, a certain degree of physical maturation must occur. Like the developing permanent teeth, which are now hidden from view and whose emergence remains years off, preparation for abandoning horizontal status and attaining the vertical state have been occurring unobserved. The skeleton must grow sturdy enough to support the body's weight; muscles gain strength and coordination suitable to the task, and the ability to balance is fine-tuned.

Most babies display a specific sequence of crawling stages before they walk. They must learn to elevate the torso and position their arms and legs properly under it. Having attained the appropriate position, they comically rock back and forth without moving an inch. Learning to bring an arm and a leg forward and then to alternate the motion from one side to the other follows. He will use the crib or play-yard rail or a handy chair to pull himself upright and move along holding the rail for support. Acquiring each step requires much practice.

These stages occur in sequence, though each baby proceeds through them at his individual developmental rate. Even for a single baby, the time period devoted to each sequential stage isn't uniform. Should a child omit one of the stages, it simply means that he never outwardly demonstrated the skill he inwardly possessed; he moved along to the next step very quickly.

Finally making a short, solo stroll won't mean your baby will completely abandon crawling, at least not for a while. Most children alternate crawling and walking, gradually decreasing the time spent on all fours while slowly increasing periods on their feet. Until their balance and coordination improve, crawling will still provide the fastest method of transportation to their destination.

Standard walking posture includes a widespread stance, flexed knees, and weight resting on the inner arch. Often arms are raised with hands outstretched until the new walker achieves some proficiency. Sometimes novice walkers feel more secure carrying an object, such as a small toy, in each hand. This cowhand-type posture provides a wide base and a lower center of gravity for increased stability.

When Rachel took her first tentative steps at nine months, her grandmother was elated. "I always knew my grandchild would be smart," she crowed. Meanwhile, in the house next door, ten-month-old Matthew could hardy crawl. Does this mean Matthew is destined to do poorly in school five years from now?

Are physical agility and mental development related? Was Albert Einstein an outstanding football player? Some studies have shown a very small statistical correspondence between the two types of skills; other studies have shown no relationship at all. As any classroom teacher can attest, possession of one skill doesn't guarantee possession or exclusion of another. Matthew may be reading up a storm in five years while Rachel still struggles with her ABC's.

Rachel may seem precocious simply because she's female. Not only is female physical growth more accelerated than male, but female development advances more rapidly as well. In walking, manual dexterity, and communication skills, as well as a host of other abilities, toddler girls usually outshine toddler boys. If your neighbor's daughter runs rings around your son in these areas, it doesn't signify that she's a genius and he's a dolt. He's simply exhibiting normal

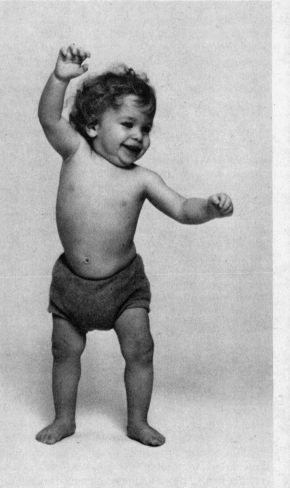

masculine development, and he'll catch up later on.

The courage or fearfulness with which your toddler practices walking depends both upon his inborn personality—shy or venturesome—as well as your reactions to his attempts. He's going to fall, and fall often, before his gait grows steady and confident. Falling usually means sitting down with a hard thump. Sometimes, however, he may pitch forward, and those upheld, outstretched hands help break the fall.

If you encourage his efforts at walking despite these setbacks, you'll help develop a secure explorer. If you overreact to his spills, you'll foster fearfulness and hesitancy.

Excessive restriction of his natural drive to explore and learn produces one of two results: The toddler rebels, and each new day offers a fresh battleground for a clash of wills—yours and his. Or he conforms to your fears and inhibits the development of his independence.

Few parents would knowingly hamper their child in this manner. Usually the situation results from an overactive parental desire to keep the baby safe. Making sure his environment is as free of hazards as possible, while keeping restriction of his activity to a minimum, provides a healthier atmosphere for your toddler.

Talk, Talk, Talk

Listening to your baby babble, you heard a variety of noises, none of which was intelligible. For the first year of his life, his babbling consisted more of vowel sounds than consonants; by the end of his first year, he has accumulated nearly all necessary vowel sounds for true speech.

Studies have shown an effect you've probably noted in caring for your child: Babies tend to "talk" more when their babbling elicits a response. When no reply occurs, their chattering dwindles.

Your response to your toddler's nonsense speech is vital. It helps him practice making and using the sounds needed for the real words he'll soon say, which is why you should avoid using baby talk. What you say is eventually what you'll hear.

When your toddler utters a noise that remotely resembles a real word, your delighted response will signal him that he's done something pretty special. Continued reinforcement whenever he happens to make that sound eventually encourages him to remember it and repeat it. Then the word must become attached to an object for it to have real meaning. For example, your baby will repeat "dada" many times before he finally associates the sound with a person, thus transforming a nonsense syllable into real speech.

Most one-year-olds possess a small spoken vocabulary— three words or so; by fifteen months toddlers average nineteen words, and at eighteen months, twenty-two words. Just a year from now the trickle of speech will have been transformed into a torrent, and spoken vocabulary will increase to nearly three hundred words.

Your child will demonstrate daily that he understands far more words than he can articulate. Often he can follow simple commands or sight particular objects in response to simple questions. If you ask "Where's your bottle?" he may bring it to you or scan the room to spot it.

As more words are added to the burgeoning vocabulary, some initially may serve to represent both the word meant as well as its opposite. "Up" may mean both up and down; "off," both off and on. Language skills are practiced in much the way physical skills are: by frequent repetition. Like the "Drop It" game, you may find the new vocabulary addition cute the first time and less cute on the hundredth repetition.

Most language acquisition throughout toddlerhood is egocentric. The child usually first learns the words for items important to his sense of security or happiness, which is why early vocabulary includes words for a bottle, pacifier, blanket, favorite toy, and, of course, his parents. As these words indicate, initial vocabulary consists primarily of nouns.

While language, like physical skills, requires a certain underlying level of maturity to develop, you can aid your child's verbal development and comprehension in several

ways. If you imagine yourself learning a foreign language as your child is, you'll appreciate how helpful clearly articulated words are to the beginner. Say the name of an item as you hand it to your toddler. Avoid rapid-fire sentences, and keep your speech simple and direct. Don't bury your meaning in a torrent of words. Maintaining eye contact when speaking helps keep your child's attention. Hearing nursery rhymes and songs will introduce your child to the pleasurable richness of speech. And very simple books—often with just one picture of some common item per page—enhance his vocabulary. At this age your toddler is too young for stories; good books for him now are really little more than catalogs.

For parents like you, who read about child-rearing in order to offer their children the best parenting skills possible, insufficient encouragement of language skills isn't usually a problem. But excessive encouragement can be. Try to imagine what life would be like if someone bombarded you with speech all day long. (In fact, in another year or so you'll have the opportunity to experience just that situation when your child goes through a stage of nonstop verbalizing.) Constant chatter overwhelms a child.

In addition, don't expect your child to sit still for very long while you "read" his picture books to him. Sitting patiently isn't the strong suit of twelve-to-eighteen-month-olds. He may want to stand up while you read, and his attention span may make reading sessions a short-lived activity for a while. Many toddlers find teething on books more stimulating than reading them. Take your cue from your child's behavior, and buy plastic-coated books that can literally take a licking.

One last, important word about a much-overused word—the word "no." Parents of toddlers often find that this word has a way of becoming a major element both of their child's speech (usually beginning about the fifteenth month or so and increasing in use until approximately the second birthday) and of their own statements as well.

Learning to say "no" is part of nature's plan for your child's emotional growth. All animal life contains an inner drive that encourages the organism to grow to physical adulthood and independence from a parent. Part of this maturity comes from exercising some control over one's surroundings. To a young child, refusal to cooperate offers one of the few means available at this time to manipulate his environment. Just as he needs food to sustain his physical growth, he needs such control to fuel his emotional growth.

The word "no" constitutes a toddler's declaration of independence. Using the negative is an assertion of selfhood, an acknowledgment that the child and the parent are actually two separate human beings. Until your child feels more secure in assessing his separateness from you, he continues to depend upon negatives.

Another reason toddlers latch on to the use of "no" so quickly is that they hear it repeatedly, perhaps more than any other word with the possible exception of their name. "No, don't touch that plate!" "No, you can't go into the living room!" "No, you musn't unravel the roll of toilet paper." "No, you can't remove all the pots from the kitchen cabinet!" No! No! No! all day long. There are so many interesting items to investigate in the average house or apartment, but most of them are off limits to your inquisitive toddler. And the more agile the toddler, the more familiar "no" becomes.

Arranging for your home to be a less hostile environment for your toddler will enable you to eliminate some of the thousands of no's you utter so frequently. This tactic will not eliminate your child's need to refuse your requests, but it can make your job simpler and establish a more positive environment for your toddler.

Personality Development

Emotional development is just as incomplete at birth as physical development. Like physical abilities, emotions make their appearance in well-ordered succession: Delight and distress emerge by three months; fear, anger, and disgust first surface at about six months. By one year a child displays reactions of elation and affection, and jealousy appears at approximately eighteen months.

Early Toddler Fears: Noise, Separation, and Strangers

Some fears, such as the fear of loud noises, are innate; the child is born with them. An infant, for example, responds to a sudden noise with a startle, or Moro, reflex, when her body stiffens almost convulsively.

This fear of loud sounds increases until approximately the second birthday. Reaction to such noise diminishes after that time, but the fear never completely disappears. The toddler's terror at the vacuum cleaner's roar, at the crash of thunder, the rush of water disappearing down the bath drain, or the noise of the toilet flushing stems from a "built-in" response to danger signals that we all (fortunately) possess.

Most of these early fears will disappear spontaneously when your child matures enough to understand that the noises imply no real threat. Eventually she will have heard many of these sounds so frequently that they will be relegated to the category of background noise, which provokes no response at all.

With growing maturation, perception, and imagination come numerous additional fears, whose frequency and strength increase with age. Both the fear of being separated from you and the fear of strangers, which are typical of this stage of early toddlerhood, require some emotional development before they can surface. Until a toddler recognizes that she is a separate person from her parents, she does not worry very much about the loss of them. Once she realizes how vulnerable this separation makes her, she becomes frightened of the possible consequences of abandonment. Then conflicting desires for independence and attachment play tug of war within her.

So your toddler demonstrates her ambivalent feelings by playing happily at some distance from you only to suddenly come running back to your side for reassurance before taking off again. The sight of a stranger can send a toddler into a panic, as can a glimpse of the pediatrician who hasn't been visited in a month or the entrance of a baby sitter whose arrival signals a parent's departure. Any unfamiliar person or sight (such as a bearded man) can make your toddler cling to you for dear life—and, indeed, that's just how extreme the situation seems to a child of this age.

As a toddler matures and her perception of threats and dangers increases, you will notice additional fears cropping up. On the heels of the departing fears she has outgrown arrive the new fears of her more mature self. A fear of animals, of common varieties she's likely to meet as well as wild ones she'll never confront, fear of personal injury, and fears about the dark will plague her. Then she'll outgrow these and respond to a new group once again.

Parents often view their children's fears negatively as immature reactions that require conquering. Fearfulness distresses us because we count it as a black mark against our parenting skills. If we were better parents, we reason, our children wouldn't suffer these fears. But this line of thought ignores the fact that children of certain ages develop particular groups of fears, just as children develop certain physical skills in specific age-related sequence. Fears function as positive milestones of emotional maturation just as crawling and walking signify physical development.

Overcome with concern that our children's fears provide concrete proof of deficient parenting, we forget that fear serves a necessary purpose: protection for survival. A totally fearless individual wouldn't survive life's hazards very long. The primitive man who had sense enough to be fearful undoubtedly lived far longer than his overly courageous counterpart.

A parent's goal in handling a child's fear is not the elimination of all fear (which is basically an impossibility anyway, since new fears continually crop up at appropriate ages). Instead, because fearfulness feeds upon insecurity, set your sights on bolstering your toddler's feelings of security. You can accomplish this goal by giving your toddler plenty of affection and attention. A child who is confident of her parents' protection has a head start in overcoming her fears.

In addition, a feeling of security also stems from a child's faith in her own powers. You will be wise to avoid over-protectiveness and to encourage your child to try her small wings. Your job is to do for her only what she cannot do for herself—and to do these things only after she has been given an opportunity to accomplish them independently. Feelings of competence inspire self-confidence.

Take your child's fears seriously. Though they seem ridiculous to you, she hasn't invented them just to get attention or for other devious motives. She is truly afraid.

However, taking her fears seriously does not mean you abandon an adult perspective and resort to pretending to lock the offending vacuum in the closet so it can't escape and frighten her again. You don't want to give her fantasy additional weight by participating in it. Turning the vacuum off and using it at another time behind closed doors to muffle the sound is sufficient. Allowing a child to examine a frightening inanimate object (like a vacuum) when it is turned off sometimes eases the fright. Playing with a toy replica of the feared item may also prove helpful.

Do not force your child to confront the object of her terror. Comfort her if she cries; hold her until she decides she can let go of you. Never threaten a child with a fearful event to encourage good behavior: "If you don't eat your dinner, the doctor will have to give you a shot" is more likely to inspire a fear of your pediatrician than a hearty appetite.

Many early toddlers combat their fears with an attachment to a favorite stuffed toy, quilt, or pacifier. This perfectly normal behavior also upsets some parents. "I can't stand that raggedy blanket of Jason's," says one parent. Another calls her daughter's pacifier her "plug."

It helps to remember that toddlerhood is as difficult for the toddler as for her parents; she needs all the support she can muster to outgrow it. Security blankets and such offer extra support. If you avoid viewing them as symbols of inadequate parenting, they will lose their power to affect you. What caring parent would deliberately remove a baby's emotional props? Eventually the child will discard them when she outgrows her need for them.

Since your child will outgrow most of her developmental fears quite naturally, there's no point in making too big a fuss over them. Your composure calms your toddler. The

test of good parenting isn't whether or not your child experiences fear but how you handle the fear which inevitably occurs.

Temper, Temper

Nature has arranged for anger and fear to appear simultaneously for good reason: They are twins of a sort. These two emotions emerge to protect us when we face possible harm. Fear makes us flee danger; anger helps us confront it. This choice of "flight or fight" aids survival.

A child's difficulty in handling both of these emotions is twofold. Her first problem lies in learning what situations appropriately require fear or anger—in understanding, for example, that a vacuum consumes dirt and not little children.

Her second predicament lies in determining how much of either emotion seems sensible in a situation—in learning, for example, that hitting another child for touching her prized toy is extreme. During the toddler years a child's internal emotional-response gauge undergoes fine tuning. Experience teaches emotional etiquette.

Unfortunately, experience takes time to acquire, so toddlers frequently display seemingly inordinate amounts of anger. One study shows the maximum frequency of angry outbursts occurs at eighteen months. Frustration causes much of this anger, and the sources for frustration during early toddlerhood seem endless.

Physical restraint causes anger even in adults. Imagine, then, the toddler's difficulty in coping with the minute-to-minute frustration of not being allowed to run and examine anything that catches her eye—and almost everything catches a toddler's eye. If she sets up a howl as you sit her down for the hundredth time in her highchair or snatch her away from a lamp moments before she would yank it down on her head, her frustration has found an outlet in her anger.

According to one study, daily routines provide the source of more than one-third of children's anger. You and your toddler may rarely agree on when and how she should eat, rest, play, have her diaper changed, get dressed, or bathe. The need to leave the playground to head home for dinner may seem perfectly sensible to you but not to the toddler on the swing. She's not interested in her stomach until hunger overwhelms her—and when it does, she will shriek for her meal, unconcerned that her love affair with the swing delayed her dinner.

Then at dinner she'll scream to hold the spoon herself and screech even more loudly when she fails to manipulate it properly to transfer the food to her mouth. As the toddler struggles toward competence in doing many daily tasks for herself, her dissatisfaction with her performance provides fertile ground for anger to thrive. "Mother, please, I'd rather do it myself" might be the universal motto of the toddler, whether she's eating, bathing, or dressing. However, her lack of coordination undermines her ambitions for independence.

Lack of language facility aggravates the problem. Though her vocabulary is growing rapidly, it cannot keep pace with her thoughts. Her difficulty in communicating these thoughts frustrates her desire to have her every wish gratified immediately.

One mother recalls doing errands with her sixteen-month-old son, who suddenly demanded, "Sing 'Winda Wanda.'" Not knowing what "Winda Wanda" was, the mother offered a variety of songs. None of them suited the child. As his frustration with his inability to communicate grew, so did his anger, until he finally threw himself down on the sidewalk and bawled. His embarrassed mother endured the curious stares of passersby, who thought that she had mistreated her sobbing child in some way. At last inspiration struck, and she realized what his request meant—a line from a nursery rhyme: "Goosey, goosey gander, *whither* do you *wander?*" For the twelve-to-eighteen-month-old toddlers, nearly half of their speech requires decoding of the "Winda Wanda" type; their anger under the circumstances is hardly surprising.

That this incident involved a boy, rather than a girl, isn't surprising either. Parents of sons may find toddlerhood to be a particularly difficult time for several reasons. Because their motor activity level is higher than that of girls, boys may encounter greater frustration from the more frequent interference with their movements. Increased frustration from such interference and restraint results in increased anger. From infancy girls are more sensitive to touch, so they may respond better than boys to comforting gestures when they are angered. And because boys are also slower to talk than girls, they face additional frustration from their greater inability to communicate.

Some children seem to tolerate frustration more calmly than others. From your first days together you've been aware of your baby's individual temperament. Several studies have shown that the intensity of infants' reactions to stress—crying, body movements, and increased pulse—differ markedly at birth. Not only are some infants more vulnerable to stress than others, but differences also exist in the ability to be soothed after stress occurs. Some babies quiet down relatively quickly, while others continue to cry and thrash about long after the source of stress has disappeared. Tests on identical and fraternal twins seem to indicate that these reactions are to some degree hereditary.

Introvert or Extrovert?

Children do not possess at birth the ability to engage in social interaction. But at two months infants smile in response to any human face; by six months they don't respond quite so indiscriminately, and as we have seen, because early toddlers are so attached to their parents, at one year a stranger's smile often provokes alarm, rather than a friendly grin.

Clearly, maturation increases the capacity for selective sociability. In an experiment that paired children between six and twenty-five months of age with both another child and a new toy which was changed every four minutes, neither the toy nor the other child much interested the six-to-eight-month-olds. The nine-to-thirteen-month-olds also proved fairly unsociable: Each child showed greater interest in the toy than in the other child. The fourteen-to-eighteen-month-olds, however, responded to the other child before they reacted to the toy.

The growth of sociability depends upon two requirements besides maturation: instruction in the skills of friendship and situations in which these skills can be practiced. Just as you provide a vocabulary for your child to acquire word by word through repetition and imitation, your example provides a repertoire of social skills that encourage emotional growth.

Your one-year-old, confronted by an older child or by a stranger who smiles at her, may turn and search your face for cues to appropriate behavior before she responds. Some of this normal twelve-month shyness will disappear as a few months pass. But your toddler needs your encouragement to learn sociability. If you isolate or discourage her from such contacts, she learns to be shy instead of outgoing.

Feelings of trust in one's parents and self-confidence play as important a role in emerging sociability as they do in overcoming early fears. Meeting adults who overdo a greeting or confronting a group of noisy children can be over-whelming; the toddler needs time to adjust. If she has established trust in herself and in you, she will.

Some children seem to be more naturally outgoing than others, just as some are more active, more verbal, more fearful or courageous. One recent study of identical and fraternal twins indicates that shyness, like physical traits, is inherited.

However, environment can modify personality traits. Studies comparing the personalities of identical twins reared apart with those of twins raised together reveal that separated twins often possess more similar personality traits than un-separated pairs. Scientists have theorized that the differences resulted from the unseparated twins' attempts to differentiate themselves from each other, an unnecessary task for sepa-rated pairs. Their environment moderated their personali-ties.

You can moderate a tendency toward shyness in your child by regularly exposing her to other adults and children. Even though she is still too young to engage in real cooperative play with others, such early social contact is important, especially for the first child in a family, who associates primarily with adults. Later-borns tend to be more sociable simply because they always have their older siblings around for company.

Until your child attends school, you have been and will continue to be in large part *both* her heredity *and* her environment. Like most parents you have probably noted some consistency in your child's temperament and are likely to have labeled her nature (at least inwardly, if not to interested relatives and friends as well) as shy or lively, brash or pensive. Little children have a way of living up (or down!) to your expectations of them, so beware of less than complimentary labels.

Even complimentary labels can straitjacket a child: Good children can have bad days; quiet ones sometimes raise the roof. Give the emerging personality room to develop its own special characteristics before you try to pin it down with a set of restrictive descriptions.

Daily Routines

Eating

Eating Less With More of a Mess

Say goodby to the logger's appetite that your baby possessed only a few months ago, for toddlers eat less than they did as infants. A little arithmetic explains why their appetites decrease. If the average 7-pound baby, who triples his birth weight at one year, continued to gain weight at a steady pace, he would weigh 1,700 pounds by the time he started kindergarten. As growth slows, so must appetite.

Not only do toddlers now eat less, but they also eat erratically. They may consume a hearty portion at one meal and little else all day. In fact, for several days they sometimes exist on what seems to be a more suitable diet for a bird than for a growing child. Or a particular food may become a favorite almost to the exclusion of all others for periods of time. Teething pain, illness, reactions to vaccinations, disruptions in the daily routines, and fatigue can also interfere with appetite.

Parents who are unprepared for the normal slackening of appetite or for the effect of these external influences worry that their child isn't eating properly. Usually this concern is unjustified. If you offer your child a variety of foods along with the multivitamin supplement prescribed by your pediatrician, you'll easily fulfill your toddler's nutritional requirements.

Actually, concern over the size of a toddler's portions can create mealtime problems where none previously existed. Problem eaters generally aren't born that way; they're created by loving, worried parents. Motivated by concern for the child's health, these mothers or fathers attempt to keep the child in the highchair beyond his endurance to sit still in one place. Then they cajole him to eat the food he would reject.

Mealtime also becomes problem time for parents who set unrealistic standards of neatness for this messiest of ages. Parents whose major concern is keeping the kitchen clean when their toddler eats or who want to rush through meals as quickly as possible to restore the kitchen to apple-pie order can expect dinnertime to be a disaster. Fine restaurants recognize the value of a pleasant, unhurried atmosphere in encouraging diners' appetites. We don't usually think of the importance of atmosphere with toddlers, but it affects them as well.

You may think that proper atmosphere includes such niceties as sitting in one's seat while eating and quietly consuming the meal. Toddlers, however, have different ideas regarding mealtime etiquette. First of all, many of them can't tolerate sitting through a meal. They resemble a passenger who has been confined to a seat for such a long time that standing provides relief. If your child has difficulty remaining seated, don't force the issue now. As long as you can restrict him to the kitchen so that he doesn't leave a trail of food from one end of your house to the other, accept his need to stand.

Every so often try the highchair again; eventually he'll sit through a meal. Do not allow him to stand in the highchair, as he could topple out or tip the chair and seriously hurt himself. A highchair should come with a combination waist and crotch strap that is firmly attached to the chair and not to the tray. This safety strap should always be used. It keeps the child seated in the chair and also keeps him from sliding out from under the tray. If your child must stand, he's safer standing on the floor.

You might also mistakenly believe that the purpose of a mealtime is to eat the meal. To a toddler eating may be a secondary mealtime activity. Playing with the food is frequently as enjoyable and satisfying as eating it.

The things a toddler can do to a serving of mashed potatoes can be so truly disgusting that childless adults have vowed to remain childfree after observing a typical toddler meal. So it is important to remember that your toddler *needs* to handle his food. All the "fingerpainting" with the potatoes and the squashing of the meat and the slapping of the spoon into the applesauce which spatters in every direction are, in a sense, scientific tests. Your young scientist learns lessons in texture, taste, temperature, color, and viscosity in his highchair laboratory. The mess he makes is entirely normal and necessary. On especially bad days it helps for you to remind yourself that he will outgrow this activity.

Bibs that cover a toddler from neck to ankles and that have a pocket sewn along the entire bottom hem to catch spills and dribbles provide the best protection during these messy meals. A plastic material will keep liquids from soaking through to the child's clothing. Even this protection will fail on days when your toddler decides to shampoo his head with his cup of milk, so never fill his cup with more than a small amount of liquid at a time. If you avoid loading his plate with too much food, he won't be as tempted to play, and there will be less mess to clean off the floor. Cover yourself with an apron as well.

Sometimes mealtime mess simply indicates that the child is no longer hungry. If he ate nothing at all, he probably wasn't hungry to begin with. When this happens, just remove the food and end the meal. Hungry kids do manage to get some food into themselves even as they pulverize the diced beets.

If your child rarely seems hungry for his meals, his bottle may be the culprit. A toddler who is still getting most of his milk from a bottle rather than from a cup is probably too full of liquid to consume much solid food.

Because milk is often labeled the "perfect food," parents don't worry about overconsumption. However, milk is a poor source of iron, and if it replaces the meat and vegetables which supply this mineral, the toddler's diet isn't well-balanced. Your toddler needs only three to four cups of milk each day, and you can meet some of that requirement with alternatives such as yogurt or cubes of soft cheese, which make a good finger food.

Finger foods can enhance a toddler's pleasure in mealtime. Cooked vegetables cut into little cubes; well-cooked meats either minced or ground; small pieces of ripe fruits—

all encourage toddler independence by making self-feeding possible. Your pediatrician is your best source of advice on which foods are appropriate for your child and the timetable for adding them to the menu.

Never offer toddlers foods that can cause choking. These include hot dogs, meat chunks, nuts, seeds, popcorn, hard candies, and lollipops. Even when you have limited the menu to safe foods and have strapped your toddler into his highchair, you should never leave him alone while he eats.

Tooth Care

The All-Important Baby Teeth

If you are one of the millions of parents who believe that baby teeth "don't count" because they'll be gone in a few years anyway, you need to learn more about these temporary but very important teeth. They are called baby teeth, but they last far beyond babyhood. Their name makes them sound unimportant, but in their limited lifetime they serve several significant functions.

These teeth allow a child to chew many of the solid foods needed to build a strong, healthy body; without primary teeth your child would be deprived of necessary nutrition. In addition, chewing builds muscles whose larger size then encourages the growth of the jaw. Baby teeth contribute to an individual's attractiveness by giving symmetrical shape and contour to the face. They also act as "place savers" that aid the proper alignment of later permanent teeth, and they allow your child to make many of the sounds required for intelligible speech.

Though the usefulness of baby or primary teeth may seem short-lived, their lifespan is brief only by comparison with that of permanent teeth. Consider how comfortable you'd be without teeth for six or seven years, the length of time most baby teeth survive. In fact, some baby teeth last *twice* as long as that.

The premature loss of just one baby tooth through an accident or disease can affect the health of a child's mouth currently and in the future as well. Trauma to the primary front teeth may delay the appearance of the permanent central incisors. Such loss can also cause speech defects, such as lisping, which will later require special speech therapy to correct. The early loss of a single tooth permits the remaining baby teeth to shift from their proper positions when they find the room to do so. Since the permanent teeth often follow the path set by the baby teeth, such shifts in alignment affect the future permanent teeth as well. The new, improper position of a roving baby tooth may also prevent an emerging permanent tooth from occupying its proper spot. Finding its reserved space filled, the permanent tooth must move elsewhere with no consideration of the aesthetics of its new position or its ability to perform efficiently there. Shifts in alignment now create the need for orthodonture later in life.

If dental disease resulting from poor sanitary conditions in the mouth causes the loss of a baby tooth, the child risks the development of gum disease, as well as increased vulnerability to cavities in both the remaining primary and the future permanent teeth. And if decay from a baby tooth reaches the roots of a permanent tooth still encased below the gum surface, the adult tooth may become fused to the bone, a condition requiring corrective surgery. Untreated dental disease jeopardizes all the remaining teeth, since disease-causing bacteria continually seek new hosts and multiply rapidly. Imagine a strong bridge which loses one supporting strut in a storm; that loss weakens the entire structure, which is less able to maintain its integrity with each new blow it receives. The same principle holds true of the mouth when just one baby tooth is lost prematurely.

Cleaning Baby Teeth

To help prevent the consequences of dental disease, baby teeth require daily cleaning. The purpose of cleaning teeth, whether baby teeth or permanent ones, is to remove a substance called plaque, a film which covers the teeth and thrives in the tissues of the mouth. When oral bacteria in plaque react with food particles on the teeth, sugar in the particles ferments, creating an acid which damages tooth enamel. Bacteria eventually invade the interior of the tooth through the resulting breach and destroy it.

The most efficient method to clean your toddler's teeth at this age is to wipe them with a piece of gauze. Toothpaste is unnecessary; just be sure to wipe the front and rear surfaces of the tooth, top to gum line.

Some dentists also recommend that you whisk this gauze over the gums as well. Since this extra touch means you are giving your child better protection against tooth decay by eliminating more cavity-producing bacteria, it is a good safeguard.

As additional teeth emerge, you may want to begin to use a little toothpaste on the gauze, since fluoride toothpaste will help offer greater protection against decay. The toothpaste will protect more effectively if not separated from the teeth by a film of saliva. So dry the teeth with a separate square of gauze first.

The best time to accomplish this cleaning is after the toddler finishes each meal and bottle; cavity-causing bacteria do most of their damage within twenty minutes after food is consumed, so it is best to schedule tooth care immediately after eating. (If, like most people, you brush upon waking and before retiring, you allow the bacteria to work unimpeded.)

Use your changing table for this routine, and position yourself either to the side of or behind your child's head. If your toddler is uncooperative, you may find sitting on a bed or sofa with the child's head in your lap more convenient. An uncooperative toddler can sometimes be induced to tolerate the tooth-care routine by being given his own piece of gauze to hold while you work and to use when you've finished. In fact, encouraging him to imitate you gets him started early on proper dental care.

Avoid scrubbing the child's teeth and gums. A light touch is all that is necessary, and too strong a hand will turn tooth-care time into a battleground.

Fluoride

The best ingredient for building decay-resistant teeth is fluoride, a chemical compound that occurs in nature. When tooth enamel incorporates fluoride as it forms, the enamel becomes harder, creating a much more effective barrier to bacteria than it could provide alone. While fluoride applied topically in the form of toothpaste helps prevent decay, the protection isn't as effective as the barrier created when fluoride is taken internally during tooth formation.

Fluorides can be found dissolved in water, among other sites. Their uneven distribution, however, means that many water sources have fluoride levels too low to help fight tooth decay. Some communities solve this problem by fluoridating their water system to protect the entire population. If the water your family drinks is not fluoridated, your toddler should be getting fluoride internally in some other form—usually it's incorporated into his daily vitamin drops. Pediatricians do not prescribe fluoridated vitamins in areas where the water supply is treated because overconsumption of fluoride causes an unsightly brown mottling on the teeth. Studies show that no side effects occur when the proper dosage is followed.

If your community water supply contains fluoride, but you always give your toddler milk or fruit juice instead of water to drink, you are depriving your child's teeth of important protection. In addition, fluoride taken internally doesn't eliminate the need to clean your toddler's teeth. Proper tooth care, good nutrition, and fluoride are all necessary weapons in defending a toddler's teeth against decay.

Sleeping

How Much Sleep Is Enough?

Chances are you worry not only whether your child eats properly but also whether he gets sufficient sleep. How much sleep is enough? The answer differs from child to child, so judge by your child and not by the clock. The best way to determine if your child receives enough rest is by observing his behavior. Crankiness, temper tantrums, and a decrease in physical coordination (especially if such problems arise early in the day) signal fatigue and the need for more rest.

Some children seem to require less sleep than others; these kids exhaust their parents long before they tire themselves. The average twelve-to-eighteen-month-old spends approximately thirteen and a half hours of every day sleeping. Children with an abundance of stamina need only one nap a day at this age; less energetic toddlers still need two, although both the morning and afternoon naps may be shorter than those of just a few months ago.

You will find that sleep patterns fluctuate as erratically as eating habits. Many of the same factors that affect appetite—teething pain, illness, inoculations, and disruptions in the daily routines—also interfere with naps and bedtimes. However, ignore daily imbalances; they appear less erratic when you consider your child's total sleep time for a week or more.

Bedtime Strategies

Most toddlers eventually reach a stage where sleep becomes an enemy they battle. Even when they are so tired they can hardly stand up, toddlers seek ways to avoid the inevitable. Since sleep means an interruption of play and exclusion from their parents' company as well as from the interesting events of the household, their reluctance to cooperate with your plans for bedtime is hardly surprising. The idea of resuming all their activities after a nap or upon waking in the morning doesn't reassure them, for toddlers have not yet developed a sense of time.

Classic toddler strategies to escape sleep include: tantrums, calling to parents, noisily shaking the crib rails, and throwing blankets and toys out of the crib and then demanding their return. You will need some strategies of your own to counter these ploys. Only the overly optimistic expect to eliminate such behavior entirely.

Sometimes a few quiet lullabies or several minutes of browsing through a book ease the separation to sleep. A record on the phonograph or the radio turned to quiet classical music may help. Some desperate parents have found that the constant hum of the fan in the room air conditioner is a hypnotic sound that induces sleep. It also muffles the wailing that every parent invariably comes up against in the battle of the bed; sometimes the only solution lies in allowing the child to cry for a time.

For some children the most effective inducement to go to sleep is the one they shouldn't have: a bottle. A bottle supplies the comfort and emotional satisfaction a child in distress wants; however, falling asleep with milk on the teeth encourages tooth decay. Some toddlers will accept a bottle filled with water, and you might want to offer that.

In the absence of a bottle, or even in addition to it, many toddlers use a pacifier or their thumb. Use of either one may continue until past the age of three, when many toddlers spontaneously abandon this activity.

Some children cannot shake the habit, much to their parents' chagrin. Though using a pacifier beyond age three and a half may indicate some emotional problem, it does no physical harm to the mouth because it is pliable. However, prolonged thumb-sucking after the permanent teeth start to surface at about age six can push the front teeth forward to such an extent that in later years orthodonture will be required to correct the damage.

Unfortunately, no really good solution to this problem exists. Cures (such as bitter-tasting medicine on the thumb or the use of a glove) can create emotional difficulties by making a child feel disobedient or unloved. Such remedies are, therefore, not recommended. You can gently try to remove the thumb from your child's mouth once he has fallen asleep. Children who persevere in using the pacifier may be encouraged to do so by parents who use it as a plug to quiet a rambunctious child. This use satisfies the parent more than the child, who usually abandons the pacifier when it isn't misused in this way.

Bathing and Dressing

Rub-a-dub-dub, the Toddler in the Tub

The twelve-to-eighteen-month-old is so spirited, so eager to explore, taste, smell, and touch, so eager to feed himself, that he generally looks as though he desperately needs a good scrubbing, even though he may just have been bathed. He gets so dirty that some days one bath is not enough.

Since he is nowhere near nighttime bladder control, he usually wakes up soaked. A quick "half bath" dunk in the sink is easier and more thorough than an elaborate sponge bath. Diaper rash can still occur, though the toddler's skin is less sensitive than an infant's. Thorough bathing helps eliminate this painful condition.

Many parents choose an after-dinner bath as the main one of the day, since that timing eliminates any possibility of a head full of applesauce or a milk shower—at least until the next morning. Bathing a toddler before dinner is usually a frustrating waste of time.

Baths, like meals, can be either a pleasure or a hassle,

depending upon the atmosphere in which they're given. Toddlers resent being hurried through any of the daily routines, so leave enough time for the bath to become an enjoyable, relaxing activity.

While a child of this age enjoys playing in the tub, he may object to washing in it. Either you can let him play with floating toys while you wash him, or you can give him his own small bar of soap and let him begin to learn to wash himself. You'll need lots of patience as well as time, for the combination of poor coordination and slippery soap can delay the bath considerably. Washing your hands may be easier for him to master at first than washing his own.

Some children refuse to sit in the tub just as they refuse to sit through meals. Don't waste your energy trying to keep your toddler seated. Just make sure you have a rubber mat on the tub bottom to prevent slipping. Of course, you should *never* leave a toddler unattended in the tub, no matter how secure his balance.

Even children who enjoy the bath can suddenly reconsider and object loudly to the whole idea. Few creatures are as fickle in their likes and dislikes as a toddler. If your child suddenly decides that baths are not one of your better notions, you may want to substitute sponge baths for tub baths for a few days and then try the tub again. Since the noise of water filling the tub or emptying from it can frighten a toddler, it's best not to subject him to either one.

Shampooing may contribute to a toddler's reluctance to bathe. Washing the hair of a child who refuses to cooperate requires skills beyond those of mortal folk. Even toddlers who agree to sit have difficulty keeping their heads sufficiently tilted to eliminate soap and water dripping in their eyes.

Some of the following suggestions eliminate headwash headaches:

1. Divert and conquer. Save an especially enticing bath toy for use only during shampoos. If it's interesting enough, your child won't notice that you are sudsing his hair. Do not let him linger with the toy after you have finished, or it will lose its appeal for the next time you need it.
2. Use a washcloth or a plastic spray bottle to wet his hair, rather than dumping a lot of water on his head at one time. Sometimes the child objects not to the water but to the amount.
3. Prepare a plastic pitcher or bottle full of warm water when you run the bath, and use it for rinsing soap suds out of your child's hair after the shampoo. This eliminates the need to run the bath itself while he's in it— which may be the source of the problem.
4. Hang an interesting plastic mobile or toy from your shower head. Your child will have to keep his head tilted up to look at it.
5. Make a headband of a rolled washcloth sewn to a piece of elastic. Position it just forward of the hairline, and it will catch and absorb the water that drips into his eyes. This solution better suits the eighteen-month-old than the twelve-month-old, who generally won't tolerate any item resembling a hat.

6. Let your spouse assume the headwash duties. Everyone's approach to a problem is different. A change of face may eliminate the difficulty.

Clothing for Quick-Change Artists

Toddlers never stand still for very long, so you need clothes that go on easily and that allow for quick diaper changes with a minimum of tussle. Overalls with snaps along the crotch make diaper changes easier than outfits that require complete removal for changing. Zippers or snap fronts rather than ones that button speed dressing time.

For a child of this age, pants with straps stay in place better than half pants, which tend to slide below the toddler's stomach. Look for shirts with stretchy necklines to accommodate a toddler's large head, and steer clear of the ones that open with three tiny buttons rather than snaps along the shoulder; they were not made for human hands to manage on a squirming child.

Avoid clothing that is too small or too large. Tight clothing restricts movement and will make a toddler irritable, and clothing that is too large can be hazardous to an unsteady walker. If overalls are too long, hemming the cuffs is safer than just turning up the bottoms because they unroll easily and can cause tripping.

Dresses for toddlers should be saved for special occasions because they leave the knees unprotected for crawling and during falls. The best dresses to buy do not restrict movement. Choose styles that fall loose from a yoke, rather than ones with a sash tie at the natural waistline.

Your toddler's clothes will remain new-looking longer if you select bright, medium-range colors rather than very dark or very pale ones, especially for overalls and outerwear like snowsuits and jackets. Pale colors show every stain, and dark ones fade after a few washings. The knees on light-colored overalls rapidly turn dingy gray, and on dark colors they lose their dye faster than the rest of the garment.

If you live in a cold climate, a two-piece snowsuit with an attached hood proves more practical and versatile for toddler needs than a one-piece suit. On milder days or on outings to the store or supermarket, where most of your time will be spent indoors, the jacket can be used without the pants. Unlike a separate hat, the hood doesn't get lost, and it keeps chilly winds off the neck.

One, Two, Button My Shoe

You don't need to rush out and buy your toddler a pair of shoes the moment he takes his first step. In fact, letting him go barefoot a while exercises his foot muscles and helps him become steadier on his feet. Unless he'll be walking on surfaces where protection is necessary—like concrete or sharp, rocky terrain—barefoot is best for beginners. When a novice walker is fitted for shoes, he may be reluctant to walk in them at first anyway, preferring to play with the laces or to remove the shoes altogether.

Toddler shoes should offer flexibility and traction—flexibility to allow for the natural movement of the foot and traction to minimize falls. Either soft leather or canvas uppers provide sufficient flexibility. Avoid buying vinyl or other synthetics because these materials do not breathe or absorb perspiration. In addition, they retain their own shape, rather than molding themselves to the walker's foot, as a shoe should.

High-topped baby shoes of the past, which were once thought necessary for ankle support, have been replaced by lower, more pliable tops. In fact, your child's first shoes needn't be shoes at all; many doctors feel sneakers will do just as well. Doctors generally reserve high tops and inflexible styles for correcting orthopedic problems.

If the shoes you choose have smooth leather soles, score the bottoms lightly with a pen knife to increase traction. Rough-grade sandpaper also works well. When purchasing rubber-soled sneakers, observe the way your toddler walks in them in the store. Rubber soles can grab the floor and trip an unsteady toddler who hasn't yet learned to lift his feet for each step. If this happens, select a different style shoe and postpone purchasing rubber soles until your child walks more steadily.

Even if you buy inexpensive shoes—and at the rate toddlers grow, expensive shoes are unnecessary—keeping your toddler well-shod can be an expensive proposition, simply because he'll need new footwear every two to three months. You should check the amount of space between his big toe and the end of the shoe every other week to make sure the shoes still fit.

Remember that canvas sneakers can shrink both from perspiration and from being tossed into the washer and dryer. They should be fitted with this factor in mind and should be checked even more frequently than leather shoes. Don't try to cut costs by purchasing shoes so big that the child must grow into them; this is dangerous to the novice walker, who needs a proper fit for comfort and safety.

To achieve a proper fit, the salesperson must measure both of the child's feet, since they are rarely the same size. In order to gauge the maximum length and width of the child's foot, the child should stand with his full weight on his feet when being measured.

Allow about three-quarters of an inch of growing room between the end of the big toe and the front of the shoe. When you push down with your thumb to check this, make sure that the toddler hasn't sabotaged the fitting by curling his toes under.

The toe box of the shoe should sit high enough above the toes to prevent pinching or rubbing. Slide your hand around the inside of both shoes to find any rough or uncomfortable spots in the seams. Your toddler won't be able to tell you if he's uncomfortable, and you may mistake his discomfort for the general unhappiness many children display at their first fitting. The combination of strange salespeople, unfamiliar surroundings, and the unaccustomed weight of the shoes themselves often causes tears. Holding your toddler on your lap during the fitting may calm him. Carry a small toy in your pocketbook to divert his attention from his fear.

Your toddler's feet are malleable, and an improperly fitted shoe can distort normal growth or cause corns and calluses. So with each new pair of shoes you buy in the coming months, your child's feet must be remeasured, and you should never buy him shoes when he isn't with you to try them on.

For the first few days limit the amount of time your child wears his new shoes to just a few hours. This allows him to become accustomed to them and to break them in gradually. If the back of the heel is too stiff, work it down with the palm of your hand a few times to soften it. Should any red, irritated areas or blisters appear on your child's toes or at the back of his heel after wearing the shoes, do not allow him to continue wearing them. Return the shoes to the store for refitting.

Socks, too, must fit properly, or they can rub enough to cause blisters. They should be large enough for the child to wiggle his toes and long enough not to pinch in the front. Socks that are too small cramp the feet and slide down over the heel, making the child uncomfortable. A blend of cotton and nylon is preferable to 100 percent nylon, which can make the feet perspire. If you do use stretch socks, pull the toe away from the child's toe slightly after you put the socks on him to make sure he has some wiggle room.

Playtime

Playing Is Fun-damental

Whoever coined the phrase "easy as child's play" didn't comprehend how much effort a child expends in playing. Social scientists call a child's play his work. In this sense a toddler is, in fact, the littlest workaholic, for his work occupies his every waking moment and often prompts him to refuse sleep, even when he's exhausted.

We view a toddler's activities as recreation because no one compels him to play in the same way that adults are compelled to work. Nevertheless, children *are* driven to play; the drive comes from within and it surfaces very early in life.

Infants play with their hands and feet almost as soon as they can spot them. Later they play with their voices, experimenting with pitch and volume. When sufficient play has taught them all they need to know for the moment about a particular subject, they progress to another topic of interest. Child's play is really self-education, a thorough instruction in the nature and properties of the child himself and of his environment.

Toddlers throw themselves into this personal schooling with great intensity. They are so overwhelmed by the wonder of everything around them that they tend to lurch wildly from place to place, drunk with the exhilaration of wanting to learn everything at once. The ability to walk excites them, for it offers them the power to satisfy their curiosity at will.

Parents often find the "at will" factor overwhelming. Allowing a toddler to satisfy his insatiable curiosity, while simultaneously keeping him safe, is exhausting, for toddlers weren't given common sense proportional to their inquisitiveness.

Few adults possess adequate energy levels to keep pace with a toddler. But your child's abundant activity should please you even as it exhausts you, for it represents an active mind seeking knowledge. Recognizing this goal, you should give your toddler as much freedom as possible to explore his environment.

For some parents allowing such independence proves difficult for two reasons, the first physical and the second psychological. If this baby is your first child, you are probably living in surroundings quite appealing to an adult and less satisfactory for a toddler. China and crystal objects, glass tables, and pale upholstery create lovely interiors — but not comfortable ones for raising children. Such rooms should either be babyproofed or closed off to your child. If he is allowed to explore, he will either hurt himself or destroy some valuable object. If he is permitted into the room and forbidden to explore, he will be (quite reasonably) frustrated and angry, and you will tire yourself out thwarting his natural instincts, for he is too young to discipline.

The psychological aspect of parental problems with independence isn't as neatly solved. Parents, naturally, want to keep their children safe, but absolute safety exists only in a cocoon. Surrounding a child with overly protective care obstructs the growth of independence. In the long run such obstruction proves more harmful than letting your child take a few spills. After exercising normal caution about where and how your child plays, *don't hover*. Your confidence in him inspires his confidence in himself.

Left to his own devices, but under your watchful eye, your child will also learn the art of amusing himself, a skill you'll come to appreciate greatly as your child grows. Ask any mother of two about the differences between her children, and one of the first traits she'll applaud is her *second* child's ability to keep himself busy. Second children aren't born with this trait, nor are first children genetically deficient in it. But second children usually learn to rely upon their own creative resources because their parents are both busier and less attentive than when the family numbered only three. Your child needs this "healthy neglect" as much as he also needs your attention.

Toys—the Tools of Learning

Whether playing by himself or with you, your toddler will benefit from an assortment of well-chosen toys. Well-chosen means safe, sturdy, and age-appropriate. Many parents ignore the age designations marked on toy packaging because they reason that a child as bright as theirs needs the stimulation of a toy meant for an older child. The suggested age designations become especially important to parents of toddlers because toys specified for children age three and younger are supposed to meet certain safety standards. A toy meant for an older child is potentially hazardous in the hands of a younger one, no matter how precocious.

When choosing toys for your child, look for and follow age guidelines. Select toys of quality design and sturdy construction, and check all toys for safety. There should be no sharp points or edges, and since any toy can wind up in a young child's mouth, all his toys should be made of non-

toxic materials, and there should be no small parts that could
be swallowed and cause choking. If a toy comes with an
attached cord or string, check its length. A long cord could
become wrapped around a toddler's neck and cause stran-
gulation. If you discover a hazardous condition in a toy you
buy, report it to the U.S. Consumer Product Safety Com-
mission in Washington, D.C.—1-800-638-CPSC.

Choosing appropriate toys for your child shouldn't be
difficult—if you remember his skills and interests. A twelve-
month-old is a perpetual motion machine, so a toy that he
can grasp and push or one he can yank along behind him
makes a good choice. Other motion toys include rocking
horses and riding toys of many varieties.

These types of toys often incorporate realistic sound effects: Horns honk, bells ring, engines make revving noises.
Pull toys in animal shapes bark or quack; some push and
pull toys sound like popcorn makers gone berserk. Decide
whether you can tolerate the sound before you buy the toy,
since toddlers love these noisemakers.

Riding toys should be built low and sturdy enough for a
toddler to mount and dismount without your help and without tipping the toy. Early toddlers especially spend much
of the time simply getting on and off the toy. Your patience
will be exhausted long before your child's interest wanes if
you must assist him each time. Avoid riding toys with pedals. Toddlers of this age do not have the coordination to use
them properly and only find them frustrating.

For quiet play stacking and nesting toys also intrigue the
toddler. It will probably be several months before he masters
the knack of arranging them in the proper order, but that
won't detract from his pleasure in them one bit. Toddlers
often enjoy teething on these toys as much as playing with
them. Rubber balls of different sizes are fun to roll at first,
then to throw and retrieve, and finally to kick.

Do not discount the educational and play value of the
toys you can make inexpensively at home from common
household items. If you have some boxes with tops, your
toddler will enjoy removing the tops and trying to replace
them. Different-size boxes can be used for nesting, which

teaches size discrimination. The boxes also make fine containers for your child to fill with safe kitchen items, such as small pots and potholders. You may think that putting items into the boxes and taking them out, only to put them in again, is a boring activity. Your child, however, will find this pastime fascinating.

An unopened cylindrical box of oatmeal makes a good roll toy, and small cereal boxes make excellent, lightweight building blocks. Toddlers also play contentedly with a pan and a wooden spoon for banging.

You can recycle cartons into several creative toys. If you remove the top, the toddler will climb in and out of the carton hundreds of times. Attach a short length of string to it, and it becomes a wagon for pulling a favorite stuffed animal. Cut a hole in the top of a sealed box and another low on its side and your toddler has a surprise box. He drops a toy into the top slot and fishes it out of the bottom by sticking his arm through the lower hole. Use another carton to make a toddler mailbox. Cut different-size mail slots into its sides. Then give your toddler your junk mail to sort. He'll have another fine lesson in size discrimination because he must match the larger envelopes to a big slot.

A good look around your home, coupled with a little imagination, will yield other equally enticing, educational bargains.

Elimination

Too Soon for Toilet Teaching

Here's a silly question: How many normal five-year-olds do you know who still wear diapers? The answer, of course, is *none*—which is why worrying about toilet teaching wastes the valuable time you could be spending enjoying your child. When the time is right, your child will need very little instruction in using the toilet.

How will you know when this time arrives? Bowel and bladder control, like other physical abilities such as walking, skipping, or hopping, depends upon physical maturation. The child must develop neuromuscular control over the rectum's sphincter muscles in order to contain and release bowel movements at appropriate times. Before age two most toddlers have not matured sufficiently to master this skill; the ability to control the flow of urine develops even later.

Whenever possible, wise parents encourage their child to learn new skills like bowel control at times so appropriate to the child's blossoming abilities that chances for failure are minimal. From such success the toddler develops a strong, sustaining sense of self-esteem.

So for now, forget about toilet teaching. You can, however, take two preparatory steps which will aid in toilet teaching later on. First, you can avoid making any negative comments or facial expressions that indicate distaste in changing diapers. These negative cues add needless anxiety to the process of learning to use the toilet. They also make the inevitable toileting accidents seem catastrophic. Any skill develops more easily when the learner's self-esteem doesn't depend heavily on success or failure.

Second, you can decide what words you will use with your child to refer to bowel movements and urination. You can use these words with him now and teach him to add them to his vocabulary. The proper vocabulary simplifies communication, making both teaching and learning easier.

Do not be deceived into believing that your toddler is prematurely ready for toilet teaching right now simply because he moves his bowels at regular intervals. Regularity does not mean that your child exercises conscious control over his bowel movements. Regularity actually occurs as a result of the gastrocolic reflex, which stimulates the emptying of the bowel in response to the distention of the stomach. Because meals distend the stomach, elimination usually occurs shortly after eating.

Rushing your child to the toilet or potty during his regular movements doesn't mean he has bowel control; it means you have trained yourself to anticipate his daily schedule. Should any of a number of common factors interfere with his regularity, his "control" will disappear along with your patience.

Guide to Good Parenting

Going With the Flow

In learning to handle your toddler, you will have an opportunity to use nearly every lesson you have ever acquired in improving human relationships. A positive attitude about the task of child-rearing helps immeasurably, of course, since events often have a way of working out as we expect them to.

Maintaining a positive attitude depends upon establishing

realistic expectations for both your child and you. Learning about toddler growth and development provides you with guidelines for determining what behavior parents can reasonably expect from a child of a particular chronological age and developmental stage. Without this knowledge parents may demand obedience and skill (in toileting, for example) which physical immaturity precludes. Without this knowledge raising a toddler becomes a most frustrating experience for parents and child.

Here's how appropriate expectations helped one hassled mother: "Every task from early morning until bedtime took far longer than the amount of time I budgeted for it. I was constantly angry at myself for taking so long getting everything done. I resented my daughter because she slowed the schedule down further by insisting on doing things for which she lacked coordination. I stupidly thought she would let me continue to feed and dress her without interference. It took far too long for me to realize that this snail's pace was what life with a toddler was going to entail for a while. Once I realized that, I reduced my expectations about how much work I could complete each day, and I stopped feeling so resentful."

Having read this chapter, you know something about the way nature has programmed your child to strive toward independence. So you encourage her desires: to remain vertical, to remain in motion, to feed herself, to explore by tasting, touching, etc., to repeat a skill *ad infinitum* until it is mastered, and to be dependent when independence proves overwhelming. Thwarting nature's intentions creates unnecessary conflict between you and your child.

You might label this philosophy "going with the flow." A Chinese fable illustrates the wisdom of this type of approach to your relationship with your toddler: Two trees stood side by side when a great storm began to blow. One tree fought to remain upright in the face of the strong winds. The winds thrashed so wildly that eventually their force snapped the rigid trunk. However, the other tree, yielding to the strength of nature, bent and swayed, but remained whole when the storm subsided.

The fable actually contains two lessons for parents. One illustrates the value of flexibility. The other shows the liabilities involved in attempting to confront an overwhelming force. The experience will certainly leave you much the worse for the wear!

This does not suggest that you should allow your child to do whatever she wants, just that you make wise use of her toddler disposition. Since a toddler is such a distractible creature, she is easily diverted from places and things that are off limits. Either offer her a substitute to engage her attention, or pick her up and turn her away from the item so that her gaze falls on some other fascinating object.

Making wise use of your toddler's disposition also means acknowledging that she is too young to discipline effectively at this age. Just because she is learning how to talk does not mean she also knows how to listen—especially when the command you want obeyed conflicts with strong inner desires unhindered by a conscience.

She may remember not to touch a china figurine or fragile glass paperweight for a few minutes after being reprimanded, but soon it calls to her again to come and examine it, and she won't be able to resist. She needs greater maturity before she'll be able to internalize the restrictions you set and to stop herself from touching what she shouldn't.

Recognizing this immaturity, you don't depend on her undeveloped moral sense to guide her, nor do you drain your own energies by constantly running after her to rescue her or your home from destruction. Instead, you make your environment as childproof as possible. The sanity you save will be your own.

Besides making your life saner and your child's life safer, childproofing offers additional benefits: gifts of independence and self-esteem. Your toddler obviously enjoys greater freedom and more positive responses from you when her surroundings are safe ones. A child whose every move provokes a rebuke will have difficulty thinking of herself positively. By childproofing your home you minimize the possibilities for failure in much the same way you do when you decide to postpone toilet teaching at this age. The whole family is happier when parents don't attempt to teach what a child isn't developmentally ready to learn.

Preparing a Safe Environment for Your Toddler

Unless you never add or subtract so much as a single item from your home, childproofing must be a continuous project as well as a thorough one. Perhaps the easiest method of insuring safety is to examine your home room by room, inch by inch. To gain a toddler's-eye view of your household, survey the rooms on your hands and knees after your initial inspection. From this new perspective you're sure to find many potentially dangerous items you've overlooked.

Toddler's Room: Toys and bumpers that could be used for climbing should have been removed from your child's crib when she learned to pull herself to standing. That was also the time to lower the crib mattress to the bottommost position and to raise the crib sides to their highest position. Even with these precautions, you must be continually alert to attempts by your toddler to climb out of her crib, with the risk of falling and being hurt.

Make sure the crib is safely situated within the room; electrical cords, lamps, appliances (such as air conditioners and heaters), wall decorations, windows, and furniture should lie well beyond your child's reach from the crib.

If your child's room has a bureau with a hutch that sits atop it or a similarly styled desk and bookcase, be certain that the two pieces are joined together securely from the back with a brace and that the corners of the top piece are screwed into the wall. Follow this procedure for any large two-piece item in any room of your home. Children have been seriously and even fatally injured by climbing on such furniture and inadvertently pulling the top piece down on themselves or by removing a book from a shelf and upsetting the entire unit.

If your toddler's toys are stored in a toy chest, check whether it has a lid support that holds the lid open in *any* position and that keeps it from dropping unexpectedly. A free-falling lid is dangerous, as it can drop not only on little fingers but on a child's head or neck, with dire results. If the chest does not have a safety lid support, you will need to install one or remove the lid altogether.

Do not store riding toys in your toddler's room if it is located on the second floor of your home. Even with a gate across the top of the staircase, the potential for a dangerous fall exists.

Toddler toys must be examined frequently, as hard use can create hazards which didn't exist when the item was new. Discard broken toys promptly.

Make sure all baby toiletries and supplies are stored well out of your toddler's reach. You know the lotion isn't for drinking, but your toddler's first instinct is to taste whatever her hands reach. Baby powder, too, is potentially dangerous in toddler hands; if aspirated, it can cause choking. Even supplies which pose no health threat can create quite a mess when examined by a toddler.

Protect your child from electric shock by putting safety caps on unused electrical outlets in her room and all other rooms of your home. If possible, position furniture in front of outlets so that your toddler will be unaware of their existence. All lamp cords and other wires should be situated out of a child's reach or tacked securely to the wall. Bulb sockets should have light bulbs in them; otherwise, they tempt toddlers to stick their fingers into the empty spaces. Blind and drapery cords should be shortened so that the loop ends are well out of a child's reach—toddlers have strangled in such loops.

Make sure all windows in your child's room and through-out your home have secure screens or metal guards to prevent a fall. Install locks that keep windows from being opened beyond a certain point. If you live in a two-story home, safety gates should be securely installed at the top and bottom of all staircases. Avoid using expansion-type wooden gates; they pose a potential hazard if a child gets her head or neck caught in the diamond- or V-shaped openings.

Be certain that the door to your child's room cannot be locked from the inside. This goes for all other rooms in your home. An adult should be able to unlock all doors from the outside.

Bathroom: When you are not in the bathroom with your toddler, keep the door closed and secured on the outside with a hook-and-eye latch installed high out of your child's reach. Children have actually drowned in the toilet bowl when they leaned over to play with the water, lost their balance, and couldn't right themselves. A diaper pail poses a similar hazard and should be covered with a childproof lid.

Never leave a toddler unattended in the bath even for a second. Unsteady balance and a slippery surface combine into a deadly twosome. To prevent the possibility of scalding, never run the hot water alone into the tub—lukewarm avoids accidents. Even with this precaution, always test the water temperature before putting your child into the tub.

Electrical appliances do not belong in the bathroom; nor do glass cups and bottles.

Lock up the medicine cabinet as well as all toiletries and cleaning supplies. Locking up dangerous items, whether in the bathroom, kitchen, or any other room in your home, is always preferable to putting them out of reach; forbidden substances are powerfully attractive, and "where there's a will there's a way" all too often holds true of toddlers who want to investigate off-limit areas.

Kitchen: You will need to install childproof safety latches on kitchen cabinets and drawers. These latches help keep your toddler from getting into dangerous untensils, breakable dishes and glassware, poisonous cleansers, polishes, detergents, insecticides, drain cleaners, and the like, as well as prevent her from emptying a cabinet's contents onto the floor, a favorite toddler pastime. You may want to assign one cabinet for your child's use and fill it with several small pots and their tops, a large wooden spoon for banging, some potholders, and similar safe items.

Isolate all toxic substances in one high, locked cabinet. Never store food items and poisonous ones near one another, and never store anything without a label—if something is accidentally ingested, you must know what it was. Keep your plastic trash bags in this safe spot too, since they can cause suffocation. When you discard a plastic bag, tie knots down the length of it so that it cannot fit over a toddler's head. Wrap sharp items (razor blades, broken glass, etc.) before discarding, and remember that discarded bottles or boxes which held toxic substances often contain enough residue to harm a small child who decides to survey the contents of the kitchen garbage can. Rinse and tightly cap such containers, and make sure your trash can is childproof and out of your toddler's reach.

If you turn pot handles to the back of the stove, your toddler won't be able to grab hold of a hot pot. As an extra precaution, use the back burners to put greater distance between your toddler and hot pots or sizzling fat. If possible, remove stove controls within a toddler's reach; otherwise, apply tape to prevent her from turning on the burners herself. Keep the dishwasher closed, especially if it is loaded with breakables or sharp untensils or contains soap.

Keep all small appliances away from the sink, and unplug them when not in use. The electrical parts in these appliances are live *even when the switch is off*. Make sure appliance cords remain well out of your child's reach.

Always secure your toddler in her highchair with both the waist and crotch straps, and make sure the chair is positioned in an area free of kitchen traffic and well away from potential hazards, such as a hot stove or an electrical appliance. Even with these precautions, your child should not be left unattended when she's in her highchair.

Finally, be aware of how easily distracted you can be while working in the kitchen. A boiling pot or a ringing telephone claims your attention for a minute, and a minute is time enough for a tragedy to happen. Locking up dangerous utensils, cleaning agents, and other household chemicals won't prevent an accident if you leave one lying within your toddler's reach while you answer the phone.

Living Room, Dining Room, Den, Master Bedroom: Inspect these rooms for wobbly floor lamps, unsecured electrical lamp cords, hanging tablecloths, fragile bric-a-brac, candy dishes containing potentially dangerous nuts or hard candies, filled cigarette boxes and match holders. Also check

the drawers and shelves of all cabinets, breakfronts, desks, and bureaus, and remove any dangerous items, including liquor bottles. If you display perfume bottles, cosmetics, and the like on an open dressing table or bureau in your bedroom, these must also be removed and put in a place your toddler cannot get into. Keep sewing supplies and knitting needles locked up. Sharp table corners should be covered with protective guards, and tables with glass tops should be removed for the protection of both the child and the table until your toddler is old enough to treat such furniture properly. Bolt all bookcases securely to the wall.

If you have a fireplace or wood-burning stove, protect your toddler by installing a fence or firescreen, and never leave your child alone in a room with either one burning. Glass fireplace enclosures keep sparks contained, but the glass gets hot enough to burn a toddler's hand. Remove fireplace equipment sets that usually adorn a hearth. The tools are sharp and heavy enough to cause injury if your child should pull them down on herself. And remember, every home should have smoke detectors, and they should be checked periodically to be sure they're in proper working order.

If your home has slippery ceramic tile, polished wood, or vinyl floors, your toddler should wear shoes with rubber soles when walking on them or go barefoot. Never allow her to walk on these surfaces in her socks. Uncarpeted wooden steps present a particular hazard; carpet them if you can.

Many common houseplants—including amaryllis, mistletoe, caladium, dieffenbachia, philodendron, to name just a few—are toxic if ingested. You best insure your toddler's safety by removing all plants from your home until your child is old enough to understand that plants are not for eating. If you choose to retain them, be sure to place them well out of reach and to frequently check areas around the plants for fallen leaves, blossoms, or berries.

Cellar: Bar access to your basement by installing a hook-and-eye latch high on the cellar door and far away from a toddler's reach. Inventory poisonous substances and dangerous tools stored in the basement and lock them up. Always keep boiler room doors closed and locked.

Car: A majority of states require that children under a certain age be secured in a crash-worthy auto restraint when riding in a car. No caring parent would ever transport a child one inch without one, and no ride is too short to buckle up before you leave.

Make sure that the seat is correctly installed in your car and that your child is always properly secured in the seat. Without these precautions, even the safest auto restraint is worthless as a protective device. It should be noted that some seats come with a top tether strap. This strap provides an extra margin of safety, but *it must be correctly anchored to the car*. If you have this type of seat, be certain that the tether strap is properly secured. If it isn't, your child will be safer in a seat that doesn't require one.

All auto restraints manufactured after January 1, 1981, must meet federal safety standards. If you are using a hand-me-down seat, you can contact either of two organizations to learn if it meets current safety requirements. Write to: Physicians for Automotive Safety, P.O. Box 430, Armonk, New York 10504, or Division of Public Education, American Academy of Pediatrics, P.O. Box 927, Elk Grove Village, Illinois 60007. Enclose a self-addressed, stamped envelope for a reply.

Once your child is properly secured in her auto restraint, never close the car door before checking to see that her hands won't be caught in the door. Do not allow your toddler to carry any toy which could cause damage to her eyes in the event of a short stop or an accident. And never let her eat or drink while you are driving. Driving an automobile safely and handling a choking emergency quickly and competently are mutually exclusive activities.

Outdoors: You can protect your toddler from the danger of wells and swimming pools by surrounding them with a fence that is kept locked with a chain and combination lock. Do not depend upon a closed but unlocked gate. Never leave a toddler unattended near any body of water or near a drained swimming pool or in-ground goldfish pond in winter, as these collect enough rainwater to create a hazard.

Automatic garage door openers also pose a potential risk. Several deaths have resulted when a child was crushed between the door and the ground. Your garage may harbor poisonous automotive or gardening supplies, as well as sharp or heavy gardening equipment. Take inventory of these items and lock them up. Generally, your garage should be off-limits to your toddler.

Toddlers who haven't yet graduated from the stage of tasting everything in sight cannot be left alone outdoors even if your yard is fenced. Many common garden plants and bushes are poisonous. Christmas rose, daffodil, Dutchman's breeches, horsechestnut, hyacinth, larkspur, lily of the valley, mountain laurel, oleander, star-of-Bethlehem, and wisteria are just a few. Depending on the particular plant or bush, it may be the seeds, bulb, or root that's toxic, or the stem, leaves, berries, or flowers. Even parts of commonly grown vegetable plants contain noxious chemicals— potato vines and sprouts, for example, and rhubarb leaves.

If you barbecue on a grill or hibachi in your backyard, take the same precautions you would near any hot surface. And don't forget that barbecues often retain heat for several hours after the cooking is done, so don't relax your guard once the meal ends. Discard hot coals where your toddler cannot get to them and burn herself.

Playground: Toddlers must be supervised in a playground; if you are talking to other parents while your child pushes an empty swing, you can expect to visit your local emergency room when the swing hits her eye or tooth. Older toddlers can usually learn to avoid playground hazards— any piece of equipment that swings freely, for example— and to use the equipment properly, such as sitting, not standing, on swings or seesaw. Of course, this instruction does not eliminate the need for constant supervision.

Constant supervision is just as necessary if you install a jungle gym in your backyard, as accidents can happen there as easily as they do at a public playground. Before you buy, inspect the slide very carefully for rough or sharp edges. Also be sure that there aren't any places where a child's head could get caught, such as in the ladder or around the hand grips at the top of the slide. Check this last point especially if you're considering getting an indoor gym house.

Proper apparel prevents playground accidents and injuries. Shoes should tie or buckle, and rubber soles grip apparatus better than leather ones, giving your child firmer footing. Long pants protect knees. And don't forget a sunscreen. Several hours in the sun will burn unprotected, sensitive toddler skin.

Safety Starts Now

Don't procrastinate in putting childproof measures into effect. The precautions which seem so unnecessary one day can become vital to your child's safety the next. New skills, advanced dexterity, seem to appear overnight; you and your environment should be prepared for them.

Post the telephone numbers for the police and fire departments, for your local poison control center, and for your pediatrician and hospital. Consult your pediatrician about accident prevention and about what steps should be taken if an accident does occur. Get a good book on child and home safety; read it through and study it. Give serious consideration to enrolling in a first-aid course. Being prepared will help you keep the level head that will be needed if your child does have an accident.

One last warning—make sure that your child cannot leave the house without you. Occasionally a toddler has managed to open a door no one realized she could manipulate and has wandered onto a nearby roadway or spent the night outdoors in subfreezing weather with predictably tragic consequences. Are the doors to your home childproof?

3. Eighteen to Twenty-four Months

How They Have Grown

Though your child is growing less rapidly than he did as an infant, toddlerhood is a period of accelerated growth. This acceleration foreshadows the growth spurt that will occur when your child reaches adolescence.

At eighteen to twenty-four months boys and girls are nearly equal in size. The average eighteen-month-old boy is slightly taller and heavier than the average girl of the same age, though her legs are longer than his. By the time they celebrate their second birthday, the average boy and girl will weigh almost four times more than they did at birth and will have grown an additional 75 percent of their birth length. At two years of age boys have attained about 50 percent of their adult height; girls, 53 percent.

Body proportions continue to change as the torso, arms, and legs grow, making the head more suited in size to the body. The torso slims down, and the neck lengthens so that the head no longer appears to sit directly on the shoulders.

This external growth reflects enormous internal changes that are occurring simultaneously. Muscle growth declines and will continue to do so until puberty. Boys, however, have more muscle tissue than girls. The percentage of body fat also declines rapidly until about thirty months of age, when this decline decreases somewhat. This reduction in fat produces the child's new "streamlined" shape and the appearance of arches in the feet, which were previously camouflaged by fat pads. Girls lose less fat than boys do, and later on they will regain it more quickly.

Because growth of the heart parallels skeletal growth, heart size continues to increase now along with the skeleton. When the general rate of body growth slows at approximately age four, heart growth will also decrease. At puberty both growth rates accelerate once again. The speed of the heartbeat, however, which began its decline in utero, will continue to decrease until maturity is reached.

Most neural development occurs between conception and the toddler years. The expansion of the nervous system, which is 60 percent complete by the child's first birthday, consists mainly of maturation of cells which were present at birth, not in the production of new cells. A myelin sheath, which aids in the transmission of nerve impulses, has begun to surround many nerves responsible for motor skills.

The various segments of the nervous system mature at different rates, and many of its reflex responses disappear when the child gains voluntary control over a particular set of muscles. For example, walking supplants some toe reflex actions. And the Babinski reflex, the turning upward of the big toe (rather than downward) when the sole of the foot is stimulated, disappears in most children by eighteen months of age.

The part of the brain which controls muscular coordination—the cerebellum—has been increasing rapidly in both size and complexity. Its growth coincides with the growth of motor skills and muscle coordination.

Understanding how thoroughly intertwined internal

growth is with the development of new abilities, how essential to development is the growth of the body's various systems, should convince you of the folly of pushing a toddler to master new skills—whether the skills are physical ones, like walking, or intellectual ones, like reading and arithmetic computation—before he has the internal apparatus to handle the task. When a child is ready to walk, he's ready from the inside out. You'd have to tie him down to prevent his doing so.

Numerous experiments have demonstrated that attempting to teach a child a skill in advance of his physical readiness to acquire it is a waste of time. Studies with identical twins involving skills of stair climbing and cube manipulation demonstrated that the twin who was introduced to the skill at a later age learned it in a shorter time period than his sibling who was encouraged to practice it months earlier.

Postponing teaching their first child a skill until he displays some readiness frequently tries new parents' patience, so anxious are they to see progress. By the time their second child arrives, these same eager-beaver parents are much less inclined to tamper with nature's schedule.

What They Can Do

New Language Skills

Between one and a half and three years of age a child's ability to listen improves rapidly. This improved skill encourages enormous vocabulary growth and the use of increasingly sophisticated sentence construction. Don't expect to hear the Gettysburg Address. However, the two-word "sentences" your toddler creates represent an enormous improvement in her ability to voice her thoughts; just a few months ago her conversation depended upon a mere three words!

You no doubt recall how often your toddler repeated those first words, and you will notice a similar approach to learning sentence construction. Her early sentences mimic old-fashioned grade school primers, with the same heavy concentration on repetition: "See baby." "See mama." "See dada." "See ball."

After the millionth repetition, she begins to sound like a broken record, and you may find your sanity in jeopardy. This is another situation in which your needs and your child's may conflict: You'd appreciate some peace and quiet; she needs the noise she makes. Once she possesses the physical maturity to combine words, as well as words to use, she is as internally driven to build sentences as she was to practice walking, and she talks to anything that will listen, including her toys when she plays and herself. The feedback provided by both your responses and the sound of her own voice improves her skill in word manipulation. To a toddler silence isn't golden; it exists as a void to be filled. Nature and toddlers both abhor a vacuum.

Typically, these first sentences are models of linguistic economy. They eliminate every part of speech except those vital to voicing the core thought, usually a verb and a noun ("See ball.") or a noun with "this" or "that" or "here" or "there": "Ball here." "Cup there." "What's that?" (or more likely, "What dat?") becomes a constant refrain.

Speech Problems That Aren't Really Problems

Don't worry if your child shortens words by omitting sounds or even entire syllables or substitutes one sound for another. She may say "duck" for "truck," "foon" for "spoon," or "fire" for "pacifier." These abbreviations and substitutions occur because the toddler does not yet possess the ability to voice all the necessary individual sounds and sound combinations to duplicate the words she hears. You will find that there are some sounds she can say at the beginning of a word but not at the end and some in just the reverse manner.

None of these habits indicates a speech problem in a child of this age; she simply suffers from immaturity. Attempting to correct her mistakes is a waste of time and may even be harmful. Since she cannot make the corrections, all you can accomplish by calling attention to her mistakes is to create frustration. Do not adopt her babyish expressions, or you will deprive her of an appropriate speech model; just continue to speak properly, and when she has the ability to imitate your speech more exactly, she will. In fact, some children will object to hearing an adult duplicate their babyish mispronunciations. Toddlers hear the distinctions between your speech and theirs, even if they have trouble reproducing them.

Toddlers will also use pronouns improperly for a long time to come, no matter how good your example. Perhaps because a toddler's sense of self is still shaky, she has difficulty distinguishing which pronoun refers to herself and which to others, so she uses some pronouns interchangeably: "I carry you," says a two-year-old to her parent; what she means as she stands on tiptoe with her arms upraised is "You carry me."

Learning any new motor skill seems to require a certain

single-mindedness of purpose. So if your child talked before she walked, as some babies do, her vocabulary growth will be delayed while she is mastering the art of locomotion. This tendency seems to appear primarily in precocious toddlers and in girls. After the child masters the skill, vocabulary growth resumes.

Just as their language grows increasingly fluent, some toddlers may begin to stutter and continue to do so for several months. Their minds may be thinking too quickly for their mouths and their still limited vocabularies to keep pace. Some experts have suggested that tense children are especially prone to stuttering. Boys suffer from it more than girls, probably because their verbal abilities and their vocabularies lag behind girls'. More left-handed children stutter than right-handed ones.

The suggested treatment for stuttering at this age is simply to ignore it. Do not urge your child to speak more slowly, to take a deep breath, or to begin her sentence again. Avoid rushing in to phrase her thoughts for her; wait patiently until she can voice them herself. If you think tenseness may be part of the problem, try to find ways to alleviate it (perhaps you are demanding too much discipline or self-control). Otherwise, time provides the best remedy.

Increasing Your Child's Vocabulary

Exposure to various experiences stimulates your child's developing linguistic ability, so this is a good time to visit a farm, the zoo, and other places of interest whose highlights will be added to her vocabulary. Use picture books and postcards that correspond to the sights she has seen on these trips to reinforce the acquisition of these new words.

Nursery rhymes and songs also encourage vocabulary development in toddlers. They are so enchanted with speech at this time that the rhythmic sound effects of these poems and lyrics cannot fail to delight them, and they will learn to say some of the words with you. Very simple storybooks that contain frequently repeated refrains become favorites too. Write your own simple story about your toddler's favorite person—herself—and use snapshots to illustrate it. It will command more rapt attention than any best seller ever generated.

A small snapshot album of her own will delight her too. Include photos of family members, pets, favorite equipment at the local playground, friends, baby sitters, and she will spend hours turning the pages and naming each picture. This type of book offers the possibility of expansion when the child makes a new friend or learns a new word.

Describe your activities and hers in short sentences that she can mimic: "I tie your shoes." "We wash our hands." "Up we go." "It's time for lunch." At first she will echo only the last word or two, but she'll be storing both ideas and grammar for later use. However, avoid doing all her talking for her. If you don't anticipate her every wish, she will need to talk to satisfy her wishes.

Toddlers enjoy naming the parts of their body. You can increase your toddler's vocabulary by teaching her the names for the ankle, elbow, shin, calf, wrist, sole of the foot, eyebrow, etc., after she has learned the simple ones, like eyes and nose, that are usually taught first. Most experts agree that children should also learn the appropriate names for their sex organs at the same time that they learn about the rest of their anatomy.

Personality Development

Mine, Mine, Mine!

The emotion of jealousy appears at approximately eighteen months, and it occurs most frequently between that time and three and a half years of age. Just as anger and fear develop simultaneously because they are opposite sides of the same coin, jealousy and possessiveness also arrive hand in hand.

Between these two ages, your toddler establishes his individual identity by collecting bits and pieces of information about himself into an internal collage that defines his individuality. And he is vigilant in guarding the ownership rights to the treasures he has assembled. Twenty-month-old Kevin, for example, became enraged when he heard his mother playfully call his cousin by the pet name she had formerly reserved for him. "Me 'Porkchop'!" he bellowed until she found another nickname for his cousin.

During this time a toddler also begins to realize that he is a separate individual from his parents, and this knowledge makes him feel uncomfortably weak and vulnerable. To offset this disturbing state of mind, he manufactures a support system for himself based upon his possessions. What he "owns" are his parents, his toys, and other miscellaneous items, such as his nickname. In his mind possession of these talismans protects his individuality and bolsters his fragile sense of self. His selfishness is a kind of psychological state of red alert against possible encroachment on any facet of his identity. It is both natural and necessary to the process of becoming independent. You've heard the saying "Get a grip on yourself"? Well, no one ever had a tighter grip on himself than the toddler at this moment. Relaxing his grip might result in a fearsome loss of self.

These feelings of insecurity make learning to share an impossible task for a toddler right now. "Mine!" means preservation. Even if he has no interest in a particular toy, his possessions are too tangled up with his sense of self at this point to permit generosity.

The arrival of a sibling at this particular stage in a toddler's life can seem especially threatening. A toddler younger than eighteen months is so egocentric and requires so much parental care himself that he doesn't take much notice of a sibling's demands upon his parents' time and attention. After age three and a half he is more independent and is increasingly interested in activities outside his home and family to want or need exclusive attention from his parents. But between these two ages the toddler is old enough to respond to the profound disturbances that a new baby creates in family dynamics and young enough to have trouble handling them.

His parents no longer belong exclusively to him, and sharing them is infinitely harder than sharing a toy. In addition, he must abandon the role of baby because now an understudy is playing that part. Since his sibling usurped both his starring role and the supporting cast before the toddler was ready to relinquish either one, jealousy results.

Jealous reactions mirror the "fight or flight" responses of anger. The child may choose an aggressive response to his problem. He may fight the intruder, his new sibling, by poking or hitting the baby, by disturbing the baby's sleep, or by suggesting as one child did, "Throw baby away." Sometimes this behavior lies dormant until the baby is old enough to steal the spotlight by gurgling and cooing or by learning to crawl. And sometimes the jealousy takes the form of overenthusiastic "loving"—hugs that are too tight, toys ostensibly tossed into the crib for the baby's enjoyment which happen to land on her head instead, or playthings appropriated from the baby because they might "hurt her." Because aggressiveness is such a common response of a child this age to a new sibling, leaving the toddler alone with the baby usually isn't wise.

Less aggressive children take the opposite approach: flight from maturity back into babyhood. "If you can't fight 'em, join 'em" seems to be the reasoning behind this solution to the loss of attention and to the parents' demands on the toddler for increased maturity. Reverting to infantile behavior garners additional attention from the parents and eliminates the possibility of complying with their expectations for more mature responses.

Increased amounts of thumb-sucking or time spent holding a security blanket or stuffed toy; more than the usual amount of babyish chatter; cranky, demanding behavior; withdrawal, and clinging may all be symptoms of this flight from maturity. Jealous reactions seem more intense in first-born children than in others, probably because they have the most to lose.

No matter how good a parent you are, you cannot totally eliminate either possessiveness or jealousy in your child. Nor would you want to, since coping with these emotions helps a child mature. Unfortunately, it is a fact of life that maturity develops from confronting misery. You can, however, somewhat defuse the intensity of these emotions through proper handling.

In public especially, a child's apparent selfishness with his possessions embarrasses many parents. They cope with their discomfort by attempting to enforce generosity before the child is ready to cooperate with the lesson. "I'll teach you to share," they mutter angrily, wresting the toy from a screaming tot and handing it to a playground friend. Usually this solution produces one enraged child and one bewildered one, who (now that he has the toy in his hand) is more interested in watching his companion scream than in playing with his prize.

Sharing toys will come more easily when your toddler is a little older and a little more sure of himself. Small playground items like pails and shovels can be duplicated to avoid unnecessary hassles. When larger items, such as riding toys, are at stake, be prepared for some unhappiness no matter how evenly you attempt to divide the time allotted each child. Toddlers this age don't understand "fair"; they only understand "mine." Sometimes the less aggressive of the children will allow himself to be distracted by another toy (which the first child will then undoubtedly take a shine to). Try to rid yourself of the notion that a child of this age should be generous, and do not make him surrender unnecessarily the items that he values.

When the jealousy arises over the intrusion of a new baby, the toddler confronts the playground drama magnified many times over. Having lost the major component of his identity—his former role in the family—as well as the undivided support of his parents, he is now in the process of reworking his identity to conform to the new situation. He isn't very confident of what new identity he'll create for himself or how he's going to set about doing it. This uncertainty naturally will affect his behavior, vacillating between babyish mannerisms one minute and more mature demeanor the next.

Make sure your expectations of your toddler don't suddenly exceed reasonable levels. After all, he hasn't grown up magically just because an infant has arrived. The contrast between his abilities and the helplessness of the new baby puts unfair pressure on him to abandon his immaturity. He may need extra attention, and if he reverts to somewhat babyish behavior, additional hugs and kisses are more likely to improve the situation than reprimands. Quite often emotional growth seems to require a step backward prior to a leap forward. If you avoid making too big a fuss over his retreat to infancy, it will probably be short-lived.

Budding Sociability

In the experiment which paired a child with a playmate and a new toy every four minutes, a sociability of sorts first appeared in the fourteen-to-eighteen-month age group. Unlike younger babies, the children in this group paid attention to the playmate before examining the toy. Then, from nineteen to twenty-five months, social behavior increased and changed; now the toy was used to initiate interaction between the two children.

Prior to this period the toddler's play has been mainly a solitary affair, for the most part unaffected by the activity of others around him. Any socializing between children resulted mainly from one toddler coveting another's toy or from curiosity about the other child's appearance. This curiosity might have prompted interaction in the spirit of scientific investigation—to get a closer look at the interesting buttons on one's jacket or the bells on another's shoes— and not as an opening gambit for making an acquaintance.

While individual play continues to occupy much of the child's time, attempts to socialize also occur. The first sign is so subtle you may not recognize it as social behavior. The toddler plays beside other children, though not necessarily at the same activity, as though satisfying the need for social contact through physical proximity. Social scientists label this behavior parallel play.

When children engaged in this parallel play have similar toys, they take another step closer to true sociality. The toddler now mimics the motions of another child playing nearby; one rolls a toy engine across the floor and makes a noise of a train, and two feet away his companion follows suit. This kind of imitation is often called associative play, and it appears frequently in nineteen-to-twenty-five-month-olds, possibly because their memory and coordination have improved sufficiently by now to reproduce others' actions.

Such primitive social interaction stimulates toddlers' imaginations, since they invent new play behavior for a companion to follow, as well as add their companion's performance to their own repertoire. It also teaches toddlers a very important lesson: that they can influence the actions of others. Such benefits suggest that children of this age ought to be exposed to play situations with other toddlers, even though they do not yet interact with one another in the way that parents usually define as play. Parallel activity usually involves very little, if any, exchange of conversation and no cooperative give-and-take between the participants.

One study found girls more likely than boys to use this device for socializing.

Some scientists have theorized that parallel play arises from a child's uncertainty of how to approach social relationships. Others think that such responses are a programmed part of the maturational process, much as many motor skills are. Interestingly, researchers studying courting patterns have recently observed that in the early stages of courting, couples tend to signal their interest in each other by discreetly imitating each other's body positions and gestures. Whether this ploy is learned or inborn, it seems to remain a permanent part of our social repertory.

Mimicry plays an equally important role in your toddler's relationship with you. Imitation is child's play, and like all play it is instructive. Your toddler will ape your use of household equipment, your telephone conversations, your use of "please" and "thank you," and a thousand tasks you do each day. (He may also attempt to use his mother's makeup, his father's after-shave lotion, or the furniture polish, so keep such supplies locked up.) Few other people will find your every move as fascinating as your toddler does. This is a time in which actions truly speak louder than words.

There are two good ways to take advantage of your child's natural inclination toward mimicry at this stage. First, if you encourage him to imitate your activities, such as stirring, pouring, dusting, sweeping, combing your hair, zipping zippers, and such, you have given him the keys to both self-esteem and increased independence. Time-consuming chores take even longer when a toddler participates, so busy parents often prefer to exclude the toddler from trying his hand at them. This is a mistake. A few minutes with the broom or a chance to pour his own juice from a small cream pitcher filled with a minuscule amount of liquid provides important experience for your child. Whenever possible, include him in your activity.

Second, his "monkey see, monkey do" mentality will reflect whatever courtesy and gentle demeanor your example provides. The child who bosses his playmates, who never

says "thank you," is often simply duplicating the kind of treatment he himself receives. A toddler of this age is a first-class student, and you are his teacher even when you are unaware of the lessons he absorbs.

Understanding Temper Tantrums

Part of the reason the "Terrible Two's" have gained their reputation is the increase in temper tantrums that occur as a child nears his second birthday and that continue for some months thereafter. Why tantrums now? Like the explosion that occurs when volatile chemicals intermix, a powerful combination of circumstances interacts during this time.

First, frustration increases sharply as your household routines begin to impinge upon the freedom of babyhood. The toddler can't do or have everything he would like at the time he would like it, and he is far from mastering the finer points of patient behavior. No matter how flexible a parent you are, families function best when some sort of schedule shapes their day: Meals are served at fairly regular times;

bedtime hours are observed; baths are a fact of life. Not one of these customs does a toddler find convenient or, indeed, necessary. So a battle of wills ensues.

In addition, his whole orientation is negative at this time as he psychologically breaks away from his parents toward independence. His inclination is to say "no" to whatever activity an adult has in mind, sometimes even when the suggested activity appeals to him, sometimes even when his negativity contradicts itself. Here's a conversation between Scott, age twenty-two months, and his mother. Mother: "Do you want to take your coat off; it's warm here." Scott: "No!" Mother: "Oh, so you want to keep your coat on?" Scott: "No!" Orneriness is his middle name.

Third, his verbal ability, which has grown enormously, still remains grossly inadequate to his desire for expression. Much of what he says only he himself can decipher, and he hasn't the vocabulary to express fully whatever weighs on his mind. See how calm, cool, and collected *you'd* remain if you couldn't give voice to your feelings and if no one understood you half the time anyway when you finally managed to state your complaint.

Fourth, the desire to perform tasks requiring superior muscular coordination far outstrips actual ability to do so. Have you ever tried to fasten a tiny clasp on a necklace or to close buttons or a zipper behind you? Then you understand the toddler's predicament in wanting to dress or feed himself and not succeeding very well.

Other factors can increase the likelihood of a tantrum: fatigue, hunger, illness, disruptions in the daily schedule, a parent's indecisive behavior, as well as the technique used to handle the previous tantrum the child had. Though tantrums, like many other unpleasant forms of behavior we've examined (such as fear and possessiveness), cannot be completely eliminated, intelligent planning and a calm response when you're confronted with one can help reduce their occurrence.

You might try to soften the blow of interrupting your toddler's play for meals, bath, or bedtime by announcing the coming event. "Lunch soon!" will eliminate the sudden annoying disruption of his activity and provide a sort of transitional buffer zone during which he can mentally begin to switch gears. This technique usually improves your chances of getting your toddler to cooperate in changing activities.

Allowing the child to carry a part of one activity into the next sometimes has the same effect: "Lunch now; bring your teddy bear with you." He will probably lose interest in the toy once the meal has begun, and you will have maintained the continuity of activity which toddlers value so highly. This technique works especially well if the toy can be transferred to the bathtub or bed next.

Capitalize on the knowledge that toddlers love to be helpful and to imitate adult behavior. If you want to lure him from his play for a bath, ask that he first lay out his pajamas and then help you put down the bath mat. Participation in preparation for a new activity often smooths the way.

If the desire to accomplish more than his physical abilities allow causes tantrums, break each task into smaller sections at which he can be successful. For example, hand him the proper side of his shoelace, but let him give the yank to undo the knot. Then you loosen the laces sufficiently for him to remove the shoe. You undo the buttons on his overalls, but he can pull them down. You pull his socks partway over the heel; he finishes the job. It helps to accompany this dual effort with comments that indicate you'll alternate in doing the job. Say, "First I undo the snaps; now you pull your shirt up." A toddler can assist in completing almost any task if you take the time to analyze the best way to divide the labor.

Tantrums that result from fatigue, hunger, or disruptions in your schedule can be sidetracked with a little forethought. Many parents find that carrying a small poptop can of juice or one of the juice boxes that come with an attached straw along with a small snack can avert an outburst. Choose items that do not require refrigeration and keep an extra in both your carryall and your car.

Obviously, fatigue-induced tantrums mean more sleep is

required. They can also indicate that your child has been involved in an activity or kept immobile beyond the limits of either his interest or his patience. If sitting in the shopping cart at the supermarket generally produces a screaming fit in your child by the time you reach the check-out counter, reducing the amount of time spent in the store or leaving him home with a baby sitter makes sense. To be successful, shopping trips generally require the preparation of stocking a bag with small toys, snacks, and other items of interest to occupy his attention. This "goody bag" also proves invaluable on days when your normal schedule can't be followed; distractions can avert tantrums.

Does it surprise you to learn that your behavior may be a factor in encouraging your child's outbursts? If you have a hot temper which often eludes your control, your child may mimic your own response to frustration. In addition, vacillation on your part in making a decision may encourage your toddler to throw a tantrum to "help" you decide. Telling a child that the hour has come to leave the playground should mean just what you've said—it's time to go. But if you make this announcement and then procrastinate while you chat with friends, you're asking for problems when you finally decide it's really time to leave. He now knows that saying doesn't make it so.

If your child then throws a tantrum because he wants to continue playing, and this induces you to remain in the playground even longer, you've taught him a lesson you really didn't want him to learn: Tantrums produce the desired result. The moral here for you is to make a decision carefully, and then stick with it. Many parents don't learn this lesson until they've already made the mistake of allowing themselves to be blackmailed by tantrums. It's much harder to retrain a child than to establish firm ground rules from the beginning.

You might also want to examine how you feel when a tantrum does erupt. Most of us become embarrassed when our children thrash around in the midst of an outburst; lack of control, even in a toddler, isn't very well tolerated in our society. If you allow your embarrassment to subvert your better judgment and capitulate to your child's demands, you're likely to confront the problem repeatedly in the future.

What you should do is pick your child up and hold him close. When he has a tantrum in public, this may be difficult, for you'll probably feel more inclined to strangle him than cuddle him. However, he needs to know that he is loved even when he is angry and out of control. Sometimes this physical contact and restraint will calm him.

Most parents try reasoning with the child: "We must leave the playground; it's time for dinner." Reasoning doesn't work well for the child. By the time he's thrown a tantrum, he's already beyond reason. Even under the best of circumstances, toddlers aren't reasonable beings. However, if making reasonable remarks helps *you* feel better, if they prevent you from voicing some time-honored principle of child psychology such as, "If you don't stop crying, I'll give you something to bawl about," then such remarks serve a useful purpose. Go right ahead and say them (while you carry your child to the car for the trip home)—just don't expect your toddler to obey the voice of reason. When you have quickly and efficiently acted on your statement, the force of the outburst abates.

Examining your feelings regarding tantrums also means taking a close look at the balance of power in your relationship with your child. You don't want to be a doormat for him, but neither should you expect him to respond cheerfully to having all his decisions made for him. When the choices aren't crucial, let him steer the boat for a change. He'll be less likely to balk at your authority if he has opportunities to exercise his own power regularly. He will also be absorbing lessons in how to lead and how to follow in social situations with his playmates.

How frequently a child has a tantrum contains a message about his daily life. If he always seems to be howling and protesting, perhaps you need to reassess all the factors that can ignite a tantrum and see whether you can further defuse them. The solution might be as simple as a longer nap or an earlier bedtime. Or perhaps you are pressuring him to mature faster than his biological clock permits.

Learning to deal with frustration is a necessary part of life. Tantrums are the first step in accommodating frustration, so a complete absence of tantrums isn't cause for rejoicing. Eventually a toddler will learn more productive techniques for dealing with interference, but right now these fits provide the immature mind's most common response to

restraint. If tantrums are missing from your child's emotional repertoire, he isn't separating himself from you as he must to mature, and some adjustments must be made in your relationship.

When properly handled, tantrums tend to decrease as the child matures. Immature behavior is, of necessity, extreme behavior. An equilibrium cannot be achieved until the extremes have been explored, so children must test the extremes to acquire information about their emotions. They are seeking answers to important questions: What happens to me when I act this way? Does it achieve my goal? How do others react to my behavior? Am I satisfied with their response? Would altering my behavior improve the response? Is this the best way to get what I want? Of course, toddlers don't phrase the problem in such sophisticated terms, but these are the questions raised when they experiment with their emotions. Your response provides the answers.

Daily Routines

Eating

Mealtime—Food for Thought

In the past the accepted wisdom about the relationship between food and exercise held that exercise stimulated a hearty appetite. Today we know that exercise helps control and regulate appetite and that an excess of exercise actually decreases appetite. You've probably noticed this phenomenon in your child: When she's enjoyed moderate activity, she gobbles her meal enthusiastically. When she's overtired, she doesn't eat well. If you remain at the playground a little longer than usual or take your toddler on a shopping expedition that continues past the hour you'd planned, your child may fingerpaint with her meal rather than consume it. Or she may sit in her highchair and whine and cry as she pushes away whatever she's offered. If you want to avoid this problem, stick as closely as possible to regular mealtimes and feed your toddler before exhaustion sets in.

Overstimulation can produce a similar decline in appetite. An event as simple as the arrival of company may over-whelm your toddler; sometimes horseplay too close to the dinner hour diminishes the desire for food. Unlike the over-tired toddler, who cries and whines, the overexcited child launches her food into outer space, overturns her cup on her head, or watches her vegetables crash land on the lin-oleum one by one. The food goes everywhere except into her mouth. Her behavior is manic, and she finds herself exceedingly funny.

If you're the sort of parent—as most of us are—who worries about good nutrition, this kind of mealtime upsets you. Perhaps you try to coax a few mouthfuls into your child while distracting her with songs or by pretending the spoon carrying the applesauce is an airplane heading for its hangar or a train entering a tunnel. Maybe you cajole her to "take one spoonful for Mommy and one for Daddy and one for Grandma" and so on. This activity continues until, by hook or by crook, you've succeeded in spooning down enough of the meal to satisfy your need to nurture or until she's managed to dump the entire plate into your lap or onto the floor.

A better way to handle the situation would be to focus on *her* needs at that meal and to fulfill *your* desire to express your love and concern in another way. We have already spoken of the wisdom in maintaining a farsighted, rather than a nearsighted, perspective of your child's food intake, of looking at the weekly consumption rather than the daily one. If she misses this meal she'll still thrive, and you will not have been a negligent parent.

You might want to examine the problem from another angle. Suppose the child in that highchair were not *your* toddler and that the parent making train whistles with the spoon were someone else. As an observer, how would you suggest this distressed parent handle an obviously tired, cranky toddler? Would you advise shoveling in a meal no matter how reluctant the diner? Of course not! If you weren't emotionally involved with the drama, you'd counsel that a tired toddler would derive far more benefit from a nap than from a meal—even one delivered by a 747 or an Amtrak express.

If you had to recommend a solution to the parent of this child, you might propose that a warm bath before dinner or a few minutes of snuggling on a parent's lap while looking at a picture book would calm her. If you weren't the parent involved, you certainly wouldn't continue to try to feed her in that condition.

This technique of pretending to be a disinterested observer rather than a participant proves helpful in many situations. It is most useful during those highly charged moments when your ideas about how to handle a situation and your toddler's don't coincide or when your child's rambunctious behavior or crying threatens to drive you to drink. Using this trick allows you the opportunity to put the wisest solution to a problem into practice, rather than the response prompted by overactive emotions.

Now, you are the observer in the following situations. As the onlooker rather than a participant, what changes would you make in these scenarios? First, Mrs. Smith wants Jennifer to stop playing so that Mrs. Smith can run some errands. Jennifer begins to cry as she is pulled away from her toys, and her mother bribes her to behave by offering a bag of cookies. Second, young Greg has demonstrated an unusual act of generosity by relinquishing an intriguing toy so that a playmate can have a turn with it. To reward Greg, his father produces some candy. Third, two-year-old Richard reclaims his strainer from Karen, who promptly begins to howl. Karen's parent offers her a cupcake to distract her from her loss.

As the parent in any one of these situations, you might have responded exactly the way Jennifer's, Greg's, and Karen's parents did. Especially when you're tired and busy, avoiding a toddler's tears seems a bargain at any price. As an observer, you'd note that hunger was not a factor in any of these situations, though food was offered in all three of them. You'd never countenance using food (especially sweets) as a bribe, a reward, or a distraction any more than you would encourage offering that airplane spoonful of applesauce as a substitute for a nap.

A good habit to teach your child early in life is to associate food with only one stimulus—hunger. Encouraging its use in any other situation begins a lifetime of poor eating habits, ones that can lead to obesity later on.

Distract with a toy, a song, by pointing out some item of interest in the immediate vicinity, or by removing your child to another spot. Reward with hugs, kisses, smiles, and compliments. And the less you bribe by any means, the better off you'll both be. Bribes teach manipulative behavior.

Healthy Snacks, Healthy Meals

Now is the time when you can encourage your child to eat the type of diet that will serve her well her entire life. Never again will you have as much control over the food your child consumes as you do now. If you put this opportunity to use, you will be teaching important lessons in nutrition.

One of the best ways to accomplish this is to set an example through your own diet. You know how fond toddlers are of copying your habits. If you constantly munch on cookies and junk food, your child will want to eat them too. "Do as I say, not as I do" isn't going to influence your toddler very well, and you may find yourself in the shoes of one mother who took her two-year-old daughter out to lunch for a special treat. As they climbed the steps of the restaurant, the little girl turned and announced, "I want soda; you have milk."

Substitute nutritious choices for foods containing empty calories derived from their high sugar content, for foods which include large amounts of unnecessary preservatives or additives (like food coloring), and for foods which are high in fat. Pay attention to protein sources. Poultry, fish, and veal provide protein just as red meat does but with far less fat and cholesterol. When buying chopped meat, look for packages marked "extra lean," as these do not contain

fat ground in to extend the meat. Processed or combination meats, such as those in salami and bologna, contain large amounts of fat, food coloring, preservatives, and salt, all of no benefit to your child. Avoid frying foods; bake or broil them instead.

Investigate nonmeat sources of protein, such as beans and whole grains. These are less expensive than animal protein; however, they should be eaten with foods that complement them nutritionally in order to increase their protein value. If you are interested in including some menus based upon plant protein into your family's diet, an excellent book on the subject is *American Wholefoods Cuisine*, by Nikki and David Goldbeck.

You might try some cheeses that are made from skim

rather than whole milk. These may taste somewhat bland to you, but toddlers, who have more sensitive tastebuds than adults, won't mind. Instead of feeding your toddler yogurt with fruit already mixed in, buy plain yogurt and mix it with fresh fruit pureed in your food processor or blender, since commercial fruit-blended yogurt often contains unnecessary amounts of sugar.

Get into the habit of reading labels, as ingredients are listed in order of their quantity in the product. If sugar appears near the beginning of the list, find a sugarless substitute or at least one with reduced amounts of sugar. Juice products such as punch, fruit juice cocktail, and fruit juice drinks generally contain generous amounts of sugar and water but little juice. Drinks advertised as having "real fruit flavor" do contain the flavor but omit the juice along with its nutritional value. Soda is equally unnecessary. Your toddler is healthier drinking juice that is labeled 100 percent fruit juice or juice that combines crushed fruit and water. For a treat try mixing pure fruit juice with a little carbonated water. Plain tap water makes a fine drink to offer thirsty toddlers; parents seem to forget that a toddler doesn't always require juice or milk.

You'd be wise to avoid feeding your toddler sugar-coated cereals. However, even noncoated cereals may contain unnecessarily large amounts of sugar, so read the ingredient information listed on the package before you buy. In addition to being mixed with milk, dry cereal makes a good snack for toddlers because it can be picked up as a finger food.

If you bake, you might try experimenting with your recipes to reduce the amount of sugar used. Often this can be done without diminishing the flavor. A marvelous source of dessert recipes for parents who care about the amount of sugar in their children's diet is *Sweet and Sugarfree*, by Karen E. Barkie.

Sweet Tooth—Sour News

Why so much fuss regarding sugar? First, doctors are more concerned than ever with the effects of being overweight, and sugar consumption encourages excess weight gain. Second, sugared foods contain extra calories but not extra nutrition, so they don't promote growth—or at least not the kind of growth caring parents wish for their child. Third, sugar consumption causes cavities, and your child needs her teeth, even the temporary baby ones.

Good nutrition is related to how *much* sugar a child consumes, but studies reveal that good tooth care is related to how *often* she consumes it and what *form* it's in. In fact, in terms of cavity prevention, your child is better off eating a large amount of junk food all at once than a smaller quantity of sticky sweets distributed throughout the day! Of course, she's best off not eating junk food at all, but if you're going to allow it, what you want to avoid is a day-long sugar bath of her teeth. The stickier the treat and the longer it remains on the tooth surface, the more time it has to work its damage.

Schedule sweets only once a day, after a meal, so that your toddler will be too full to consume large amounts of sugar. Another reason for scheduling sweets after a meal rather than as a snack is that chewing generates saliva, which can help neutralize the sugar. Sugary snacks require little chewing and don't produce sufficient saliva when eaten to wash sugar off the teeth. Brushing immediately after finishing sweets should be a family habit.

Traditional advice has been that dried fruits can be added to a child's diet at about age two, and many parents view dried fruits as a compromise between letting their child have a sweet snack and insuring wholesome nutrition. Dried fruits, however, contain high concentrations of sugar and are sticky as well, so they're really not as good a compromise as believed. If you allow your child to have dried fruits, her teeth should be brushed promptly afterward.

There is surprising evidence that sugar may be beneficial in one particular circumstance: getting your toddler to fall asleep. In an experiment conducted by doctors associated with the Boston University School of Medicine, researchers found they could count on babies falling asleep about fifteen minutes faster than usual when they drank formula that contained sugar and the amino acid tryptophan. The old habit of milk and cookies before bedtime may induce sleep. If your child suffers insomnia, try having her get more fresh air and exercise to promote sleep before you increase the sugar in her diet.

Tooth Care

On to the Brush

At eighteen months your toddler's smile reveals approximately a dozen teeth. Sometime in the next few months the four cuspids will appear, filling the spaces between the incisors and the first molars. The more teeth your toddler has, the more tedious using a gauze pad to cleanse them becomes. Allow your toddler to watch you brush your teeth as a preparation for your substituting a toothbrush for the gauze pad on hers.

When she seems ready to accept the brush, buy a child-size one with a small head and soft bristles. If you say aloud what area you are cleaning and follow the same order each time, your child will begin to memorize a total tooth routine. As you're brushing say, "First we clean the bottom back teeth on the left side; we brush the inside, we brush the outside, we brush the top of each tooth." Then move the brush to the opposite side of the mouth and explain, "Now we brush the bottom back teeth on the right side—inside, outside, and top." Next do the bottom center teeth, then repeat the routine with the upper teeth.

Count a dozen or so strokes aloud for each front, back, and top surface as you carry out this routine. When your child is able to brush her own teeth, you will have guaranteed a more thorough job if she has an idea of how many strokes constitute a proper cleaning.

You should repeat the description of your actions and follow the identical order of steps each time you brush. Continue to count out each stroke. Stress that the front, back, and top surfaces of each tooth must be cleaned. Emphasize cleaning the tooth surface near the gum line, an area most children miss when they begin to brush independently.

Once your toddler has absorbed the steps in the tooth-care regimen, let her direct your cleaning and see if she remembers each of the steps. After you've finished, let her give a demonstration of how she brushes her own teeth. (If you can arrange for her to use a mirror while she does this, she will be able to do a better job. Unfortunately, most bathrooms aren't arranged for the convenience of toddlers.) With this kind of training, your toddler will learn how to do a thorough job of tooth care when she becomes solely responsible for it.

Like any other routine, brushing will become second nature if you insist on your child's performing it at regular times, as you do eating, sleeping, and bathing. Daily dental care is every bit as necessary as the daily bath, to which parents never give a second thought. For some reason, even the most fastidious of parents often overlook early tooth care.

Mother, Please, I'd Rather Do It Myself

Although independence in handling daily tasks and personal hygiene is a most desirable trait, it is *not* desirable in tooth care. A toddler's coordination is simply inadequate for accomplishing the task well, and she lacks the necessary dexterity for reaching inaccessible spots in the back of the mouth. She also lacks the judgment to assess whether she's cleaned her teeth thoroughly.

The more successful you have been in encouraging independence in handling the other daily routines, the more difficult a time you will probably have convincing your toddler to relinquish this particular responsibility. Your best bet is to establish the routine so that she becomes accustomed to having you brush her teeth until she has the skills to handle this responsibility alone.

Sleeping

Nap Knacks

Your toddler may be down to one nap a day and seem ready to abandon that, or she may still be snuggling down both morning and afternoon. There's a wide variation in the amount of daytime sleep toddlers need and no rule for conforming. Whatever pattern supplies your child with enough energy to get her through her wakeful periods alert and in good humor is the proper amount for her.

Overstimulation can affect naptime in the same way it plays havoc with meals. A child who is all wound up from roughhousing or other high-level activity usually won't drop off to sleep without a struggle. She needs time to unwind before she is able to relax and drift off to sleep.

Planning your child's day as a sequence of different types of activity helps to create problem-free bedtimes: active play first, then a quieter activity, which leads into rest. If your child still takes two naps a day, simply repeat this routine morning and afternoon. Periods of high activity are vital to sleep because without them the toddler doesn't expend sufficient energy to tire herself enough to sleep.

You may find that on days when your schedule or the weather restricts outdoor activity, your toddler may experience some trouble in settling down and may nap less than usual. How soundly she slept the previous night, teething, the first stages of a cold, etc., can all affect the length of a nap. As with meals, keep an eye on the overall sleep picture, not on the daily one.

Try to establish a naptime routine, for then your toddler's expectation that a nap follows a story, which follows lunch, accomplishes part of your job for you. Another routine that seems to work well in establishing naptime is letting the child arrange a bed for a favorite stuffed toy; then she can play the role of parent in putting the toy in for a nap before she is settled in for her own. Keeping a special toy aside for napping with also encourages cooperation. Or perhaps your child can assist in the preparation by helping you lower the window shades.

Your attitude can make a difference too. Don't ask whether she wants to nap because her negativism will probably prompt a "no," no matter how tired she is. Say firmly, "It's naptime now," and, as you did when leaving the playground, suit your actions to your words without delay. You don't want to teach her that it can be postponed.

Giving Up a Nap

Eventually you'll begin to see signs that the nap has outlived its usefulness. Your toddler may spend the entire time talking to herself in the crib if she's docile, or she may raise a big fuss every afternoon when you begin the nap routine. Another sign of outgrown naps is the inability to fall asleep easily at night, especially if your child has dropped off quickly in the past. When daytime rest interferes with evening sleep, changes must be made in your daily routine.

Here comes what looks like contradictory advice: You must now be flexible about naps. If you expect your usual routines and schedules to fall apart during this period, as they undoubtedly will, then you're less likely to be upset by the upheaval in your life.

Giving up the morning nap is easier on a parent than saying goodby to the surviving afternoon nap. To ease the transition from two naps to one, you'll have to juggle naptime and mealtime. The best way to accomplish this change is to serve lunch earlier than usual (before exhaustion sets in and eliminates the meal altogether). Move it up by an hour or more, and schedule the remaining nap immediately following this early meal. The nap may last a little longer than previously. When your toddler wakes, she may want a small snack if she was too tired to eat a complete lunch. Then she's ready for an afternoon of activity, which you will again end earlier than you did before. Prepare dinner early as you did with lunch, and allow for some quiet play after the meal if she doesn't seem ready for sleep yet.

On paper the switch sounds relatively simple. Real life is more complicated because on some days this schedule just won't work all that well; your child may be at the stage where one nap is too little, but more than one allows too much daytime rest. One way to counteract this is to try every few days to sneak a day in with two naps. Then revert to your new schedule again for a day or so before another day that again includes the extra nap. One surefire method of sneaking in the second nap on alternate days is to put your child in her carseat and take a drive. The motion of the car will induce sleep, and you can time your excursion so that this nap does not interfere with bedtime. On days that include two naps, you can also increase the opportunity for extra active play in preparation for the additional nap.

If your child has already progressed to one afternoon nap and is now ready to forgo that, your organization of the day is somewhat similar. Try not to let your child exhaust herself during play periods, and schedule more quiet playtime into her day. Prepare dinner an hour or so earlier and move up bedtime too. Expect fluctuation between no-nap days and days that include them until the transition is fully accomplished.

Like all maturation processes, the change in sleep patterns is a gradual process, and to expect a simple, easy solution is unrealistic. Try to get extra sleep yourself while this changeover occurs because you're going to need all the patience you can muster during this period; your child's cranky periods are likely to be more trying than usual due to her increased fatigue.

Bedtime Bedlam

Your routine at night should resemble the naptime schedule: Allow for a period of unwinding before sleep. At night this is easily accomplished with a bath, which is relaxing. Allow time for whatever sequence of habits calms your child, and read a book or two. Try not to let the number of items in the bedtime routine grow to uncontrollable levels, or you'll be spending half the night trying to get your toddler into bed.

It's a good idea to get all the little rituals out of the way before you begin to read and to set a limit on the number of books you complete each night. All drinks of water, the selecting of toys to sleep with, the tucking in of toys and dolls, should end before settling down to a story. In that way all the preparations have been completed, and your toddler can predict with great accuracy when her day is absolutely, positively finished. If you leave the number of bedtime stories open, you prepare the stage for a battle each night for "just one more." Your toddler finds comfort in the constancy of this routine, and you can put her into bed immediately after you finish the last book. One trick that makes her want to stay in bed after you've finished reading is to use a heating pad to warm the bed before putting her in. The warmth is soothing and can help a child drift off to sleep with a minimum of fuss. Never leave the heating pad in the crib with the child; use it only to prewarm the sheets.

Jailbreak

At some point your child may discover how to climb out of her crib. This tactic is, after all, the perfect solution to the problem of being left all alone in the boring, and perhaps increasingly frightening, darkness. The consensus of most experts is that the child should be led firmly back to bed. If you are very pleasant and reasonable about the situation, you may encourage the addition of this activity to the others in her nightly routine, and a very unwelcome addition it becomes. Let her know from your tone of voice that you are not pleased to have her reappear before morning. Your toddler will probably respond to your displeasure. Leaving a hall light burning outside her room can be reassuring if disapproval alone doesn't work. There are also stuffed toys which double as nightlights; when the toys are squeezed, they glow. Having the power to control the light sometimes offers enough reassurance to promote sleep. If the problem continues, a gate across the doorway of the room makes your message concerning bedtime unmistakable and also restricts unsupervised wandering. Another safety measure is to put pillows on the floor next to the crib to cushion a possible fall.

Sometimes all your child wants is a response that indicates that you care—an extra kiss and hug, for example. Try giving her a kiss to hold in her hand or her pajama pocket until morning. To a toddler the solution itself is often of secondary importance to the demonstrated concern for her feelings.

If you send your toddler to bed as a punishment during the day, you attach unpleasant memories to being there that may encourage nightly "jailbreaks." Using bed as a punishment is unwise; find some other means to express your disapproval.

Bathing and Dressing

Fun in the Tub

The older your child gets, the more she enjoys bathtime, and well-chosen bath toys offer opportunities to play and learn at the same time. Well-chosen doesn't mean expensive. In fact, some of the best bath toys are ones you can make or purchase inexpensively in the hardware store or the housewares section of your supermarket. For example, buy the largest brightly colored sponges you can find and create several different playthings with them. First, cut some into the simplified shapes of familiar animals. Your child can learn the names for each and their distinctive sounds while she scrubs the soap dish clean with them. You can help her use them as puppets and make up a small dialogue between them, which will increase her vocabulary and improve her ability to create sentences.

Make other sponges into puzzles by cutting large-size shapes out of their centers. If you cut the same size shape from different-color sponges, your child can learn to make a fit based first on color coordination and then by matching the shapes. This is an activity that she will repeat many times over.

Soap crayons make a good bath toy for a two-year-old. She can enjoy scribbling wildly on the tile and then cleaning off her handiwork with one of the sponges. A paint brush for water painting would be useful too. Your total investment so far is just a few dollars for hours of bath fun.

Next, purchase a plastic measuring cup with a spout,

some plastic cups of different sizes, a plastic and rubber turkey baster, and an unbreakable camp mirror made of aluminum. Learning to pour is an all-time favorite toddler activity, one that goes on interminably if time permits. And what better place to learn to pour than in the tub, where spills don't matter? The baster is fun to fill and squeeze repeatedly, especially if the child can rinse the soap off Mommy's hand with it. And the mirror is useful for observing a headwash.

If you have some plastic containers with lids and plastic jars and bottles in different sizes, each with its own screw top, you have created another puzzle for your toddler to solve by matching the proper top to the right size container. As an added bonus, your child will enjoy learning how to screw and unscrew the tops, an intriguing activity for a child of this age.

A doll with washable hair makes a terrific bath toy, especially for a child who is shy of having her own hair washed. Add a washcloth, and your child will enjoy being the parent washing the baby. Your child might like scrubbing some of the doll's clothes along with doll, and a hand towel functions as the doll's bath towel when the bath ends.

You should, of course, never leave your child unattended in the tub. If she is engrossed in her activities, you have time to clean the bathroom while she plays or to remain in the room and read a book.

The Littlest Swimmer

Before you enroll your child in any program—whether for swim instruction or play group—you should decide what benefits you want your child to gain from the group and what approach to providing those benefits best suits you and your child. Then visit several class sessions to evaluate whether this choice is the right one for you.

These precautions apply especially to swim programs for toddlers, as a wide variety of approaches and goals exists among these classes. Class sizes range from individual instruction to large groups; programs exist for swimmers as young as two months old. Some gyms encourage the parent's participation, while others frown upon it, claiming that "a parent in the water is an emotional situation." Presumably the emotion isn't positive. Instruction runs the gamut from no-nonsense serious to fun and games. And getting the child into the water may be as pleasant as enticing a child to paddle toward a toy or as unsettling as "sink or swim" with the instructor nearby as a rescue unit.

One swim club describes its curriculum as a "survival program" and claims the skills it develops would give the parent extra rescue time if a child accidentally fell into a pool or off a boat. You should be very wary of programs that claim to make your child water-safe. As the coordinator of a YMCA Gym-Swim Program noted, "Toddlers don't possess enough judgment to be water-safe. They're too young, even if they can swim."

Other drawbacks to diaper-dipper swim classes include a possible increase in respiratory or ear infections during the winter months in cold-climate areas and the possible ill effects of swallowing large amounts of chlorinated pool water when learning to submerge.

Despite these liabilities, a properly chosen program does offer toddlers and their parents several important benefits. It encourages a joyful communication between parent and child, as well as promoting fitness by strengthening and stretching young muscles. It provides an opportunity for practicing gross motor coordination. Psychological benefits can be an additional dividend: "Our toddlers don't necessarily swim sooner than others," says the swim coordinator, "but they do become water people later on due to their early, happy exposure to it."

Dressing Difficulties

Not too long after a child learns to take her clothes off, the idea occurs to her that it would be nice to reverse the procedure. The toddler's dressing problem, as with so many difficulties in life, is that the spirit is willing, but the flesh is weak. Dressing herself requires more coordination than

the child possesses. Failure equals frustration, and we all
know by now what the end result of frustration is. You
won't hear: "Mother, I'm having a small problem with these
overalls; could you please help me?"

Some wise clothing choices coupled with a few time-
tested techniques can prevent a hopping mad, Rumplestilt-
skin-like rage. First, schedule enough time for dressing.
This may seem a minor point, but it's really one of the most
important techniques. Nothing ignites a situation faster than
urging a toddler to hurry a task which gives her difficulty.

The only course of action that makes matters even worse
is attempting to exclude her from the chore and doing it
despite her efforts to participate. Allotting extra time helps
both of you remain calm.

As suggested in the section about tantrums, try to break
the larger task of dressing into smaller parts that she can
accomplish: "I'll hold the pants; you put your leg in this
side." When both legs are in: "You pull the front up; I'll

pull the back up." Make it a partnership instead of a competition.

Getting dressed in front of a mirror can help the situation, since your toddler's interest in watching the reflection helps keep her temper under control. You might also play mini-magician: "You hold this ball; let's watch it disappear into your sleeve. Abracadabra! Here it comes!" Then it disappears into the other sleeve. If you own a large, easily manipulated doll, she can dress the doll while you dress her.

When you buy clothes, select those with the features that make this struggle easier for both of you. Front closings, large buttons or zipper pulls, elastic-waist pants, and sneakers with Velcro straps instead of laces help avert frustration.

You'll probably often find yourself tempted to ignore your toddler's desire to dress herself and to accomplish the task single-handedly in as little time as possible. Constantly distracting a child to prevent tantrums, making the simplest of chores a game of strategy, becomes wearing after a while, and the straightforward approach seems very appealing. ("I don't care what you want; I'm tired, and this is what *I* want for once!") However, try to resist the impulse to speed up the procedure. The dividends won't materialize immediately, but they *do* eventually appear, in the guise of increased competence, increased self-esteem, and less work for the parents because practice does make perfect. If you always dress your toddler, she can't learn how to do it for herself. You'll have saved a few minutes, but you'll have wasted a magnificent opportunity to help your child mature.

Playtime

What Makes a Good Toy?

If you consider the needs you want your child's toys to fulfill, you'll discover the characteristics that good toys share. Toys ought to encourage your child's physical development by providing opportunities to use large and small muscles. Toys should supply sensory stimulation that fosters the development and appreciation of the work of the senses.

Toys can stimulate dramatic play so that a child can try on different roles and different emotions, as well as learn the give-and-take that social relationships require. They can promote the ability to reason and to understand the principles of cause and effect. They should offer an outlet for creative impulses and impart to the child a sense of mastery over her environment. The better a toy can fulfill any one or a combination of these functions, the more enjoyable playing with it becomes.

Toys are generally classified as either structured or unstructured. Structured toys are those whose wealth of detail or narrowness of function limits (except to those with very unusual imaginative powers) the kinds of play to which they are suited. A spinning top, for example, won't be pressed into play much beyond the first day a child sees it, when its newness makes it desirable. Familiarity with such toys definitely breeds contempt; they're the ones that gather dust on a shelf by the second day or lie buried at the bottom of the toy chest replaced by more useful toys.

By contrast, unstructured toys serve a variety of needs and uses and can become whatever the child's imagination makes them. Some unstructured toys provide a *decade* of enjoyment for a child. This is not an exaggeration. A child can play with a set of blocks from the time she is a toddler almost to her teen years. She may need additional sizes and shapes to construct the ever more intricate designs she creates, but contained within that set are the few blocks she uses to make her first "building."

This does not mean that you should buy only unstructured toys. It simply means that if you are aware of the relative play value of your selections, you will invest more money in the unstructured, long-lasting choices than in the ones whose popularity wanes quickly. A battery-powered monkey that plays a drum costs as much as a good-quality soccer ball which your child will enjoy for years. Battery-operated toys, in general, lack the versatility of unstructured toys.

Good Toys for Eighteen to Twenty-four Months

Because the toys suggested for twelve-to-eighteen-month-olds fulfill so many of the criteria for good toys, your child will continue to enjoy them now that she is a little older. However, she will probably begin to use them in more sophisticated or rambunctious ways than in the past. Her skills in throwing and catching will improve, and she will begin to ride her rocking and riding toys harder and faster as her coordination matures.

Increased maturity also makes some new playthings appropriate now. Many of the best toys for this age engage a child in doing what comes naturally: imitating others. A toy telephone, a tot-size sweeping set, a little grocery cart and some empty boxes to fill it with, a doll carriage with baby doll, a simple hammering and pounding toy, all offer a toddler opportunities to mimic the rhythms of life around her.

A beginner set of wooden blocks is a good choice now. If you buy a large set, avoid giving your toddler the entire set at one time. The largest pieces are unwieldy for a child of this age, and she'll be overwhelmed by the amount anyway. She'll play with a small number and make a mess with the rest. Instead, select a small group of various shapes for her to use at eighteen months and put the rest away for now. Offer her some more in a few months when she needs them. Several companies make plastic blocks that interlock when pressed together. These are good choices as your toddler approaches the two-year mark. Interlocking blocks minimize the frustration of collapsing buildings and allow your toddler to stack more than the few wooden blocks she can balance. Be sure to buy those made for this age and not the ones for older children.

The sandbox at the playground will probably claim much of your child's time there. Though at first many toddlers are content just to sift sand through their fingers, toys for sand play enhance their enjoyment. Buy a large pail to accommodate your toddler's unsteady aim and a large shovel too. Your toddler is too young to use a sand mold for its intended purpose, but she'll enjoy burying one and finding it again. You might want to bring along some plastic cups or containers and an old plastic pitcher. Your toddler will practice pouring sand for hours. Save the strainer for a few months; toddlers of this age don't appreciate the principle of it yet. (Don't forget to shake out your child's shoes and socks before she leaves the playground; otherwise, she'll transport large quantities of sand into your home. Carry a small container of baby powder in your tote bag and put some on her feet when you're removing sand. The powder loosens the sand more quickly, thoroughly, and gently than just brushing it off with your hand.)

This is a good time to introduce your toddler to music. Though she's too young to handle a record player, she's not too young to enjoy music. Don't make the mistake of re-stricting your child's music appreciation to only those records that are marketed for children. Folk songs, jazz, and classical music aren't for adult ears only. Your public library's record collection is a wonderfully inexpensive way to expose your child to many kinds of music.

Make use of a tape recorder if you have one. First, record your toddler talking or singing and play it back to her. Second, tape your own rendition of her favorite songs and rhymes.

Increasing your visits to the public library and adding to your toddler's own library are important during this period because her ability to improve her use of language and the size of her vocabulary depends upon such stimulation. Do purchase some of your toddler's books. Even if she still doesn't treat her possessions with the gentlest hand, she takes great pride in ownership. You want to encourage the attitude that books and the pleasure they bring are every bit as important as owning toys. For some reason parents who are willing to spend small fortunes on toys labeled "educational" are less open-handed about buying books. While many toddlers amass far too many toys, nobody ever owned too many well-chosen books.

You can select somewhat more complicated books than would have interested your toddler only a few months ago. Picture dictionaries expand her vocabulary; you might try Richard Scarry's *The Best Word Book Ever*. In this case the title is not an overstatement, for the drawings are so richly detailed that you and your toddler could spend a long time talking about each individual illustration.

Very simple storybooks with perhaps one or two lines of print per illustrated page increase your child's ability to use sentences. Toddlers especially enjoy books that have a single line repeated frequently in the story. *Good Night Moon* is a classic of this type, and the books about the Smalls—Farmer Small, Fireman Small, the Small Family, etc.—have simple story lines which describe the daily events in the lives of these little characters that toddlers find extremely appealing. The simpler Dr. Seuss books make for good toddler reading too. *Green Eggs and Ham*, for example, has great aural appeal now and will continue to be a favorite later on, when your child begins learning to read. Many children seem to memorize Dr. Seuss books and pretend to be able to read them long before the actual event occurs.

Other good choices include counting books and books that tell a story through pictures alone without any text. Count the items on a page slowly with your child, and point to and touch each one as you say its number. Use wordless storybooks to encourage your child's powers of observation. Let her describe what the characters are doing and wearing, etc.

When Is a Toy Not a Toy? When Is a Book Not a Book?

Once you have stocked your home with toys and books, you have accomplished two things. First, you have given your toddler the potential to widen her horizons. Second, you have the makings for the messiest house this side of the equator. When is a toy not a toy and a book not a book? When you own and display so many of each that they function merely as distractions, as items to be pulled off shelves, examined momentarily, and discarded in favor of exploring and discarding another toy just as quickly.

If you want your child to make the best possible use of all you have gathered for her, do not present her with all these treasures at once. Her attention span is still short, and her senses are easily overwhelmed. Instead, rotate the toys, perhaps every week or so, to keep her interest in them fresh and to foster new, creative uses of each every time it returns to circulation. Follow suit with her books as well, but if she becomes attached to one particular book as part of her bedtime routine, do not rotate it until she is willing to part with it.

You will also need proper storage for toys and books. The best arrangement is a set of shelves low enough to the floor for your child to reach easily. One father built his own shelves and stenciled the names of the toys on the wide front edges of the shelves, where the names could easily be seen. When he and his son put the toys away together, the father pointed to the words and said them as he put the toys in their designated places.

Toddlers relish such organization, for it makes some sense out of what is to them a very confusing, distracting world. Encourage neatness by making a game of finding the proper spot for every toy, and always follow a play period immediately with clean-up time so that your child associates the two. If one *always* follows the other, you will have fewer arguments as she grows older about the necessity of straightening up the room after play.

You will probably be doing 99 percent of the clean-up to your child's 1 percent, but make sure that your child participates to some extent. She is not mature enough yet to put one toy after another away. You'll have to get her started by saying, "I'll put away the telephone; you put the ball on the shelf." Then ask, "What will you put away next?" When she gets the hang of this, increase her responsibility by asking, "What *two* toys will you pick up and put away now?" Later on make this a memory game by asking, "Can you remember to put away the doll, the car, and the fire engine?"

Just as with dressing, this procedure takes longer than simply doing it yourself. However, unless you want to be picking up after her playtimes for the rest of her childhood, the time to start teaching neatness is now.

Elimination

Toilet Teaching Now? Perhaps

The time *may* now be right for teaching your toddler to use the toilet. Two factors *may* work in her favor: She *may* have matured enough physically to gain bowel and bladder control. And she *may* be verbal enough to tell you when she needs to use the toilet.

With the heavy emphasis on the word "may," you have probably gathered that successfully teaching a two-year-old to use the toilet is by no means a sure thing. The most important implication of the word "may" is that using the toilet, like walking, talking, or riding a two-wheeler, is a learned skill based upon a foundation of physical maturation. If a child has reached the appropriate maturational level and *if she is sufficiently motivated to learn*, toilet teaching is a snap. The absence of either one of these conditions dooms the entire experience to failure.

Is Your Toddler Ready for Toilet Teaching?

You need some guidelines to help you judge whether your child is physically ready to learn. The child who asks to be changed when her diaper is soiled, who stops her play activity while urination or defecation is in progress, whose elimination occurs on a fairly regular schedule, and who imitates your other daily activities with gusto is probably ready to be taught. Without some of these signs you'd be unwise to start yet.

Even if your child meets all these criteria, there may be some compelling reasons for you to postpone toilet teaching. If you are nearing the end of a pregnancy, you might as well save your strength. The chances are that all your child's wonderful progress in this area will disappear with the arrival of a new baby. Other upheaval in your life at this time, such as a move to a new home, your return to a job, or a change in caretakers, all militate against initiating toilet teaching now.

How to Begin Toilet Teaching

Introduce the idea of using the toilet by commenting on your toddler's soiled diaper when you change her. Say, "I make a BM in the toilet." You might want to vary this for the next few days by telling her each time you change her about a different relative or friend who uses the toilet too. Avoid making other gratuitous comments because you don't want your child to feel pressured. Pressure brings out her negativity, which is no asset in this situation. You want the desire to learn to come from her.

If being observed doesn't bother you or your mate, let your toddler watch the same-sex parent use the toilet. Just as your child wants to imitate the way you sweep the floor or use the telephone, she'll want to mimic this activity as well.

Next, if you are planning to use a potty chair that sits
on the floor, leave it in the bathroom so that your child can
examine it. She may ask to use it herself, even if she doesn't
need to at the moment. Let her try it out and get comfortable
with the idea. The decision whether to use a potty or a seat

that fits on the adult toilet is a matter of personal preference. Because of its small scale and lack of flush mechanism, many toddlers do find the potty chair less intimidating. Others, though, have no qualms about using a seat on the regular toilet. If you decide on a seat, you'll need to provide a sturdy step stool for your child.

Both potty chairs and seats often come with a detachable shield designed to deflect the stream of urine downward when a boy urinates. This shield should be removed. Frequently boys scrape themselves on it, and an injury on the toilet isn't likely to improve your chances of getting your child to return to use it again. Either teach your son to hold his penis down or let him watch and imitate his father.

Try reading to your child whatever selection of toddler books your local library stocks on the topic of toilet use. One of the most popular because it speaks to both sexes is *No More Diapers!*, by Joae Graham Brooks, M.D.

Because you want the whole procedure to be relaxed, you'll need to remain housebound for a week or more when you decide the time for toilet teaching has arrived. If you plan trips, you'll confront the unpredictability common to the early stages of toilet learning. Once she is free of the diaper, the toddler is often concerned enough about having an accident to feel that she needs a bathroom when she doesn't have to go and not to realize enough in advance to get to one when she does. She may run back and forth to the bathroom a million times a day in the beginning until she gets the physical signals under better control. Don't add to her insecurity by expecting her to accomplish this feat in the midst of outside distractions.

Many parents have found that toilet teaching is easier on them in the summer than in the winter. Children can run about with little or no clothing, which facilitates the many trips to the bathroom. If a child has an accident, there is the advantage of having fewer clothes to change and wash. Obviously, though, it makes no sense to wait until summer if your toddler has expressed an interest in using the toilet.

If you manage to catch your toddler just before she has a BM, put her on the toilet or potty, and praise her when nature takes its course. Sometimes you may be a little late, but let her finish on the toilet nevertheless. It will encourage her to try to earn all the wonderful praise the next time the urge strikes.

Unless you have good reason to believe that your child is about to defecate, sitting her on the toilet or potty just to see if anything happens may make her feel she has failed when she doesn't produce. As with all other forms of teaching, you want to maximize chances for success and minimize possibility of failure.

Bladder control follows bowel control, so don't expect complete compliance all at once. Most children will not develop bladder control at night yet, so revert to diapers at bedtime. This tactic allows for more relaxed learning.

Some parents have found that giving the child extra liquids to drink during the teaching period facilitates bladder control because increased liquid consumption makes frequent visits to the bathroom a necessity. At first, this may mean lots more wash for you to do, but it also means increased opportunities for using the potty or toilet and getting a round of applause for even partial success.

Accidents are bound to happen during this teaching period and beyond, so be prepared to remain calm when they do occur. Say something comforting like "Everyone has an accident sometimes." Then clean up the child and ignore it.

The Reluctant Learner

Suppose your child expresses no interest in using the toilet even after all the demonstrations and praise. Or suppose she uses it successfully for a day or so and after that she's just not interested. What then? Leave her alone. Do not pressure her. Just return to diapers and tell her that she can tell you whenever she changes her mind and decides that she is ready. This unemotional response avoids making the procedure into a battle of wills. If she doesn't broach the topic at all in the next few days, forget about toilet teaching now and try again in a few months.

Guide to Good Parenting

Great Expectations

What makes parenting such a hard job? To begin with, parents follow a schedule that no union would ever endorse for its members—twenty-four hours a day, seven days a week. Then there's the matter of a difficult "boss," a two-year-old tyrant who doesn't know his own mind very well yet. But most of all there's the problem of great expectations, which unfortunately so often diverge widely from reality. The day-to-day drudgery of parenthood is all the more overwhelming and disappointing to parents who filter their vision of parenthood through a rose-colored lens.

Part of the problem stems from expecting our children to be better than other kids simply because they're ours. Our imaginary kids don't have tantrums, don't make a mess of the household, don't have problems sharing, and certainly don't need any discipline. They're naturally even-tempered, neat, generous, and good. They are, in fact, too good to be true.

But when we notice the discrepancy between our fantasy and reality, do we acknowledge that the dream doesn't exist and, more important, can't exist in real life? Unfortunately, most of us don't. We go right along believing that if only we were better parents, they'd be better kids. Our sense of failure in not living up to our own expectations creates a pervasive feeling of frustration and depression.

The worst part is that our toddlers' imperfect behavior demonstrates our inadequacies to the world at large. Jacqueline, age nineteen months, pulls every toy she owns off the shelf and makes a huge mess. What can you expect from a child with an incompetent parent? Cary, twenty-two months, creams another toddler in the sandbox because he doesn't want anyone touching his pail. Another sign of incompetence. Caroline often balks at cooperating with her mother's directives—deficient discipline from a deficient parent must be the cause. Katie, age two, shows absolutely no interest in using the toilet. Chalk up another black mark against poor parenting.

It's very easy to feel guilty when you're the parent of a toddler, not only about your child's behavior but about your own. You yell; you feel resentful; you feel overwhelmed, and you blame yourself for not being a more perfect parent. And then you blame yourself again for feeling this way. After all, good parents cope better than this, don't they? .

Well, not really. Only in our dreams and maybe in a TV sitcom as well. But not in the supermarket or at five o'clock in the afternoon when patience wears thin. And hardly ever with our first children, when we are as new to the game as they are and nervous about the correctness of our technique and the quality of our effort.

So, what can we do about this sad situation? Like Dorothy in Oz, we can remove the distorted lenses which conjure up fairy-tale families behaving in fairy-tale ways. We can understand the forces that motivate a toddler to behave the way he does, and we can cease to blame anyone (except maybe Mother Nature) for perfectly normal, if difficult, behavior.

And as a result of this understanding, we stop expecting the unreasonable. At this age the unreasonable includes a desire to clean up the mess one has made, an ability to share toys or parents with another child, and a tolerance for following instructions. We also put an end to the ridiculous notion that we ought always to have the patience, ingenuity, and sweet nature of Mary Poppins. All this really means is that living with a toddler becomes far more manageable when we accept our toddlers and ourselves as we really are.

Big and Little

One very special application of the problem of unrealistic expectations concerns parents of toddlers who are either much taller or shorter than the average child of the same age. Because their size makes these children appear older or younger than their chronological age, adults tend to make inappropriate demands of them. They expect these children to exhibit behavior more suited to their size than their age. Tall children are pressured to behave more maturely, while less is expected of small kids whose appearance is especially babyish.

These unrealistic expectations may become self-fulfilling prophecies, and the child, whether tall or short, is deprived of his right to age-appropriate behavior. The tall child loses an important part of his childhood when he is pressured to attain an advanced stage of emotional development prematurely. His fears may be summarily dismissed, his forms of speech found inappropriate, and his normal lack of bowel and bladder control unacceptable. Such disapproval either may make him feel a failure or may prompt him to struggle to behave in the desired manner. But the latter response can create a nervous, unhappy child.

The exceptionally small child retains his babyhood longer than he should. He doesn't develop emotionally because everyone continues to baby him. He isn't expected to achieve the same levels of competence as an average-size toddler, so he misses out on establishing the sense of confidence in himself so vital to self-esteem. Such treatment can create an exceptionally dependent individual.

If you are the parent of a child whose height sets him apart from his peers, you must make a special effort to treat him appropriately yourself and to insure that the other adults in his life do so as well. Do not pressure the tall toddler or baby the short one. One mother recalled her child's being teased by a cashier at a supermarket register. Noting the box of disposable diapers among the groceries, the clerk chided the child, "You're too big for diapers." Responded a very wise mother, "She may be too *big*, but she's not too *old*."

4. Twenty-four to Thirty Months

How They Have Grown

From the moment an American child is born, her height becomes a topic of conversation and is likely to remain so throughout her childhood and adolescence. She will be measured against her siblings, her friends, and that mythical beast "the average child." Her height will play an important role in determining her self-image, her view of others, and others' opinions of her.

Growth depends upon the interaction of the hypothalamus, a portion of the brain, and the pituitary gland. The hypothalamus secretes into the bloodstream a growth hormone-releasing factor, which signals the pituitary gland to release its growth hormone.

Appropriate growth indicates that the body's systems are functioning properly, which explains why infants must be weighed and measured during their monthly examinations.

However, once a child reaches toddlerhood, there's little point in measuring her monthly, as her growth has slowed. You're more likely to note changes at six-month intervals now. Lack of growth much beyond that time period may indicate the need for your pediatrician to examine your child more thoroughly to find the source of the problem.

Greater growth occurs between the first and second birthdays than between the second and third. Between ages two and three your toddler will grow approximately the same amount she grew during her first three months. This deceleration of the growth rate continues until about age four, when increases in height and weight slow to a steady average of approximately 3 inches and 6 pounds yearly until adolescence.

Your child's center of gravity changes with growth and altered body proportion. Until the toddler adjusts to her changing body, her movements will seem clumsy and uncoordinated. (Many years from now when your child begins her adolescent growth spurt, she will encounter similar difficulties in coordinating her movements.)

A variety of hereditary and environmental factors influence your child's rate and amount of growth. Family growth patterns, race, nutrition, access to fresh air, exercise and rest, as well as the quality of family relationships, all affect growth. A firstborn child generally arrives both shorter and lighter than her siblings but won't necessarily remain so. Even seasonal influences on growth and weight gain have been charted: The time between April and June is the season of greatest growth, while greatest weight gain occurs between October and December.

Studies of height indicate that infant and toddler size offers a rather good, though still imperfect, indication of adult stature. While a small correlation exists between a child's height at twelve months and her adult height, it increases at age two and continues to do so in succeeding years. The correlation between toddler and adult height is higher for males than females. Parental height provides another fairly reliable predictor. In general, tall infants and toddlers, whether male or female, do tend to become tall adults.

Beyond providing beneficial conditions for physical growth, a parent can do little to influence a child's ultimate height. You cannot make your child any taller than nature programmed her to be.

Big, Strong Boy; Fragile, Little Girl

If growth were merely a handy indicator of a healthy body or just a measurement on a yardstick, few parents would waste much time worrying about their children's ultimate height. But height subtly affects a child's life in many ways. Many parents believe "bigger is better" and then unconsciously behave in such a way as to make the motto true.

Preoccupation with large size is built into our language. "Nice and tall" is a compliment; who wants to hear that their child is "nice and short"? We admire men who are tall, dark, and handsome, people who sit "tall in the saddle," who can fill a "tall order." Would you want to be "shortsighted" or "short of cash" or "short-changed"?

This mindset ultimately influences our behavior with our children and consequently their self-image. Both size and sex play a part in how children are handled. Babies that are large, robust, or male generally receive more roughhousing than their smaller, frailer, or female counterparts. People tend to view male babies as big but female babies as pretty or cute. Bigger children come to think of themselves as strong and capable because they have been treated as such, and so early handling contributes to a self-fulfilling prophecy.

Studies have shown that the effect is perpetuated throughout life. The double standard continues to apply, since early maturation is a positive force for males. They tend to be more social than their shorter, more physically immature peers, to assume leadership roles, and to benefit from the edge that advanced physical maturity confers in the sports arena. Girls do not derive the same benefits from early maturation and are likely to become less social with their peers rather than more so. Early-maturing boys and late-

maturing girls garner more attention in school newspaper articles. Tall adults were found to be paid more than short ones performing the same job; salespeople wait on tall customers before short ones; tall presidential candidates usually triumph over their shorter opponents.

While parents cannot stretch short youngsters, they certainly can stretch their self-image. If you indicate your pleasure in your child's body, she will construct a favorable image of herself. If you are distressed by your son's lack of height or your daughter's abundance of it, you encourage your child's dissatisfaction with his or her appearance. And to belabor a point, teaching your toddler to be a competent, self-reliant individual adds inches to her self-image.

Overweight Woes: Even Toddlers Have Them

A child's weight carries social implications far beyond a simple set of numbers on a scale to determine physical fitness. Self-image and social consequences step onto the scale along with the child.

As you might expect, fat children and fat adults suffer discrimination from many different sources. Fat children find themselves excluded from play groups even at an early age. They become the butt of other children's jokes. Other children stand further away from fat youngsters than thin ones! One study showed that normal-weight children preferred handicapped or disfigured children to obese ones.

Obesity reduces a child's chances for college admission and interferes with her ability to find employment, especially in jobs which require public visibility. Fat executives earn less and advance to the top ranks less often than thin ones. Adults who were obese as children have difficulty perceiving their size accurately.

Would you believe that even parents discriminate against their own obese offspring? A study done by University of Cincinnati psychologists revealed that parents allowed photographs to be taken of thin offspring but refused permission for photographing of obese ones. Overweight parents, unhappy with their own size, may have difficulty accepting a child who exhibits a trait they dislike so much in themselves.

Finally, nature, too, discriminates against the obese. Fat individuals suffer more accidents than thin ones, and obese boys have a higher incidence of burns in accidents involving fire. An overweight individual's lack of agility has been blamed for this phenomenon, but self-hatred may play a hidden role in such events.

What Can a Parent Do?

The scientific evidence strongly suggests that parents can play a vital role in combating obesity in children. One of the first steps parents can take is to overhaul outdated attitudes. If you have difficulty discarding the notion that a fat toddler is a healthy toddler, you may need to remind yourself frequently of the potential health hazards: high blood pressure, heart disease, diabetes, and arthritis. Is this the legacy you want your child to inherit from your care?

Revamping your standards of beauty may also be necessary. Do you think a fat toddler is cute? Try imagining that fat toddler as a fat teenager; do the rolls of fat still seem appealing?

Consider how your statements about food affect your child. Parents who overfeed their toddlers or who encourage their toddlers to use any gauge other than hunger to stimulate appetite initiate a lifelong problem for their children. Do you applaud when your child joins the clean plate club? If you can't restrain yourself from this practice, and you are encouraging your child to consume larger amounts than she actually hungers for, serve smaller portions. Do you use sweet dessert as a bribe to get your child to finish her meal? Are you teaching your child to assess food intelligently? Even a two-year-old can understand that "milk makes bones strong" and "sugar weakens strong teeth." (Thirty percent of all three-year-olds have cavities.)

If you are in a hurry to get your child out of the kitchen, you may be encouraging obesity. Leisurely meals prevent your child from overeating; shoveling food in at breakneck speed overfills the stomach before it informs the brain of its capacity, a communication which takes about twenty minutes to occur. If you continually rush your child, the food lands in her stomach before the message arrives at the brain.

Encourage your toddler to get plenty of exercise. If toddlers spent as much time in the playground as they now spend in front of the TV, they'd grow to be healthier, thinner adults. "Don't fence me in" is a fine motto for both cowboys and kids.

If you suspect your toddler has a weight problem, discuss the matter with your pediatrician. Do not put your child on a diet without such consultation. Most physicians favor modifying an overweight toddler's menu rather than severely restraining food intake. Substituting healthful, lower-calorie foods for high-calorie junk foods allows the toddler to grow into her weight gradually without sacrificing the nutrition she needs.

What They Can Do

Influences on Speech Development

A two-year-old's vocabulary can range from only six words to more than eleven hundred, but most children's vocabularies fall somewhere between these extremes. Though toddlers will have acquired all the vowel sounds during their first year, at thirty months many can articulate only two-thirds of all letter sounds (or phonemes) an adult can make. Obviously, the clarity, complexity, and amount of communication a child can initiate depend upon the number of sounds he can create.

Toddlers acquire phonemes at different rates, though studies have shown that even newborns can discriminate between contrasts in the many different sounds that they hear. One child may have learned to make all sounds necessary to his native language by eighteen months. Others won't complete the process until an additional eighteen months—or more—have passed.

Several factors determine the rate at which a toddler acquires the sounds for speech: gender, individual developmental rate, family size, birth order, home atmosphere, techniques of child-rearing, and his family's socioeconomic group. Some researchers have linked female infants' greater oral activity (such as smiling and putting objects in their

mouths) to female verbal superiority. A more likely explanation, however, is the difference in interaction between parents and their sons and daughters. While parents roughhouse with their sons, they're more likely to talk to their daughters. In one study of two-year-olds and their mothers, for example, mothers addressed their daughters more often, asked them more questions, more frequently echoed their daughters' statements, and used longer sentences with them than with their sons. Mothers are also more likely to talk face to face with their daughters than their sons.

Individual developmental rate also favors girls, since they mature more quickly than boys. The influence of physical maturation can be seen in the fact that the development of consonant use correlates with ability to bite, chew, and lick. Immature speech and immature eating behavior coincide.

Family size and a toddler's position within the family affect the maturity of his speech. Probably reflecting increased parental attention, firstborns speak sooner and articulate more distinctly than later-borns. Small family size favors advanced speech development, and on average, twins lag six months behind singletons in speech development.

Studies generally show that socioeconomic status affects verbal ability, since children in impoverished homes speak less, use shorter sentences, and don't articulate as well as those from families with greater resources. However, such variables as the use of positive child-rearing techniques and intellectual stimulation, which occur with greater frequency in homes of higher social class, probably account for the difference in verbal ability more than the economic distinctions. Other factors, including family mealtimes (a prime conversation period) and use of verbal rather than physical punishment, were also found to encourage vocabulary development.

Why Is Verbal Ability Important?

Perhaps you are wondering why research into child development devotes so much study to the growth of verbal skills and why so much of this book suggests ways of encouraging and improving your child's speech. After all, most children do learn to talk sooner or later. However, advanced speech skills and a large vocabulary do provide many benefits for your child both presently and in the future.

Delayed ability to speak means living with frustration. Hand gestures and grunts simply cannot communicate desires and emotions as clearly as speech can. Any parent who has ever struggled to find the source of a screaming child's discomfort recognizes the value of verbal communication. A child who can say "ear hurts" saves himself hours of pain and his parents hours of distress.

By giving a toddler the power to control his environment, the ability to speak significantly reduces the amount of frustration the toddler confronts daily. In doing so, the power of speech can transform a child from a difficult handful into pleasant company. It gives him a far more socially acceptable and useful way of handling his anger than tantrums or biting and hitting. Indeed, most parents find that the "Terrible Two's" abate as speech skills increase.

The phrase "power of speech" is a telling one, for speech does confer powers of protection from pain and frustration, as well as social power, on the speaker. Competence in every sphere, including speech, improves a child's image of himself and improves his relationship with his parents.

The ability to speak improves other relationships as well. Watch any group of toddlers play, and you will be struck by the activity that centers around the child who chatters incessantly to others around him, even if he is only describing his own actions aloud. A nonverbal child is an isolated child. Talk attracts company and abets socialization, giving the verbal youngster a head start in practicing skills he'll need in nursery school and beyond.

In addition, language makes learning easier. Numerous experiments reveal that learning occurs more quickly when a child knows a name (even a nonsense name) for a shape or an object; finding differences in items and generalizing about similarities in shape are only two of many language-aided abilities.

Performance in school provides another incentive for early concentration on a toddler's verbal ability. The language arts are not individual entities but an interrelated whole. The child who speaks well is the child with the skill to become a good reader. Both speech defects and speech retardation have been related to inferior reading ability.

The Chatterbox

Remember how delighted you were when your toddler spoke his first word? If your toddler has reached the chatterbox stage, as many do at this time, the constant sound of his voice may at times fill you with feelings other than delight.

The constant repetition of words continues, for this is how toddlers commit to memory the many new words they hear. You'll be hearing more two- and three-word sentences now as your toddler begins to express his thoughts more completely. "Cookie all gone," "Roll truck," and "Honk horn" expand upon earlier communication of "cookie," "truck," and "horn," which forced you to decipher his complete thought.

Constant jabbering serves other purposes as well. Often such talk accompanies intense activity, as if the activity itself cannot exhaust all the energy the toddler generates during play. In addition, the compulsive talk provides a kind of printout of the mind's activity. Every thought is a verbalized thought. The toddler at this stage finds thinking to himself an impossibility, so the chattering continues even during solitary play. Some researchers believe that this kind of thinking aloud aids a child in organizing his thoughts and in solving problems. With greater maturity comes the ability to keep his thoughts to himself.

The natural curiosity of a two-year-old fuels the tendency to chatter. When your child wanted information before he was able to ask for answers, he ran every which way at once trying to learn about his environment. He was thinking with his feet because he lacked other means. Now he is thinking with his mouth. Your toddler wants information, and the brighter he is, the more questions he asks. Typically, questions of the "what" and "where" variety now test parental patience (and often find it wanting!). Bothersome as the barrage of questions may be at times, it indicates a growing understanding of the laws of cause and effect. A two-year-old will make an attempt to answer the same kinds of questions he asks, though the answers may not make much sense.

Along with "why" and "where" and "because" (or, more likely, "'cause"), toddler speech relies heavily on the child's name or the pronoun "me" coupled with his activity: "Todd run." "Me splash." Most children have not mastered the pronoun "I" yet, or they use it inconsistently at best. Because pronouns shift their frame of reference depending upon the speaker, mastery proves elusive. Misuse gives toddler speech much of its cockeyed charm, and there is little point in correcting mistakes, as the corrections often only confuse the child. Continue to use pronouns appropriately yourself and eventually your toddler will too.

If Your Child Isn't Talking Yet

Delayed speech may indicate hearing problems. Since toddlers may compensate for a hearing loss through superior development of sight or other senses, this deficiency may not be readily apparent. A hearing test can determine whether hearing loss is the cause of the speech problem. If your child does speak, but his speech is mainly monotone and lacks the inflection of normal conversation, you should also suspect hearing loss and have his hearing tested. An unimpaired sense of hearing is such a vital asset to a child that any sign of a problem should be promptly investigated.

Personality Development

The Good Side of Bad

"I don't know what's gotten into Lisa these days," says one mother. "She consistently does the opposite of what I want her to do."

These are the times that try parents' souls, especially those parents who can remember when they looked at the angelic newborn in their arms and vowed, "This baby will be different from other children. She won't ever talk back or misbehave." So much for the dreams of yesteryear. Eventually every parent confronts a disobedient child.

Despite the evidence that your child frequently strives to please you and that she values your approval, you've probably noticed the perverse joy she now takes in defying you as well. Remember when your year-old toddler delighted in tossing all her toys out of the play yard? Such behavior seemed defiant, since she continued to throw her toys long after you'd lost patience with her. However, revolt never entered her mind; she was merely practicing her manual skills as nature programmed her to do. In addition, she was too young to control her behavior and probably didn't understand your reprimands anyway.

The difference between your child's past behavior and her current mutiny is that now her actions are both intentional and meaningful. Your toddler is a year older, she understands what "no" means, yet she continues to defy you anyway. For many toddlers such defiant action peaks at this time. In addition to overt misbehavior and saying "no" themselves, some children protest parental authority more covertly—by deliberately slowing their pace when conforming to your demands.

Three motives explain the two-year-old's obstinate disobedience. As we've noted, such defiance actually represents a step toward autonomy and maturity, the exercise of control over decision-making (even if the decision only entails such monumental questions as whether to stop playing and take a bath). While this uncooperative behavior erodes your sanity and your patience, it does benefit the toddler's emotional growth. In order to practice being independent, she *needs* to defy you just as much as she needed to toss those toys out of her play yard a year ago. If she were always obedient and cooperative, she'd never learn to operate without your guidance.

Second, misbehavior sometimes functions as an attention-getting device. A child who longs for parental attention often prefers negative attention to none at all, and the toddler whose family now includes a new sibling may use this ploy to divert as much of the fuss as possible from the baby to herself. Misbehavior can deliver a message that a toddler's emotional needs aren't being met.

Third, your toddler uses this behavior to test you and the limits you set. She is like a scientist examining the laws of her universe to see whether they hold under a variety of circumstances. Do you *really* mean what you say? her misbehavior asks. Or can I get away with what I have in mind to do? And if you really meant that I couldn't run into the street yesterday, does that mean I have to remain on the sidewalk today as well? Walking takes practice, talking takes practice, and learning to obey simple rules takes lots of practice too, so you can expect this testing to continue until the scientist has concluded her experiment. *No skill, especially an emotional one, is learned overnight. All learning requires much repetition.*

When your toddler's behavior drives you crazy, some comfort exists in the knowledge that this type of behavior will diminish shortly unless the toddler has reason to retain it—if, for example, she isn't allowed sufficient emotional distance from her parents, if she is never allowed to make any decisions for herself, if her needs for positive attention are not met, or if discipline is so inconsistent that she cannot determine through her testing what rules she must follow.

The Parent as Magician: Changing Bad to Good

As the parent of a two-year-old, you face a continuous dilemma: how to discipline your toddler while simultaneously nurturing her emotional development. You don't want to quash your child's independence, but neither can you permit your child to run the household according to her whims.

The very word "discipline" makes parents quail and blanch, probably because few parents give thought to discipline until they actually need it. Then they're forced to make snap decisions under the pressure of the moment. Making disciplinary decisions in a pressure cooker seldom yields satisfactory results. If you want to be a good disciplinarian, you need to establish your disciplinary goals before you act.

First, consider what discipline means. Many parents define discipline as punishment, but this is not its primary meaning, and punishment should constitute a very small aspect of discipline. Discipline really means instruction. One dictionary definition reads: "training that develops self-control, character, orderliness, and efficiency." It doesn't even mention punishment until several definitions later. Every child needs such discipline because it protects her from possible harm resulting from her own impulsive behavior. It also smooths a child's relationships with adults and children, thereby making her life more pleasant and rewarding.

By developing a close, loving relationship with your child and by giving her the attention she needs, you have already begun to discipline. Her admiration and affection for you encourage her to cooperate with your wishes. Her desire for your continued love, esteem, and attention provides the strongest motive for obeying you.

Once you think in terms of discipline as education, you can begin to plan the best ways of teaching your child the rules of civilized behavior. The goal, of course, is the internalization of those rules so that your child's conscience replaces you as her guide.

If you wanted to teach your child to say "please," think about how you would begin the lesson. Probably you'd use the word frequently yourself because you've already noticed how important repetition is to learning and because you also have seen the value of your example to your child.

Once she'd actually used the word in the correct context, you'd reward her with a smile or a kiss and a comment about how wonderfully polite and smart she is. You'd continue these rewards until you were certain that "please" was firmly entrenched in your child's social vocabulary. If your toddler suddenly substituted "Gimme that!" for "please," you'd remind her of the correct way to ask for something. Your response would probably be, "We don't talk to people so rudely; we say please."

These same three rules apply to disciplining a child:

modeling and repetition of the appropriate behavior, reward for demonstrating it, and reminder and substitution of the proper behavior when the lesson goes awry. Too many parents neglect these techniques. For example, do you remember to praise your child when she manages to share a toy? Or do you take generosity for granted and only reprimand her when she is selfish? If so, you may be reinforcing the selfishness, since only that behavior elicits your attention. The same lesson applies if you respond only to her no's and never comment when she does cooperate.

A parent who considers the word discipline to be synonymous with "praise" generally raises a far more cooperative child than the one who thinks discipline equals punishment. If you remember to compliment the positive far more than you punish the negative, you're on your way to becoming a good disciplinarian.

Must You Be Consistent?

Formerly child guidance experts rated consistency right after godliness and cleanliness in the hierarchy of child care. Then the rules relaxed a bit, probably as a result of parents who found consistency a difficult goal to meet. Circumstances may change from day to day, and so do parents' moods. Behavior you accept with equanimity one day can make you furious on another occasion when everything else has gone wrong in the moments preceding the offense. How important is a consistent response?

Perhaps more than any other age group, the toddler needs consistent responses from her parents. The world is still a pretty bewildering place to her, and consistent reactions diminish some of the confusion she confronts daily. A slightly older child, who has learned some of the important patterns of her universe, can handle inconsistencies better than the two-year-old.

The fastest way to get a two-year-old to follow the rules you set is to reward her when she follows them and to react consistently when she breaks them. If you decide that a meal ends the minute a plate gets dumped on the floor, and you always remove your child from the table the minute her plate lands, your toddler soon learns that she'd better not fool around with her dinner if she expects to continue eating.

Your consistency in this situation demonstrates very clearly that you won't tolerate such behavior. Then your young scientist needn't continue to experiment by throwing her plate onto the floor because she knows *without a doubt* what to expect as a response to her action. Obviously, "without a doubt" provides the key, for if you sometimes laugh at her behavior, other times ignore it, and still other times punish her for it, the consequence of her behavior is in reasonable doubt, and she will continue to test for a predictable response.

The promptness of your response is also important. If you delay ending the meal while you reason with your child about the inappropriateness of throwing her food on the floor, you have weakened the impact of the message you send. If you want to offer your reasons ("Throwing food shows bad manners. It also wastes money and makes a mess to clean up.") while you remove the child from the table, go ahead and do so. However, do not separate the consequences of the action from the action itself if you want the lesson to be learned as quickly as possible. (After you've demonstrated the consequences of such behavior by removing the food, always offer a better alternative for the future: "The next time you don't want to eat anymore, say 'I'm full, Mommy.'")

Can You Be Too Consistent?

It is possible to follow the rules too well and become too consistent. If you have a rule for every situation and a consequence for every infraction, you'll wind up either with an automaton who obeys all your rules blindly or a rebellious toddler who follows none of them. And even the automaton is likely to rebel against so many rules eventually. You don't want to turn your home into a military academy.

The best way to achieve a delicate balance between too many rules and too few is to consider what lessons have prime importance to your family and be consistent in enforcing those. Planning ahead keeps you from being too authoritarian, as well as from being too permissive.

What lessons will your discipline stress? Perhaps treating others with care and concern and learning to eat like a person, rather than an animal, will be two lessons you'll emphasize. Deciding what values you'll stress means you won't drive yourself and your child crazy by trying to teach her all the finer points of behavior in one confusing jumble. You'll be saving your energy for instilling lessons that truly matter.

Some Ineffective Disciplinary Techniques

The technique of reasoning with a two-year-old, if it remains your only reply to a dinner that lands on the floor, makes a poor response to misbehavior from a toddler, though it works very well with older children. Most toddlers haven't yet reached the age of reason where behavior is concerned. Because toddler thought is so egocentric at this point, a toddler's main concern is how an event affects her. "Don't dump your meal because you won't get any more" impresses your lesson upon a two-year-old with far more lasting impact than "Don't dump your meal because wasting food is wrong."

Try to avoid spewing out a stream of words when you're angry. Too much talk, especially combined with a loud voice and an angry expression, overwhelms a toddler and drowns your message in a sea of words. You may *feel* better for having given an impromptu lecture, but your child will have absorbed little, if any, of your message. Parents should follow the example of advertisers, who long ago found that short, pointed slogans are learned fast and recalled easily. Try to be specific in your criticism. "Bad girl!" doesn't explain what you find objectionable; "Don't grab; ask nicely!" does.

Does the phrase "I've told you a hundred times not to do that!" sound familiar? There's little point in repeating it. You probably *have* restated the lesson a hundred times or more, but that's how toddlers learn. Expect to repeat yourself quite a few more times till the message sinks in. You'll feel better if you remind yourself that no toddler ever internalized a rule the first, second, or even the tenth time she heard it.

Neither threats nor bribes work well as disciplinary techniques. Do you find yourself threatening, "Do that again and you won't be able to sit for a week!" only to witness your toddler repeating the very act you prohibited? Threats seem to challenge a toddler to learn if the punishment you promise is certain, so making a threat almost guarantees misbehavior. Bribing your toddler to cooperate ("If you leave the playground without a fuss, you can have a cupcake.") may achieve your objective initially, but you are teaching your toddler how to blackmail you. Eventually she'll up the stakes, and you'll have to promise to buy her a Rolls-Royce just to get her to leave the swings and come home to dinner.

Hitting a child to discipline her also makes little sense if you remember discipline's original goal: developing self-control and character. You cannot beat self-control and character into a child, but you can make her want to develop these traits through the emotional rewards she receives for doing so. And having seen how quick your child is to emulate your behavior, would you want her to emulate hitting? If instructing your toddler in appropriate ways of interacting with others is one of your disciplinary goals, spankings defeat that purpose by teaching just the opposite—inappropriate aggression.

Finally, spankings prove ineffective because they omit the crucial third step in discipline: replacing the inappropriate behavior with an appropriate one. A spanking tells a child she is doing something wrong but doesn't offer guidance for improving the behavior. Even if you offer a suggestion for improved behavior immediately after the spanking, your child's attention is riveted on her injured ego and not on your lesson.

At some point all parents eventually lose their temper and spank. Only a saint completely avoids the spontaneous spanking when words and patience fail. But no good disciplinarian includes much spanking as part of a preconceived disciplinary plan, for it teaches bad behavior well and good behavior poorly.

Among the few times when spanking is justified as an instructional device occurs in situations where the possible consequences of a child's action are life-threatening, and she cannot comprehend the threat. Telling a child not to run into the street again because a car will hit her fails to strike fear into a toddler's heart. She simply doesn't understand the danger. The same is true when she tries to stick objects into an electric socket. Merely removing her from the source of the danger and reprimanding her probably won't get your lesson across. In these types of situations spanking will probably be the most effective teacher.

Should You Ignore Bad Behavior?

Ignoring bad behavior fails as good discipline because, like spankings, it doesn't offer an appropriate substitute. It also may mislead a child into believing that you condone her actions.

However, a low-key response to misbehavior, when it initially occurs, can keep poor behavior from escalating. For example, Tara pulled another toddler's hair in order to gain possession of the other child's doll. Since she got the toy she was after, she will be tempted to use this strategy again. If her mother ignores the behavior, Tara has little reason to change. If her mother spanks her, Tara has lost the doll, but she has managed to get her mother's undivided attention, and she has been treated to a front-row seat to view adult aggression. However, if her mother says quietly, "This is how we ask to use someone else's toys," and then demonstrates, Tara has learned to substitute an appropriate response for an inappropriate one.

You'll have an uncomfortably long wait if you expect your toddler to create an alternative response when her first impulse is blocked. Instead, most will cry and attempt to continue to use the strategy that failed the first time *unless the parent demonstrates a better way.*

Totally ignoring bad behavior can also encourage the child to escalate the misbehavior, especially if she used the action as an attention-getting device. The dinner plate that's flung to the floor is often followed by the cup, the spoon, and any other handy item if the parent ignores the first throw. This is another of those test situations. The behavior says: If you ignore the plate, how many things must I drop before I get a response from you?

Effective Disciplinary Techniques

Ask yourself two important questions before you attempt to teach a lesson: Is my child old enough to understand this lesson? Can she comply at this moment? If the answer to either is "no," then the lesson will frustrate both of you. When the answer to either question is negative, restructure the situation rather than the child. If, for example, Erin is throwing sand in the playground because she's so tired that she's out of control, you would do better to take her home immediately than to instruct her in sandbox etiquette. At that moment she can fulfill only one of the two requirements; she's old enough to understand the command, but she cannot obey it due to fatigue. Save the lesson for a more appropriate time.

Be generous with your praise, but do not use praise to manipulate your child. Praise that's earned is cherished. If you indiscriminately praise everything your toddler does, you've devalued your currency.

Learn to praise specific, rather than general, behavior. "Good girl!" is nearly as ineffective as "Bad girl!" Instead, comment, "I liked the way you shared your pail with Betsy." Such compliments develop pride and self-esteem. Use them wisely, and you show your child how very much she has to like about herself.

Beware of what you say about your toddler when she's within earshot. If you discipline your daughter for throwing sand but later proceed to tell your spouse about how assertive your child is, you can bet that the sandbox psychology has been wasted. After all, she'd heard you compliment her actions, and she knows where your true feelings lie. The old saw about little pitchers having big ears is especially true of discipline. If you don't want your child to continue throwing sand, fighting, screeching, or whatever, don't ever brag about misbehavior when she's listening. Otherwise, be prepared for the misbehavior to continue. Keep in mind that what's cute at two can be obnoxious at four, so think before you speak.

The more out of control your child acts, the more controlled you should be. One way to stay in control of your own anger when your toddler won't behave is to ask yourself: What do I want my child to learn from this incident? What's the best way to teach that lesson?

Toddler, What Big Teeth You Have! Handling a Biter

Biting constitutes an immature response to frustration and anger. Its frequency is probably related not only to an aggressive temperament and an inability to tolerate frustration, but also to the lack of sufficient verbal skills and maturation to substitute speech for physical violence. As verbal skills mature, they provide an escape valve for temper so that biting becomes unnecessary.

Some toddlers rarely, if ever, bite, while others seem distinctly carnivorous. Many parents find that biting occurs when a toddler is overwhelmed by a situation. Too many people, too much confusion, too much noise, unfamiliar surroundings, fatigue, etc., may help trigger an episode of biting.

Whenever your child demonstrates such sharklike behavior, immediately remove her from the situation to give her a chance to calm down. You may have to hold her mouth closed to keep her from biting you until you can get her off to a quiet place. Isolation usually works well to quiet a child who has lost control of her emotions.

After you've separated her from the crowd, you can discipline her. "Don't bite; biting hurts" might be your opening. Then suggest a more acceptable alternative: "Use your words; say 'I am mad. I want the shovel.'" Always show her how to translate anger into words so that she can eventually learn to substitute language for aggression without your help.

Do not expect to eradicate this response immediately. As always, learning more mature behavior takes time; teaching it requires patience. Some misguided parents attempt to discourage a biter by bitting her back. By imitating such behavior, you serve as a very poor role model of self-control, and you fail to provide the important alternate response which will allow her to outgrow such babyish behavior.

Daily Routines

The Tyranny of Routines

Daily routines grease the household wheels and make family life run more smoothly. They free our minds to concentrate on a myriad of other important matters. But routines can become more confining than liberating in the hands of a toddler, for, as usual, the toddler carries a good idea to extremes. Food must be placed a certain way on his plate and eaten in a particular order. He doesn't like the washing machine to separate him from his favorite outfit. He demands the same bedtime stories *ad nauseam* despite your efforts to introduce some new tales. Omit a single "and" or "the" at your own risk.

Sound logic motivates this seemingly bizarre behavior. Routines create order in what the toddler sees as a chaotic, sometimes threatening, world. The more predictable and enduring the routine, the more secure a toddler feels. Even adults find security in predictability. In order to maintain the comfort of the familiar, some live in the same space all their lives or never risk changing jobs. Adhering to a routine diminishes the anxiety produced by confronting the unknown and allows the individual to relax his guard against the possibility of sudden disaster.

Children lack many of the defenses available to adults for support in new situations, so they are less prepared than grown-ups to tolerate flux. First, adults have the benefit of experience. We know that new situations don't necessarily produce discomfort; they can be pleasant, exciting, or instructive. This knowledge reduces anxiety. Just as your child learned from experience that a loud vacuum cleaner or a running faucet wouldn't harm him, he will eventually learn that the unexpected needn't be alarming. However, accumulating the experience that tempers fear of the unknown takes time.

Second, adults understand the laws of cause and effect, so we can accurately estimate the outcome of many unfamiliar situations. We can determine when our safety is truly threatened and when our fears are groundless. Toddlers are just beginning to understand "why" and "because." The enormous increase in questions beginning with "why" during this period indicates how reassuring can be the kind of knowledge we adults take for granted. Lacking such interpretive power, toddlers find all change in routines alarming, even enjoyable ones like outings to the circus or birthday parties. While watching a wild animal act in a circus, for example, two-year-old Todd shrieked to be taken home when the trainer lit a fiery hoop for the animals to jump through. No amount of reassurance could convince him that neither he nor the trained tigers were in danger.

Finally and most important, adults have power to affect their surroundings. They can choose to stay or go; they can control the pace of events, and they can ask questions and act upon the answers they receive. Toddlers recognize the vulnerability inherent in their powerlessness. They cannot outfight or outthink a larger foe; their protests are often ignored or overruled. They are hurried into situations though they would prefer to observe at a distance at first rather than participate. By creating order out of chaos, routines offer toddlers an illusion of control where, in fact, none exists.

Routines act as a kind of invisible security blanket, which your toddler will eventually discard when he no longer requires the kind of comfort they bring. The parent who acknowledges this need raises a more secure child.

Eating

Hamburgers Every Night?

Amy had hamburgers last night, the night before, the night before *that*, and she'll probably want them tonight too. Many toddlers go through a similar stage. Some will demand the same food at only one meal a day; others want the same breakfast, lunch, and dinner until their parents blanch at the sight of yet another hamburger or peanut butter and jelly sandwich. Such eating jags demonstrate again the ridiculous extremes of toddler routines.

Examining the reasons for this compulsive behavior should convince you of the wisdom of humoring your child in this area. For many children fickleness in food preferences simply indicates the presence of a mind that doesn't know itself well yet. Amy dotes on hamburgers for several weeks but may suddenly decide that she hates them. Then she'll find a new preference for a few weeks until she tires of that.

While you and I might sample a food to determine our opinion, a toddler often adheres to an "all or nothing at all" philosophy. As usual, the toddler must test the extremes before he can settle down to a reasonable compromise— hamburgers once a week or so. Extremes in food preferences are symptomatic of a galloping case of immaturity, which time undoubtedly will cure.

Some toddlers will refuse a dish when they feel overwhelmed by the large quantity set before them or when a previous bad experience makes them cautious—once burned, twice shy. Some suddenly will eat only foods which require chewing, while others accept only strained or mashed items for a while. These also are immature reactions that a toddler will overcome if no well-meaning adult intrudes on the situation to force the child to eat what he doesn't want.

Sometimes, however, demand for a particular food has little to do with nutrition and everything to do with psychology. It may indicate a desire for attention or another skirmish in the ongoing war for independence. By forcing your child to eat what he doesn't want in either of these situations, you will win the battle but lose the war. You don't want to focus upon negative behavior unnecessarily, which is just the effect of allowing mealtime menus to become attention-getting situations. If it's independence your child desires, you can afford to fulfill his wish at the table. An argument makes sense only when the item consumed is harmful. What you want to avoid is having food become a weapon used by either parent or child to control the other.

The Sneaky Parents' Guide to Fooling Picky Eaters

If your child's food jags worry you, you have several methods to guarantee that, despite his strange menus, he is getting the nutrition he needs. If you put a variety of foods on his plate, he may try them if he thinks doing so is his idea, not yours. That means serving a minismorgasbord and resisting the temptation to urge him to sample the feast. The minute you comment to a fussy eater that the broccoli smells delicious or that cauliflower is Daddy's favorite dessert, your strategy becomes apparent. You must pretend disinterest in the whole situation.

Most parents find that telling a child not to do something often results in his doing it, which is why reverse psychology works so well on the picky eater. Use his negative tendencies to accomplish your goal. Put a little of whatever food he resists on his plate and mention casually that he probably shouldn't eat it, since most people consider that food suitable only for grown-ups. Chances are that he'll at least taste it, if not devour the entire portion.

Allowing your toddler to set up his own plate and serve some of the food himself, deciding how much to ladle out and where to place it can also help. By doing so, you've given him the illusion of independent choice, so he may not be as ornery about consuming what he's put on his plate.

It is impossible to name one food that is the single available source of any vitamin or mineral. Substitutes are available in every food category. If you'd rather fight than switch, you're wasting time, energy, and probably a good many portions of broccoli as well.

Even if your child has rejected every vegetable known to man, you can probably still work them into his meals by grinding them in a food processor and adding them to the chopped meat for hamburgers or to scrambled eggs or any other food in a disguised form.

Tooth Care

Visiting the Dentist

Sometime between twenty-four and thirty months, the four second molars usually appear, completing the set of the twenty primary teeth. The time may have arrived for your toddler to pay his first visit to the dentist.

Most dentists recommend that a child have his first checkup between the ages of two and three and receive dental examinations twice yearly. You will be the best judge of when your child can handle a trip to the dentist's office most successfully. A negative two-year-old isn't an ideal patient, so if your child is ornery, you may want to wait a bit before scheduling an appointment.

The advantages to scheduling the initial visit closer to age two than to age three if your child is cooperative are early diagnosis of any dental problem and the chance to introduce your child to his dentist before an emergency forces the issue. Meeting a dentist for the first time when the child is injured or in pain from a toothache gets the relationship between patient and dentist off to a very poor start.

Many parents simply have their own dentist treat their toddler. If your family dentist strikes you as an individual with the patience, ability, and gentle, low-key manner to handle a young child well in the dentist chair, then there is no need to look further.

However, if you feel your family dentist and your child do not make a good match or if you have recently moved to a new community and need to locate a new dentist, you may want to explore the idea of using a dentist who specializes in the care and treatment of children's teeth, a pedodontist. There are several advantages to making this choice. A pedodontist, like a pediatrician, chooses his specialty because he likes children. He expects to spend time helping his nervous, young patients relax and is trained in techniques to help them do so. He is not unnerved or annoyed by crying or by a patient who needs to hold his parent's hand. Because he constantly treats children, he is likely to be more adept at handling the kinds of problems most common to young children's teeth.

You should make an appointment for a consultation with the pedodontist before you bring your child for an examination. You will want to assure yourself in advance that you feel confident in his abilities, even if the pedodontist has been recommended by your pediatrician or a close friend.

The consultation is a good time to ask questions about the kinds of treatment he most commonly performs and the fees charged for those procedures. Look for an emphasis on preventive dentistry, catching problems before they begin in order to eliminate future decay, pain, and more complicated and expensive dental procedures. Ask about emergency treatment; can the pedodontist be reached during nonoffice hours, or will you be expected to use a hospital emergency room? How does he handle reluctant patients? Does he allow parents to remain in the examining room, or does he prefer to work with the patient alone? Is he tactful but truthful about the discomfort a procedure might cause? A dentist who tells a child that "this won't hurt" when it obviously does hurt damages the credibility of all medical personnel in a child's eyes.

Many parents are reluctant to ask for a pre-exam consultation. They worry that they will be wasting the dentist's time or that they haven't the courage to ask for information about fees or lack the knowledge to ask intelligent questions about types of treatment. However, the consultation is an opportunity for you to act as your child's advocate and insure that he gets the best care possible. It is an opportunity you shouldn't miss. In addition, it gives you a chance to learn about the dentist's philosophy and office routine and to see if they are agreeable to you.

Whether you decide to use your family dentist or a pedodontist, be sure to schedule your child's checkup for the time of day when he is at his best. Many toddlers are most congenial early in the morning after breakfast; a late-afternoon appointment often taxes the patience and graciousness of a tired, hungry child.

Prepare your toddler for the visit by announcing it a day or so in advance. Try not to make it sound momentous. The best technique is simply to explain that the dentist helps people keep their teeth healthy. Do not go into extensive detail about the possible treatment or the dental equipment, since you don't want to overwhelm your toddler with too much information or alarm him in advance. Your library is a good source for books that explain a trip to the dentist, and the illustrations help make the experience less mysterious. Also, dentists who specialize in the care of children's teeth usually distribute booklets or coloring books that acquaint a young child with dental checkups.

Sleeping

"And the Gobble-uns' at gits you ef you Don't Watch Out"

Until now exclusion from evening activities caused your toddler's distaste for bedtime. Now bedtime upsets him for different reasons: Many toddlers develop a fear of the dark and experience nightmares.

Some parents find that their toddlers slept better as infants than they do as two-year-olds. One study of restlessness in youngsters twenty-one months to fourteen years found that such habits as waking caused by minimal noise was common in the younger children in the study and occurred more frequently among boys than among girls. The problem diminished at age three. The occurrence of nightmares, however, continued to increase at age three and beyond. Since nightmares at any age seem related to anxiety and tension, toddlers' bad dreams are understandable as children leave babyhood behind and attempt to meet the challenges of their new maturity.

The increase in fears which require an active imagination (such as fear of the dark or of wild animals or monsters) indicates maturation. Though the toddler is a champ at imagining the possible dangers lurking in the darkness—ghosts or robbers, for example—he lacks sufficient creativity to calm himself by conjuring up effective, protective responses to these threats. Inability to distinguish between the real and the fanciful compounds the problem.

Daytime diversions distract a toddler from many fears. After all, the sunlit world bursts with wonders to discover and explore. Nighttime conceals the diversions and magnifies frightening shadows and sounds.

In addition, during the daytime the toddler controls his periods of separation from his parent. If playing in another room frightens him, he can touch base with a parent for reassurance. Confined to his crib at night and forbidden to make forays in search of congenial company, he is deprived of the comfort such control offers.

You can help your child overcome his fear of the dark in several ways. Avoid ridicule, which never cures fear but merely forces it into hiding. Ridicule deprives your child of the comfort of confiding in you. A feeling of security depends upon his belief that you will protect him. If you laugh, he cannot count on you as an ally. Never threaten a child who is afraid of the dark with its use as a punishment for misbehavior. Doing so violates your child's trust in you as much as ridicule does.

Be vigilant in monitoring a fearful child's television viewing and choice of picture books with frightening illustrations, especially near bedtime. An active imagination needs no outside assistance to invent things that go bump in the night. And keep in mind that cartoons can spark fears as easily as more realistic TV fare in a child who cannot yet differentiate between fantasy and reality.

Because favorite toys and bedtime routines often serve as a toddler's talismans, humor his need for them. This is not a good time to attempt to eliminate any part of the bath-stories-lullabies-drink-of-water scenario. Recognize and accept that physical thirst has little, if anything, to do with the universal toddler request for water.

Adults reduce their own fears by controlling some of the surrounding circumstances. When we install smoke detectors in our homes, we worry less about our safety. Burglar alarms minimize our fear of robbery. You can help your child conquer his fear by giving him some control over the situation. Let him regulate the lamp and/or nightlight. Very fearful children often request that the overhead light burn all night, and there really is no good reason to prohibit this. You may want to change the light switch in your child's room to a dimmer and allow him to establish the light level he prefers.

Teach your child to sing one simple lullaby repeatedly to himself, and he possesses the toddler equivalent of whistling down the dark and counting sheep all in a single song. Or try dressing him in superhero pajamas to overcome his feelings of vulnerability.

You might also pay close attention to the words of comfort he gives his toys when bedding them down for the night, since he is likely to transfer the fears to his possessions. If he promises his stuffed dog that no monsters will appear, you have an opportunity to ask what these monsters might look like, what they want, and so on. Putting fears into words can help banish them and can show you what kinds of reassurance will help your child.

Check the library for books with plots about kids who feared the dark and overcame their fear. Or, better yet, tell your child an original story about a child like him who discovered several solutions to the problem of bedtime gremlins. It may become his favorite bedtime tale.

Midnight Visitor

"Getting Erica to bed is no problem at all; I do it hundreds of times a night!" says one mother. If your problem lies in getting your child to stay in his own bed throughout the night, you're not alone. One study involving over four hundred families with children ages two to ten reported that 82 percent of these parents allowed a frightened or sick child into their bed. The children were returned to their own beds once they quieted down or fell asleep.

Talking about the problem with any group of parents reveals, however, that a child who is returned to his own bed doesn't necessarily remain there until dawn. Many toddlers find the comfort of their parents' bed so appealing that they return for more snuggling. How should you handle a persistent midnight visitor?

Many parents, desperate for an uninterrupted eight hours of sleep, simply roll over and make room for the child. "Most evenings I'm just too tired to get up and put Alex back in his own bed," says one mother. These parents often admit that capitulation doesn't provide a real night's rest. "Toddlers have a way of commandeering huge amounts of mattress and blanket far out of proportion to their small size," notes an exhausted father. Restless sleepers, kids who can only sleep crosswise, those who bring an entire menagerie of stuffed animals along with them, make for tired, stiff-backed parents in the morning.

Parents whose children share their bed every night might want to examine their own motives in permitting this practice, since exhaustion may not be the only factor which prompts it. In some cases encouraging a child to remain in bed with a parent prolongs the child's babyhood. The child's independence is stifled so that his parent's unfulfilled need to nurture or to remain in control can be satisfied. A child in his parents' bed may also be used to camouflage problems in the marriage. His presence may provide an excuse for his parents to avoid sex. In both of these situations the family bed serves needs other than overcoming the child's fear of the dark.

While the occasional visit can be tolerated, a family bed as a nightly habit benefits neither parent nor child. Since there is no easy way to break the habit once begun, the best way to handle a nightly visitor is to continue to put the child back into his own bed *immediately* and to comfort him there. Use the strategies suggested previously to give your child some control over the situation.

You may have to grit your teeth and do with interrupted sleep for a few weeks until your toddler learns to handle this fear with less help from you. You may need to go to sleep earlier yourself while this situation persists so that you'll have the strength to keep returning your child to his own bed. But a few sleepless nights now make for restful nights in the future and help your child gain emotional maturity.

Night Terrors

Night terrors differ from nightmares in that they seem to occur before the child falls soundly asleep, and he appears to be in some sort of trance while having one. He may kick and continue to flail about long after you've picked him up to comfort him. In fact, he hardly seems to be aware of your presence, though he may indicate that he sees objects or people in the room which aren't there.

Often children in the throes of a night terror scream themselves out even while being held and then fall asleep again without ever having fully wakened. (When having a nightmare, however, the child will wake, will appreciate your presence, and will have some idea of what his dream was.) Night terrors often leave no recollection in the morning.

Many children experience night terrors, and you need not be concerned over an occasional one. However, if they occur repeatedly, you should have your child examined by your doctor. One mother whose son experienced night terrors over a period of weeks found that a bedtime snack of milk and cookies eliminated his problem.

Bathing and Dressing

When Bathtime Ends

By this time you may find that the only way to separate your toddler from his beloved bath is literally to pry him loose. Toddlers rarely leave any enjoyable activity willingly, so you'll need some ploys to end bathtime on a happy note.

You will make this chore easier for yourself if you establish a routine of washing your child first and permitting play only after washing is completed. If you allow play first, he won't want to put his toys away when it's time to wash. Keeping the tub clear of toys until the sudsing is

finished usually guarantees a cooperative child when you need one.

Announcing the end of tub playtime with an impartial signal, such as a kitchen timer, can make the bath routine proceed smoothly. Another good technique is switching off the lights to signal the bath's end; they go back on once your child is out of the tub. Many toddlers object to the change in the lighting level and leave the bath willingly in order to have the lights back. This is not a good technique if turning off the light plunges your bathroom into darkness; you just want to dislodge your toddler, not terrify him. In this situation try rapidly flicking the light off and on two or three times.

These kinds of signals help sidetrack protests. They usually generate less antagonism than an announcement from you that bathtime is over, since many toddlers never think to argue with an inanimate timer the way they would with a parent. Using these devices daily will accustom your child to a bath routine that he will eventually accept as inevitable.

When protests do occur, you will be wise not to spoil an established routine by allowing an extra five minutes in the tub. The principle is the same as the technique for leaving the playground or for teaching any household rule. If your behavior suggests that negotiation is possible, you'll be fighting the battle of the bath every single night when your patience and energy are already exhausted. So don't end the bath until you're absolutely certain it's over; when you do sound the signal, don't vacillate.

You can make the end of the bath more palatable by incorporating some attractive features into the after-bath routine. Reserve some especially popular toy for postbath minutes, and your toddler won't object to leaving the tub. The toy you select should be one that isn't available for everyday use if it's going to retain its novelty. This might be a good time for enjoying the photo album you've made him.

Make postbath time pleasant by scheduling low-key playtime with the parent who has been absent all day. (However, avoid roughhousing at this hour if you want your child to

settle down quietly when playtime ends.) Having this parent
read to the toddler ends the day on a loving note, and the
child who knows he'll be allowed to select two books for
bedtime stories abandons the bath more willingly than the
one who's expected to go straight to bed.

Some diehards will continue to resist all blandishments,
no matter how attractive you make the rewards for cooperation or how pleasant the postbath period. In this situation
you'll have to assert your authority and forcibly remove
your child from the tub despite his resistance. Reasoning
with him is a waste of time, for he doesn't much care if his
skin shrivels or if everyone else is going to sleep or for
anything but his own enjoyment. Simply lift him out, pull
the plug, and try to distract him from his anger.

If your toddler finds the bath energizing, rather than
enervating, do not expect him to settle down quickly. Instead
of fighting his energy level, try scheduling his bath a little
earlier. Reduce the amount of time spent in the water and
allow more playtime after the bath in which to wind down.
This should eliminate postbath hassles.

Safety Note

Though your child is older and steadier in the bath than
he was previously, he should still not be left alone in the
tub. Many toddlers manage to move quite actively even in
the confines of the tub. They risk a fall on a very hard
surface if you aren't there to supervise. If your child slips,
he may have difficulty righting himself or he may panic if
his face goes under water. In addition to the drowning hazard, the possibility of flooding is a real one, since many
toddlers will use a bath to dump or squirt water onto the
floor if no adult prevents their doing so.

Outerwear for the Independent Toddler

A wise choice of outerwear and some tried-and-true nursery school techniques can make your toddler more independent as he approaches thirty months. Tell your toddler
that you're going to show him how the "big kids" in nursery

school put on their coats and you'll have an attentive audience. Place his jacket *face up* on the floor in front of him and open it wide. Then have him stand behind the hood or collar. He must bend down and thrust his arms into the sleeves. With his arms deep in the sleeves he raises both arms upright at the same time, and the coat slides over his head and into position. If he lays his coat out this way on the floor before he begins and then stands behind it, getting the jacket on backward or putting the left sleeve on the right arm becomes impossible. This technique works equally well with shirts, blouses, and cardigan sweaters.

Like any other skill, manipulating the jacket will require some practice until it slides on easily. Your toddler will repeat the procedure dozens of times until he can manage it easily and will crow with delight once he masters this technique. You should not be surprised to see him buttonhole any interested visitor into watching and applauding his accomplishment. (Once he has mastered this skill well enough to avoid any confusion, you can then show him how to lay out polo shirts and crewneck sweaters *face down* and slip them over his head. Mastery of this skill is probably several months down the road, though you can position the polos for him to slide into.)

If you can buy your toddler a jacket with toggle-button and loop closings, he'll be able to button himself up as well as put the jacket on—no small achievement, that! Raincoats with toggle or large buckle closures can be operated by toddlers, but you may have to search for this type, as many sport snap closures which may require more strength or coordination than a toddler of this age possesses. An excellent alternative which a toddler can manage alone is a rain poncho.

If a hat and gloves are necessary in your climate, buy a hat that can be pulled down without needing the brim turned up. Such niceties as positioning the brim to avoid impairing vision are beyond the manipulative powers of your toddler. If you can't locate a knitted hat without a brim, try stitching the brim permanently in place with heavy gauge nylon thread or fishing line. The sewing should be secure because toddlers know only one way of getting a hat on firmly—by yanking. Your toddler will be motivated to use his mittens if they are decorated with faces like hand puppets or if they are the kind that change color and reveal hidden designs when exposed to the cold. Mittens are preferable to gloves because a toddler can manage to put them on independently.

One style of sneaker or play shoe that aids independent dressing closes with wide straps that have Velcro fasteners. Put a tiny dot of nail polish or piece of colored tape on the arch or big toe of each sneaker and instruct your child to position the pair of shoes so that the two dots lie next to each other. This trick insures that he will always put his shoes on the correct feet.

The best cold-weather footwear or galoshes are boots that have the shoes built in; these make winter or wet-weather dressing less onerous. One good boot style to look for has small rubber handgrips or handles rising from the top of the boot on the inside and outside of each calf; these enable a toddler to grasp the boot firmly and pull it on. Remember to mark the boots with polish as you did the sneakers so that they wind up on the correct feet.

Playtime

Toys for Twos

Adult activities fascinate a two-year-old, and there is nothing he likes better than to be able to mimic them. Toys that contribute to his ability to do so become favorites now. A toy lawnmower and gardening set, tot-size kitchen equipment such as a stove and sink, plastic toy dishes and picnic basket are items a two-year-old uses with enthusiasm. Play-scapes which allow your child to manipulate an entire environment, such as a farm, zoo, airport, or garage, also prove popular. If you are able to visit a real-life counterpart of one of these playscapes, take the time to identify for your toddler the many different activities occurring around him. He will transfer the information he absorbs into his play.

One play set you can create inexpensively at home is a small supermarket. Use a large carton for a counter and another as a shelf to hold the items for sale. Empty boxes and containers which have been cleaned and checked for rough or sharp edges can serve as your child's inventory. A small wagon makes a good shopping cart (or simply tie a short length of cord to another carton), and a toy cash register completes the set. You and your child can take turns at being storekeeper and customer; once he learns how to handle these roles, he'll introduce his playmates to them.

Similarly, a child-size table and chairs and a toy tea set

provide the basis for a playroom tea party. The addition of some old adult clothing, such as a hat and pocketbook, enhances the pleasure of pretend.

Toy vehicles—a bus, truck, fire engine, train—are also good choices for a two-year-old, who will use them more and more for imaginative play. As with all toys, be sure to check the age guidelines on the package and choose only those toy vehicles made for this age. As for your child's own means of transportation, he may now have the coordination to use a riding toy with pedals.

Art materials—crayons, finger paints, poster paints, clay—can be used in supervised surroundings. For a child of this age, choose jumbo crayons and be sure that all art materials are nontoxic. Buying the largest, sturdiest easel you can find is a good investment, for your child will use it right into elementary school. Look for one with a deep tray to hold supplies; a shelf type allows crayons and brushes to roll onto the floor. Some easels come equipped with a blackboard on one side, which is helpful. If the easel you select lacks this feature, consider mounting a blackboard on the wall of your child's room. Again, buy the largest size you can because toddlers need lots of space for wide arm movement.

Is This the Time for Play Group?

When a toddler reaches thirty months of age, many parents consider the advantages of enrolling their child in a play group or a nursery school program. The combination of increased linguistic ability, successful toilet teaching, and blossoming sociability makes some toddlers good candidates for organized group play. Others may need a bit more time before being thrust into this kind of activity.

To determine whether your child would benefit from a play group, know his temperament and observe his behavior in situations with other children. If he is exceptionally fearful, if he still needs you within sight every minute, if his vocabulary or physical coordination appears markedly less mature than the majority of children his age, you might consider delaying anywhere from just a few months to an entire year before enrolling him in a formal school setting.

However, participation in a small group that rotates sessions among its few members' homes might serve the shy or immature child's needs very nicely. Such children can also gain confidence from play-group interaction with children younger than themselves.

Any major changes in your family life or routine also indicate that you probably should postpone play group or nursery school enrollment until life settles back to normal. These changes include such events as the addition of a new baby to your family, divorce, or a parent's return to work outside the home. Coping with one major event at a time offers all the challenge any toddler needs. It is easy for a toddler to misunderstand your motives in sending him away from home at such an emotional time. During such events your toddler needs *more* of your time and reassurance, not less.

As long as your toddler has opportunities to play with other children in his home and theirs or in a playground setting, do not feel pressured to enroll your child in an organized group or class at this time. There is no shame in a child's lack of readiness for this milestone, and if you want your toddler's first school experience to be successful, you will need to match the timing of his enrollment to his ability to separate from you and to participate in a group. Your toddler is still quite young, and while play group at this time is an enjoyable activity, it isn't essential if other social contacts are maintained.

Parents sometimes feel that they might deprive their children of future academic achievement by postponing play group or nursery school. This simply isn't true; in fact, the kind of learning that occurs in these groups is essentially social and emotional, rather than intellectual. So you needn't worry that you've ruined your child's chance for Harvard by bypassing organized groups at thirty months.

The Benefits of a Play Group or Tot Class

Why bother with play group if it doesn't lead to Harvard? Because, in addition to the opportunity for social interaction, other children and an impartial teacher will help your child discover a wealth of important information about himself and about friendship that he can't learn from his parents.

First, having a group of other children to study offers your young scientist a firsthand look at how he stacks up against his peers. Is he shorter, taller, fatter, thinner, quieter, or noisier? Finding others with similar traits enhances his image of himself. Mingling with children who differ from him gives him the opportunity to try new forms of behavior and learn if they suit him. This new perspective widens his horizons in choosing friends and learning about others.

First or only children have no one of comparable size and ability on whom to make such comparisons at home. Second children may be pleasantly surprised to find that the world doesn't consist entirely of older, stronger, bossier children. This is a good setting for a second child to practice some of the leadership skills he's observed in his older sibling.

Colin's mother was reluctant to enroll him in a tot group, for example, because she felt that he probably wouldn't derive much benefit from it. After all, Colin had two older brothers at home and a house full of toys to play with. She was further convinced that enrolling Colin had been a mistake when Colin chose the most timid child in the group as his best friend. "All Colin does in school is order this other little boy around," she says. "I didn't send him to school to learn to be a bossy tyrant!"

But Colin *is* benefiting from the group, despite his mother's doubts. As the youngest of three siblings, he certainly won't have an opportunity to exercise much authority at home; his older brothers are unlikely to pay attention to his demands. His need for dominance is being filled by his passive class friend.

Second, participating in a group teaches your child to solve his problems independently. Though the teacher acts as a parent substitute, the child quickly learns that a teacher is a far more impartial adult than his mother or father; the teacher is not likely to think he is cute when he hits a schoolmate. The teacher also will not have the time to give him undivided attention, a particularly good lesson for only children of doting parents.

Third, as part of a group he'll hone his rudimentary social skills. He'll learn to initiate the kind of interaction that leads to friendship, to moderate aggressive behavior in order to remain part of a desirable clique, and to respond to the overtures and the rejection of his classmates. Such skills won't get him into Harvard; nevertheless, they are important factors in your child's social development.

How to Choose a Nursery Play Group

Before you select a nursery school or home group, you can simplify the choice by considering the criteria for a good group. In doing so, you'll have equipped yourself with some guidelines for comparison when you observe school classes or talk to other parents about forming your own group.

For children so young the size of the group often determines how comfortably they adapt to the new setting and to the separation from you. An unfamiliar classroom jammed with noisy or aggressive children can easily overwhelm a shy toddler. Home groups offer a definite advantage in this respect because participating parents can limit the number of children involved. Two or three other children make a nicely rounded group for toddler introverts. Gregarious children may find a larger, noisier group more appealing.

A good teacher-student ratio for toddlers age two and a half is one teacher for every four or five children. (A teacher can effectively handle a slightly larger proportion of three-year-olds—one to six or at most one to seven.) Few nursery schools can survive financially on limited class enrollments, however, so you will rarely find a class comprised of fewer than a dozen or so children. Beware both of overcrowded classes and of schools which presume that a teacher and an aide can safely supervise more than twelve children at once, especially during playground activities.

You should also consider how class time is organized. What you don't want and what your child certainly doesn't need is a totally regimented routine in which every child must do the same activity at the same time. Look for a balance between individual play and group activities like sing-alongs or story time. Good schools also try to achieve a balance between active play and quiet periods. Constant activity will leave you with an exhausted, cranky toddler when class ends. Overinsistence on quiet play produces a wild child later in the day.

Beware the school that stresses academic achievement of its toddlers. Many schools cater to parent demands for superbaby curricula in order to maintain high enrollment. They do so at the expense of the child's development in other areas. (For further discussion of the superbaby question, see the "Guide to Good Parenting" section of Chapter 5.)

You'll want to know the policy about toileting ability before you enroll your toddler. If the school requires children to have bowel and bladder control before enrollment, do not sign up your diaper-clad child and hope that peer pressure will work the trick. Remember that you want this experience to be as positive as possible; don't sabotage your child's chances for success by rushing him into a situation which can make him feel inadequate.

Survey and examine the equipment available. Is there enough variety? Are toys and blocks provided in sufficient number to supply the needs of the class? Is the equipment in good repair? If you have a gregarious child, a well-equipped schoolroom may meet his needs for variety in play better than a small home group which is less fully stocked.

Observe the teaching staff. Warm, caring teachers go a long way toward overcoming any shortcomings in the physical plant of the school. Do the teachers circulate among all the students in the room and on the playground, or do they lavish their attention on a lucky few and ignore the rest of the class? Is their time spent in caring for the children rather than in making conversation with their colleagues? Do they often take the time and trouble to bend down to their students' level to encourage conversation? Are they aware of loners, and do they make an effort to help these children spend some time as part of a group (even just a small group of two)? Do they encourage both boys and girls to sample all different types of toys, or are they subtly encouraging sexual stereotyping by steering the boys to the trucks and blocks and the girls to the dolls and finger paints?

The class population is another important factor in making a choice. Least confusing for your child is a class with the same group of children participating each time. Some schools accept children on a number of different schedules in the same class, so your child may not find his favorite people there each time he attends. To a child this age such constant change is upsetting. Whenever possible, avoid an open-class policy and choose a fixed-schedule group.

American parents generally avoid mixed-age school groups, although this prejudice doesn't necessarily work in the best interests of their children. Some parents are quite willing to have their toddler associate with older children because they hope their youngster will assimilate the more mature aspects of an older child's behavior. These same parents, who believe that isolation from younger children will protect their toddlers against regression to more babyish behavior, would prefer to exclude children younger than their own from the group. However, a toddler often benefits at least as much from playing big shot to a young admirer as he does from being a follower of an older child.

The only important caveat for enrolling your child in a mixed-age class is to make certain that the class truly contains several children of each age group. You don't want your child to be the only younger or older child in the room.

Make an appointment to visit the schools you are considering. Try to pay several visits to the school or schools which seriously interest you, and attend a different class each time for more accurate impressions. It is a good idea to observe an entire class session if possible, rather than just a few minutes. A school that will not permit you to observe a class in session is a school to avoid; good schools are anxious to show off their superior staff and equipment. No well-run nursery school expects a parent to entrust a child to its care without a careful, firsthand look at the environment.

Having your child accompany you on these preliminary trips isn't a good idea because close observations will be difficult while you attend to your child's needs. In addition, such visits can become confusing to a child who doesn't understand their purpose. There's time enough to introduce your toddler to the school or group you've selected once you've made your choice.

If you're establishing a play group, you will avoid many future problems if all possible topics from type of play and type of snack to handling disputes and toileting are discussed and agreed upon in advance. Recording all major points of discussion in a charter or contract can keep misunderstandings to a minimum.

Matters of Timing

Most schools offer a choice of morning or afternoon classes. Your decision should be based upon your child's peak energy level. If he is a morning person—up with the birds but fades fast after lunch—he will probably enjoy an early class and adjust better then he would when tired. A toddler who picks up steam as the day wears on is a good candidate for an afternoon play group. Sessions limited to two and a half hours two days a week usually fill a toddler's needs nicely.

Getting Off to a Good Start in School or Play Group

Once you've chosen the school or group your child will attend, you can make his adjustment to this new situation run smoothly with a minimum of anxiety and tears. First, give him time to adjust to the idea of attending a school or play group by telling him about it a week or so in advance. (Since a toddler's sense of time is still shaky, informing him about the coming excitement too far in advance will make the wait seem endless.)

A good way to introduce the topic is to tell your toddler that soon he is going to do something he will enjoy—attend a nursery school or play group. Next, tell him who will be there: his teacher, whose name is Mr. or Mrs. Whatever, and other children. Mention the names of any children in the group that he already knows. You might also want to tell him about some of the activities: "In school the children play with blocks and trucks. They can paint with a paintbrush on paper. Sometimes they sing songs."

That's plenty of information for him to absorb initially, and you want to avoid confusing or upsetting him by overwhelming him with details. You'll probably need to restate this information several times throughout the day until he feels comfortable with it and absorbs it.

In a day or so when you feel he's ready for more information, tell him about some of the special toys or activities the nursery school offers. Highlight the ones he doesn't have access to at home—the water table, a special jungle gym, clay, etc. Again, don't expect him to absorb the information on the first go-round.

The next step is to describe what your routine will be on school or play-group days, for the more predictable you make the coming event, the more easily your child will adjust to it. A good way to illustrate the school-day routine is to make a little book about it for your child and to read it to him. Draw simple stick figures and limit your description to one or two lines of print per page.

If your child will attend a morning session, begin your narrative with your regular morning routine of waking, getting dressed, and having breakfast. For an afternoon group start your story with a brief description of your lunch together. Make sure you describe the means of transportation to the group. (Are you driving him? car-pooling? school van? He should know what to expect.) Include a page which shows you kissing him goodby and identifies your location and activity in his absence: "Mommy says goodby to Darren. She goes to the supermarket (or the office or home) to shop (or work or clean) until nursery school ends." Knowing that you haven't dropped off the face of the earth in his absence will be very comforting to him.

Describe your child at the water table and at one or two other activities. Mention some playmates. Show him having a snack and juice. *And be sure to mention that when the class or group ends, he comes home.* Tell how he gets back home again. This last bit of information may seem superfluous to you, but it is of prime importance to your child. He will not automatically assume he'll return to you, so he must be reassured that the group exists for a limited time after which the children always come home to their parents.

Putting this information in a booklet that can be read and reread will begin the adjustment process even before he enters the class or group. If the school or group you join doesn't offer any orientation program, make an effort to drive past the building in which the class is held. Allowing your child to see his classroom and meet his teacher before the first day will also calm his fears.

If you can arrange for your child to bring a small snack for the entire group on his first day, you will be helping him feel special within the group. Such gestures will add to his positive feelings about beginning this venture. Another way to help him feel secure is to let him choose some extra clothing (including a set of underwear and socks) and to let him pack them in a shoebox to take to school and keep there in case of overexuberant water play or an accident before he reaches the bathroom.

The Long Goodby

Despite all you do to help prepare your child for school, you may find that he is reluctant to let you go when the actual moment arrives to do so. The best way to handle this

situation is to announce firmly, "I'll see you as soon as playtime ends." Kiss him goodby and walk out the door. Most crying stops as soon as you are out of earshot.

Parents who linger, hoping that additional hugs, kisses,

and reassurance will improve the parting, usually find that the child only works himself up more. If he feels his screams will detain you, the crying is sure to increase with every class session.

If after ten days or so your child still becomes upset when you leave, you may want to reconsider his participation in the group and postpone it for a while. Crying for long periods of time after you've left and refusing to be distracted by the toys and the children is another indication that he simply is unready to separate.

Becoming an Advocate for Your Child

Your toddler has many years of schooling and group activities ahead of him. It is to his advantage and yours for you to speak up promptly when you feel uncomfortable with any aspect of a group in which he participates.

For example, one mother enrolled her child in a community nursery school and was dismayed later in the year to find that several teachers had begun bringing their newborn babies to class with them. Because these teachers could not adequately control a class while caring for their own infants, several accidents occurred, at least one serious enough to require a student's hospitalization. Yet the mother hesitated to object to this obviously unsatisfactory supervision.

In another instance an emotionally disturbed child was admitted to a tot class. His uncontrollable behavior required the constant supervision of one of the class's two teachers, leaving only one teacher in charge of the other ten children. Parents of children in the class complained to one another that their children were being deprived of a teacher, but not one voiced a complaint to the school administration.

Some parents hesitate to express disapproval of a school policy or group activity because they are intimidated by a school setting. (Old memories of childhood trips to the principal's office for detention linger long.) Some feel unqualified to judge a school: Teachers are trained, these parents reason; who am I to say they're wrong? Still others fear that the teacher's resentment of criticism will adversely affect her response to their child. Such fear is usually unjustified and should not keep you from voicing your concern when your child's health, safety, or emotional well-being is at stake.

No one knows your child better than you. No one can care more about your child's welfare than you. He is too young to speak for himself, so you, as his chief advocate, must learn to speak for him. As any honest teacher will admit, schools are imperfect institutions at best. To help your child benefit from them, learn to speak up in his behalf from the beginning of his school career.

Possessiveness and the Play Group

Thirty-month-olds are still quite a possessive bunch when their toys are at stake. Even if they've learned the rudiments of sharing, allowing others to touch or use their possessions is a short-lived accomplishment at best. Learning to share school toys is difficult enough; sharing one's own toys with a play group presents special problems. For some toddlers being the host child to a play group is an especially difficult experience, since both his turf and his toys are under attack.

To help counteract the feeling of helplessness which can enrage your toddler when the other children in the group begin to maul his playthings, find ways to help him protect some of his possessions. Perhaps he will want to select a few toys which will remain out of sight during the group playtime. Or he may want to fill a carton with the toys he'll allow the others to use. Some groups encourage the visiting children to bring one toy along with each of them to contribute to the group's supply for the day; then the host child isn't the only one expected to share. This lightens his social burden.

It may help to explain that when toys are shared, the owner does reclaim his possessions when playtime ends. Part of a toddler's problem with sharing stems from his fear that a toy shared is a toy forever lost to him. Another way to ease the pressure is to include some activities in which each member of the group has his own personal set of supplies. For example, planting seeds in paper cups labeled with the toddler's name allows each child a respite from the difficult task of sharing. If an art project is planned, don't put a community crayon supply in the center of the work table. Instead, distribute several crayons to each child individually so he can relax his guard on his booty. You'll exhaust yourself and the children if you expect sharing to occur continuously throughout the meeting.

Try to remember that such behavior is perfectly normal for a child of this age. Gentle persuasion—distraction, for example—will work better during group sessions than forcing the toddler to give up what he grasps for dear life. Learning to share both home territory and toys all at once is rough. It will help your toddler if you can acknowledge that fact.

Elimination

How to Botch Toilet Teaching

Many parents grow anxious if their toddler still wears diapers as he nudges the two-and-a-half-year mark. Even patient parents become impatient when their youngster shows evidence of maturity in every aspect of his development except bowel and bladder control: physical growth, language development, and social ability. They assume that toilet learning should keep pace with these other advances.

In addition, other children (especially girls) may already be toilet taught, perhaps for several months. Parents who compare their youngster to others want reassurance that their child is developing as normally and as quickly as his peers.

A new baby, too, can put pressure on the parents' formerly understanding attitude toward diaper changes (and pressure on the family budget for additional cartons of disposable diapers as well). The infant catapults his unsuspecting sibling into a new role as big brother or sister, a role which seems to demand advanced behavior and toileting skills, whether or not the older sibling is ready to exhibit them. We parents tend to label our children as "the big boy or girl" and "the baby," and we expect behavior appropriate to the label even when the older child is still a baby himself in many ways.

The problem at this point is more the parents' than the child's, for the toddler remains unconcerned with the entire situation—unless the parents unwisely transmit their anxiety to their child. Parents who pressure their toddler to become toilet taught before the toddler is physically and emotionally ready to comply open a Pandora's box of problems, for parental pressure retards effective toilet teaching. It adversely affects both the parent-child relationship and the development of the child's self-esteem.

Some parents feel that their own self-esteem is at stake when their child lags behind others in any way. The more confident the parents, the less they worry about when their child learns to use the toilet. Confidence is contagious; children catch it from their parents. Says one mother, "I've noticed that the kids who are pressured to walk to talk or use the toilet early are usually first children. By the time parents get to their second child, they've learned to relax and let nature do its job."

Other parental hang-ups, such as a desire for excessive neatness or a tendency toward perfectionism, also interfere with effective toilet teaching. A child absorbs his parents' negative attitudes toward a mess or a toilet accident and can become preoccupied with the possibility of its occurrence. When a toddler focuses on such worries, the entire teaching period becomes a nerve-wracking experience filled with fear of failure and punishment.

Children who are pressured to perform on the toilet often react by refusing to use it at all. Fearful of further failure, they no longer try for success. Thus, pressuring a child could cause toilet teaching to be delayed beyond the age where the child, if unhurried, would have succeeded. The child's self-esteem suffers because he has failed in an undertaking which his parents deem important.

Toddlers who still respond to every request and demand with an unequivocal "no!" make poor candidates for toilet teaching at this time. Successful toilet teaching requires that a child derive more pleasure from pleasing his parents than from defying them.

In a poor parent-child relationship toilet teaching may become a child's weapon to punish an overly demanding parent. This is one area in which the child obviously has the final say. If he has no opportunity to exercise any control elsewhere in his life, he may choose the bathroom as the battleground for independence.

Deliberately withholding bowel movements can cause constipation, which then begins a vicious cycle. The more constipated the child becomes from refusing to cooperate, the more painful having a bowel movement becomes. The pain provides further incentive to avoid another B.M.

Rebellion against excessive parental demands for toileting manifests itself in other disguises as well. Some children who seem to cooperate in their use of the toilet become obsessed with keeping their clothes clean and get upset over the tiniest dirt mark. They may refuse to get their hands dirty and avoid opportunities to use messy play materials like finger paints or clay. Or their rebellion may take other, completely unrelated forms, such as problems at meals or at bedtime.

Obviously, the key to botching toilet teaching is to become uptight if your child doesn't adhere to the timetable you'd prefer, to ignore his internal schedule, to rush into teaching when your child is at his most negative stage, to create tension and anxiety over the use of the toilet, to punish failure—in short, to force an issue which should never have become an issue in the first place.

Rebellious reactions, such as those described above, simply cannot occur in the absence of parental pressure. If toilet teaching has become an issue in your home, you need to assess why it means so much to you. Then defuse the conflict by postponing toilet teaching for a few months until you can handle it calmly.

What About Rewards?

Anxious parents often latch (or, for the more desperate, grab) on to the idea of speeding up the toilet teaching procedure by offering rewards beyond the usual attention, affection, and applause for successful use of the toilet. Among the more common items offered are sweets, toys, and grab-bag gifts.

Generally, offering material rewards for mastering skills that depend upon maturation and growth makes little sense. Have you ever known a family that cajoled a toddler into getting up and walking with the offer of a toy or a sweet? Promising a toy or other reward for toileting is just about as silly unless you've botched the whole toilet teaching process so thoroughly that you now feel the only way to undo the damage is to focus on an attractive present. Rewards carry with them the unspoken message that the accomplishment is not worth achieving for its own sake.

For children whose parents haven't entangled their adult egos in the teaching process, signs of maturation generally provide their own built-in rewards. "I'm grown-up; I'm not a baby" is the reaction of the exultant toddler to every new milestone he achieves. There is no greater joy for a human being than to learn something new.

A much better response to a reluctant or slow learner than the offer of a bribe is the comfort of a single sentence: "Soon you will be able to do it." This approach eliminates the element of manipulation from the toilet teaching process: You don't hold a reward over your toddler's head; he doesn't withhold the proper response to spite you or cooperate only when a prize is at stake.

Regression

Some situations will cause a toddler who has learned to use the toilet successfully to regress. Any emotional upheaval in the toddler's life is likely to affect his use of the toilet: tension at home, starting play group or nursery school, arrival of a new baby, moving to a new home, or even an illness. One parent reported that her child began to have toilet accidents when a bedridden grandparent moved in with the family. You can expect the regression to last as long as it takes the toddler to get an emotional handle on whatever is bothering him.

Unfortunately, toddler regression often occurs when parents, too, are under pressure, and tempers naturally flare when a household is in upheaval. A new baby, for example, throws established household routines out of kilter for parents as well as toddlers. No parents are overjoyed to find that they must deal with toddler toilet problems in addition to the new responsibilities an infant brings. Frequently, the parents' first instinct is to punish the toddler for his lapses.

Punishment won't solve the problem. It neither eliminates regression nor addresses its underlying cause, which is usually insecurity. However, your ability to remain calm and understanding *will* help your toddler overcome these emotional setbacks and regain his confidence.

Dryness at Night

The ability to remain dry throughout the night is generally the last step in the toilet teaching sequence. Since the average age for dryness at night is three years, many children, and especially male children, will still require diapers at bedtime. In fact, wetting at night to ages four and five isn't uncommon.

Remaining dry from bedtime till dawn or responding to physical signals for urination by awakening to use the toilet requires physical maturation. Some parents try to hasten night dryness by restricting liquids for several hours before the child's bedtime or by rousing the toddler to use the toilet before the parents themselves go to bed. Parents who rely on these methods are probably the very ones who conditioned themselves to put a child with predictable bowel habits on the toilet at the same time each day and then proclaimed him "trained." The trained persons in both instances are actually the parents.

The best method for achieving night dryness is simply

to wait until the child matures enough to stay dry. Keep your toddler's room warm at night, since a cold room may encourage bed-wetting. If night dryness has become an issue in your home, eliminate any belief that your child does it deliberately. He has no idea of what he is doing when he is sound asleep. Consider why you are so concerned about a situation that Mother Nature will address on her own if you just give her time.

Guide to Good Parenting

Burn-Out

What do you call a parent who expected to be the first perfect parent to raise the first perfect child? A single phrase accurately describes many parents who aspire to this unattainable goal: burned out. As in: exhausted, disillusioned, fed up, and disgusted.

Social scientists have documented the burn-out phenomenon in the workplace, and they agree that workers in the helping professions in particular—teachers, social workers, police, doctors, and nurses, among others—are most susceptible to burning themselves out on the job. No one acknowledges that helping people is the world's toughest task, requiring prodigious amounts of physical, mental, and emotional strength. The job of being a parent contains many of the liabilities common to these professions: long hours and little free time, frustrating and often repetitive tasks, heavy workloads, little prestige and even less appreciation.

Parent burn-out is symptomatic of a separation problem in reverse. Instead of the child refusing to part from the parents to establish her autonomy, the parents refuse to separate from the child. The parents, motivated to raise a child who will attain the successes they failed to achieve, severely limit the amount of time their child spends out of their sight and control. Parents and toddler are like people in protective quarantine. Separation is barely tolerated; baby sitters are virtually taboo. Eventually the destructive nature of such an arrangement to the parents and the child becomes clear. Excessive togetherness and superhuman energy investment exhaust the parents' vitality. Overfueling any fire smothers its flames.

Victims of parent burn-out usually approach their responsibilities with great enthusiasm, at least initially. "When Sharon was born, I produced a terrific movie in my imagination of what our days together would be like," recalls one young mother. "In my dream world our time together was idyllic. I was going to teach her all sorts of things. I would be patient, she would be cooperative, and we would be the greatest twosome since ham and eggs. I couldn't wait to get the show on the road."

Problems arise when reality fails to meet these unrealistic expectations. "We turned out to be the most mismatched mother and daughter in the history of the entire world," says Sharon's mother. "She doesn't sit still for two seconds, and I'm a whole lot less patient than I thought."

In this family, as in many others, somebody forgot to program the child properly for her role in the family scenario, and often she refuses to follow the script her parents have dreamed up. The playwrights are confronted with a character who has a mind of her own. Even the parents have difficulty following the script they themselves wrote.

To be fair, they didn't write it all themselves. From a thousand different sources—the movies, television, advertisements, other family members—we assimilate messages of what's expected of good parents. The messages translate into a job only a saint could fill, and we all know how few saints exist in the ranks of parents.

Gradually, confrontation with reality teaches parents how very difficult child-rearing is. One can only do so much, and when the "so much" falls far short of satisfying the initial expectations, parents become disillusioned. They dismiss their contributions as worthless and feel that their time has been wasted. This feeling of uselessness is one of the prime symptoms of parent burn-out. Often fatigue accompanies it, for mustering the energy to carry on a seemingly thankless, fruitless task takes some doing.

Fatigue is also a by-product of the "everything counts" syndrome. Parents who suffer from this syndrome worry so about doing a perfect job of parenting that they believe that *everything* that touches their child matters greatly. When this happens, they are constantly torn in a thousand directions, unsure of which task or worry to confront first. They spend the day mentally jumping from one problem to another. Did the toddler get enough sleep? Why did she eat so little for breakfast? Is she coming down with a cold? Why must dressing be a battle? Why can't she cooperate? Why can't I be more patient? How can I manage to fit both the supermarket and the playground into this morning's schedule? And so on into the night. Parents who also work outside the home can bear a double burden, concerned with occupational as well as parental inadequacy.

Such constant pull and tug are exhausting, and the stress they cause creates another classic symptom, the "short fuse" syndrome, a state of constant agitation in which the parents suspect that all they do all day long is yell. All too often their suspicion proves true. The more the parents yell, the more a toddler is likely to turn a deaf ear to the shouting. As you might expect, having one's explosions ignored does little to improve the situation. And when all the shouting dies down, the parents are consumed with guilt that their child will be emotionally harmed by living in an atmosphere of constant conflict.

When perpetual fatigue sets in, burned-out parents search for ways to dredge up enough energy to get themselves through yet another trying day. "I graduated from smoking half a pack of cigarettes a day to a two-and-a-half-pack habit in the two years since Bobby was born," says one mother as she pulls yet another cigarette from her pack. Other burn-out victims overeat, spend a large part of each day sleeping, or immerse themselves in television soap operas. Some victims turn to drug and alcohol abuse as "cures."

For several reasons parents of toddlers more than parents of any other age group seem especially susceptible to burn-out. During toddlerhood parents first confront the tug of war between dependence and autonomy and the chasm between expectation and reality. Also, a toddler requires parents to expend more *physical* energy in her care than the child has needed before or will ever need again: Infants can't run, and preschoolers don't need you trailing along behind them every minute. But for the moment you are constantly on the run, constantly straightening up. A toddler's energy level far exceeds any adult's, and her battery needs far less recharging than her parents' when it does run down.

Handling a toddler requires greater *mental* energy expenditure too. Parents with a toddler can never switch their mind to automatic pilot; dealing with a toddler means living in a constant state of red alert, of anticipating danger, of answering questions, of dealing with negativity and rigidity, altogether an exhausting situation. Toddler care rapidly depletes parental reserves of time, energy, and patience, and burn-out victims don't make adequate provision for restoring these exhausted accounts.

Combating Burn-Out

Burned-out parents resemble, in a sense, their own toddler. Like the child who wants hamburgers every night or
the same bedtime stories for months on end, the parents
have carried good qualities—enthusiasm and ambition—
to extremes. Like their child, burned-out parents haven't
learned to moderate their desires and expectations; they
allow their emotional pendulum to swing wildly from enthusiasm to its opposite, hopelessness, without pausing to
halt in the comfortable middle. Unable to wring perfection
from themselves and their child, they exhaust themselves
in the attempt and then, motivated by an instinct for self-
preservation, finally put some distance between themselves
and their child. Only sheer exhaustion breaks the strangle
hold of smother love.

To regain an even emotional keel, burned-out parents
need some perspective on their situation. But perspective
isn't gained by remaining smack in the middle of the problem. Part of the solution lies in taking time off from the
constant demands of caretaking, and this means time off
within each day for recharging yourself. If you do not work
outside your home, nursery school or play group will allow
you some respite. If neither is available to you, a baby sitter
or an exchange arrangement with another parent can serve
the same purpose.

Many burned-out parents started their own blaze by refusing to entrust the care of their child to another individual
for any period of time. They feel guilty when another caretaker watches the child. Often they worry that a hired caretaker can't or won't give the same high-quality care as a
parent.

However, burn-out and high-quality parent care are mutually exclusive. Burned-out parents cannot offer high-quality
child care. And hiring a baby sitter has its positive side,
which burned-out parents seldom consider: Every caretaker
has something unique to offer a child. Far from being deprived, the child benefits doubly from the time spent away
from her parents. She learns from a new relationship, and

she acquires more rested, patient parents.

Burned-out parents often view vacations as unnecessary extravagances. But parents need time alone together. The old saying about two being company and three being a crowd certainly holds true here. A trip with a toddler can be enjoyable, but it's really not a vacation for parents, since child care must continue nonstop, and caring for a child away from home generally proves more difficult in comparison with the convenience of home care. There would be far fewer burned-out parents if pediatricians prescribed regular vacations for parents along with vaccinations for their children.

Hiring a Baby Sitter

A good baby sitter is one who makes both parents and child comfortable. The parents must feel confident enough to leave their child for a few hours without fearing for the child's well-being, and the child must feel relaxed with the sitter as well.

One good way to locate caring, competent sitters is to ask teachers in your local high school to recommend some of their students. Teachers will be able to offer unbiased assessments of the reliability and maturity of teenagers in their classrooms.

Once you've located a prospect, hire the student first for an afternoon when you can discuss your child's habits and establish your "house rules." Then on future occasions you can feel carefree when you leave the house. This arrangement also provides an excellent opportunity for your child to get to know the sitter in the security of your presence, and you can determine whether you feel confident leaving the sitter with your toddler.

Your sitter should know your child's name, her favorite activities, her bedtime routines, and your policy about snacks before bedtime. Mention the specific activities you expect the sitter to perform, such as reading bedtime stories or singing a lullaby. If your child will have an opportunity to play with her toys before bedtime, let the sitter know you expect the toys to be put away before you return. Otherwise, you're likely to return to a house that looks as if it's been bombed. The sitter should know in advance if your child habitually wakes at intervals and your methods for getting her resettled.

No one expects emergencies to occur when parents spend a night out. But because that possibility always exists, you won't adequately protect your child if you haven't prepared your sitter in how to handle the most common ones.

Post the telephone numbers of the police, fire department, and your pediatrician near each phone in your home. On the same sheet of paper write your address and home phone number. If any of these services are needed in an emergency, the sitter will need to know the address where the emergency service should be sent.

The telephone number of your evening's destination should be added to these; if you will not be able to be reached by phone, you should substitute an emergency number of a trusted friend or relative as a back-up.

Tell your sitter that the numbers are there to be used if needed and not to worry about the possibility of a false alarm. You would rather have a needless call than an emergency that ends in tragedy because the sitter worried about appearing foolish.

Try to alert your sitter to the idiosyncracies of your household, so she or he won't become unnecessarily alarmed if noises are heard emanating from the heating system or air conditioning. One family neglected to warn a new sitter that their infant wore a special brace on his legs at night, and when she heard the brace crash against the crib bars, she was convinced that a burglar was attempting to break in, and she summoned the police.

Acquaint your sitter with all possible exits from your home in case of fire. Your policy for handling a fire should be: The sitter removes the child from the house immediately and makes a call to the fire department from a next-door neighbor's home or apartment. The sitter should leave with the child as soon as the fire is discovered and should not attempt to extinguish it. Make sure your sitter understands these important instructions thoroughly. There have been house fires in which the sitter panicked and ran out, leaving the children behind.

Tell your sitter what she or he is permitted to do, use, or eat in your absence. Smoking should be prohibited, as it increases the possibility of fire hazard. A good rule to which you should allow no exceptions is that the sitter is not permitted to have company. You are paying the sitter to give undivided attention to your child and her safety. With a friend around, a teenager will not remain as watchful or as attentive to your child's needs. Under no circumstances should the sitter open the door to anyone in your absence unless she or he has called for emergency services. To keep your television, stereo, and other appliances in working order, show the sitter how to use them properly.

Decide what your policy for the use of the phone will be and then tell your sitter. You should call during the evening to make sure that everything is running smoothly, and if the sitter knows you expect to check in, she or he will be less likely to spend the entire evening on the phone. A sitter's calls should be restricted to the hours after your child's bedtime.

Mommy, Don't Leave

The question of whether to leave while a child is awake or to exit after she is sleeping especially plagues parents whose toddlers become upset by an evening's separation. Though leaving a crying child is unpleasant, leaving a sleeping child who might wake to find you gone is unwise. A toddler who finds only a stranger to care for her when she expected her parents will feel betrayed and insecure.

If your child tends to carry on and create a scene in the hope that her tantrum will convince you to stay, learn to say goodby firmly and quickly. Give her a good-night kiss and say, "Daddy and I are going to the movies. When the movie ends, we will come home. Karen will take care of you while we're gone." Then go. The longer you linger, the worse the weeping becomes. Don't feel guilty. You need an evening to yourselves. The sobbing usually stops shortly after you are out of sight. If not, the crying is tiring, and your toddler will eventually fall asleep. She will not hate you when she is grown for having left her with a sitter when she was two; try to keep that in mind.

5. Thirty to Thirty-six Months

How They Have Grown

What vast changes you have witnessed in your child between the time he entered toddlerhood and the present. In just the past eighteen months he has progressed from infancy to childhood—from crawling to walking, from babble to speech. He can think and question. Truly he has grown by leaps and bounds physically, mentally, and emotionally.

However, the physical growth that will occur in the coming months is far more subtle than the obvious growth spurts of the past. This new growth refines proportions and contours more than it increases overall size. You might miss much of the physical transformation of toddler into preschooler if you didn't know what specific signs to watch for.

At birth some parts of your child's body were far closer to their adult dimensions than others. Before maturity an infant's head must double in size, his torso triple. However, an infant's arms measure only a quarter of their adult size and his legs a mere fifth. The body's extremities obviously have some catching up to do. For this reason much of the growth of late toddlerhood concentrates on these extremities.

As you might expect from the fractions above, much of the growth of late toddlerhood increases the length of the legs. At age three a female toddler's legs are approximately half their adult length; for boys the halfway mark is reached a few months later.

The growth of the legs' long bones is not accompanied by a corresponding increase in weight, so this lengthening delineates both the knee and ankle bones. Your toddler's legs assume a slimmer, more shapely appearance than their former chunky, solid look. Unless your child is obese, the fat folds or creases in the thigh disappear forever.

Changes in body proportion aren't merely aesthetic. They affect posture, stance, and coordination. The pot belly, a trademark of early toddlerhood, begins to recede into the flatter stomach of the preschooler. The belly won't disappear entirely for a while yet; it simply won't protrude as much. As the balloon belly recedes, the pronounced curve of the spine straightens, reducing the swayback effect so apparent in younger toddlers.

Both the widening of the pelvis and the lengthening of the legs combine to produce a lower center of gravity and a steadier base. As a result, your toddler will be more sure-footed and less prone to falls. These changes, along with improved coordination, transform the wide-legged, sailor-style toddler walk into a more adult gait.

Improved muscular and hand-eye coordination reduces the frustration that accompanied many tasks only a short while ago. Dressing and undressing, using a spoon, and pouring liquids are all accomplished with improved dexterity. By age three pedal toys become enjoyable because your toddler's coordination has advanced enough for him to use them properly.

What They Can Do

Encouraging Listening Skills

Now that your toddler has grown old enough to be successful at listening and at reproducing what she hears, encourage her development of this important skill. Play a simple version of the game "Grandmother's Trunk" this way: You begin by announcing that together you and your child will pack a silly trunk for Grandma. Everything that goes into the trunk will begin with the sound "s." Then ask, "Can I put a salad in the trunk?" Your toddler must answer yes or no depending upon whether the word you choose begins with the sound you've chosen. When you exhaust one sound, move on to another. This game encourages careful listening and sound discrimination, an important skill for learning to read later on. It's a good game to play when you are riding in the car.

You can also promote listening skills by playing rhyming games. In the simplest version, simply ask your child if two words rhyme—fat and hat, for example. When your child becomes proficient at recognizing rhymes, let her create a few of her own: "Can you think of a word that rhymes with 'big'?" Then let her name a word and you find a rhyme.

Tell your toddler stories as a change from reading them to her. Let her fill in details to visualize an illustration to accompany your words. For example, you begin, "Once there lived a chicken in the land where rain fell all the time." (Ask, "What color was the chicken? What color was the rain?" Then incorporate her answers into the next sentence.) "The purple chicken wore a favorite rain hat in every orange thunder shower." (Ask what the hat looked like. Again incorporate the answer into your next sentence.) "The purple chicken with the big, flowered, holey hat also owned a raincoat." And so on. She'll have to listen carefully in order to participate.

Sing to your toddler as often as possible, since she is most receptive to learning songs at this age. Your library has picture books with the words to many songs nicely illustrated, and these add to the pleasure of harmonizing together. Three good ones are *The Fox Went Out, Over in the Meadow*, and *Froggy Went A-Courting*.

Play a junior version of "Name That Tune." You hum the tune of a familiar song, and your toddler supplies the title. Then let your toddler hum and you identify her tune.

Use imaginary or toy telephones to encourage both listening and social skills. An old-fashioned, homemade telephone contraption of two empty juice cans connected by a short length of string delights toddlers playing this game. Cans with peel-off tops should be used, as ones opened with a can opener may have sharp edges.

Designate some time during each day—mealtime is a good choice—as "whisper time." Your child will learn to modulate her voice as well as pay careful attention to what is said when all conversation is held at whisper level.

The Age of Why

Perhaps more than any other yardstick, language development charts your toddler's maturation. At about thirty months you'll notice your child begin to use the pronoun "I." It's the smallest word in the English language, but its appearance marks an important emotional as well as linguistic milestone: Your child sees herself as a separate individual. "I did it!" she crows when she climbs to the top of the jungle gym. "I drew it!" "I painted it!" "I can jump!" She shouts her accomplishments to the world at large. And her smile now when she accomplishes a goal further marks her growth; in the past smiles have been reserved for social interaction or in response to a surprising event. This new grin signifies pride, an addition to her emotional repertoire.

At this same time the toddler gains a greater understanding of the laws of cause and effect. The world is no longer quite so bewildering and inexplicably complex. Now much of what she sees makes sense, can be predicted, and is therefore less alarming than in the past. Life is calmer. Perhaps the combination of establishing her independent identity and better understanding events around her helps make the three-year-old much improved company over her earlier, cantankerous self.

The age of why—questions, questions, and more questions—follows closely on the heels of the toddler's individuation and newly developed reasoning skills. Studies of toddler speech have recorded nearly four hundred questions a day, enough to drive even the most patient of parents crazy. Earlier questions depended heavily on "what" and "where." Now "why," "how," and "when" questions proliferate.

The very fact that she asks such questions indicates some ability to comprehend both logic and time, incomplete though that comprehension is. Her sense of time still depends on a sequence of events ("We can go to the playground this afternoon—*after* we straighten up your room and *after* we eat lunch.") rather than on the clock, and the idea of yesterday and tomorrow is confusing. She probably won't add future tense verbs to her speech for another year yet.

While the bulk of toddler inquiries are posed for gathering information, toddlers also have other purposes for asking questions. Understanding some of your child's less apparent motives makes the task of answering over thirty questions an hour more bearable.

The toddler asks some questions just to keep the communication between the two of you going. She doesn't know how to hold a conversation any other way. It will be another year or two before she learns to make a statement and wait for a response as a conversational pattern. For now questions provide the means for social talk.

Some toddler questions are designed simply to get attention. These are the nonsense questions or the ones which have no possible relation to what was asked immediately before or after (unlike a series of information-gathering questions, whose logic might be strange but in some odd way coherent). They are a sign that your child wants more of your time than you seem willing to give at the moment, and she's found a way to get her wish. She has learned that you can't ignore a question. So sometimes a hug and a kiss and some cuddling is the answer to one unasked question buried among a thousand inane queries.

Not all of those four hundred daily questions are original; in fact, they might be somewhat more tolerable if they were. Many of them are repeats of a question asked only seconds before. Repetition occurs because the toddler is seeking some response beyond the actual information contained in the answer you gave. There is an unvoiced, still unanswered query hiding behind the one she is capable of verbalizing. The child who asks "Are you going to the store?" five times in the space of thirty seconds perhaps wants to know and be reassured that you plan to take her along, that you are not going to leave her with a baby sitter.

The parent who fails to interpret the underlying demand

for emotional reassurance ends up shouting, "I SAID 'NO' FIVE TIMES ALREADY." What the child wants to hear from you is, "I'm not going to the store without you; I am not planning to leave you. I'm staying right here with you and in a few minutes I'm going to make dinner."

The questioning then ceases because the child no longer feels insecure. She knows you're not going to abandon her which was her chief worry. The toddler is so concerned with her own emotional state at these moments that she fails to notice that such pestering makes you remember a long-shelved plan for abandoning her in a basket in front of a church door.

Toddlers also repeat questions or rephrase your answer as a question in order to verify information received. Your toddler asks, "Where does rain come from?" and you answer, "From the clouds." Then your child queries, "Rain comes from the clouds?" and awaits verification of your original statement. She may ask several more times until she is satisfied or repeats the question as a statement, signifying her acceptance: "Rain comes from the clouds." This type of repetition resembles the way in which she added individual words to her vocabulary by repeating them over and over. Toddlers seem to absorb bigger pieces of information by much the same method.

Answering Tough Questions

Some toddler questions—those about sex or death especially—tend to strike some parents deaf and dumb, either because they feel uncomfortable discussing those topics or because they are unsure of how much information to give a toddler. Toddlers have the disconcerting habit of asking sensitive questions at top volume as you stand on the checkout line at the supermarket or on a crowded city bus. Physical infirmities or deformities fascinate them, and they do not hesitate to seek answers from you or the invalid in question.

Parents often try to push these difficult questions under the rug. They attempt to distract the child or to postpone answering in the expectation that the toddler's short attention span will shift to a new line of thought. By ignoring the question, they hope it will disappear. Usually it does—at least for a while—but not without some undesirable consequences.

By refusing to provide any answer to a child's reasonable question (even if the refusals take the guise of distraction, lack of time, etc.), you erect a barrier to honest, easy communication between your child and yourself. Sooner or later your toddler understands your reluctance and stops asking you for information. The next step is for her to stop sharing her information with you. What you want to establish from the very beginning of your relationship together is that your child can come to you when something—anything—troubles her.

In a short while you'll need to teach your child how to keep herself safe from molestation. How will she be able to broach the topic of improper advances or uncomfortable feelings about an adult to you if you make sex a subject you cannot discuss together? As a teen your child will be exposed to peer pressure for many forms of behavior which you disapprove. If you want open, easy communication with your child when she's a teen, if you want her to value your judgment then, you must begin to establish that relationship by answering her questions now; it won't blossom suddenly when she's on the verge of adulthood.

In addition, children rarely give up easily in their quest for knowledge. They'll keep asking until they find someone who will answer them, and you may be less than pleased with the misinformation other adults or other children dole out.

If the question your child asks is an embarrassing one because the object of her curiosity is present—i.e., "Why is that man in a wheelchair?"—tell the child that this is not the place to answer it but that you promise to explain it as soon as you are alone. When you are alone, answer the question even if your toddler doesn't remind you of your promise.

After you have finished telling her that people use wheelchairs because their legs don't work well, explain that when she sees a person she has a question about, she must whisper the question in your ear or save it until you are alone together to avoid hurting the person's feelings. Three-year-olds can be quite sympathetic to others' feelings and usually cooperate very well with this request. Do not make her feel guilty for having asked; you want her to come away from this experience feeling she can trust you with her thoughts, not feeling anxious. When she does remember to save such questions for private conversations, praise her for being so considerate.

Questions about sex generally come in stages. Your child does not want nor could she absorb much detailed information all at once. A popular first question is, "Where do babies come from?" A good answer is that babies grow inside the mother in a special place that's called the uterus. Experts recommend specifying where the baby grows so that the child will not confuse pregnancy with any function of eating. And from the outside it looks to the toddler as if the fetus is in the mother's stomach. Just because you have answered the question doesn't mean your child won't ask it again; until the information is absorbed, she will.

It is not necessary to wait for the child to pose this question. If the opportunity presents itself for you to pass this information along naturally—when you see a pregnant animal on the street or an obviously pregnant woman—take advantage of the situation.

A good rule of thumb is to answer your toddler's difficult questions with only as much information as you can fit into a short sentence or two. More than that is confusing. Give the child time to absorb what you have said, and don't rush in with more chatter or turn your attention to another task which will cut off a follow-up question before she has time to frame it. You need to follow her lead here and let her set the pace of the exchange.

If you find that questions about sex make you so uncomfortable that you have difficulty answering your child, the solution might be to choose some of the many books in your library meant to be read to a toddler. Read them to your child when she asks her first question because before long she's going to want to know how the baby got into the uterus and how he's going to get out. A defensive, anxious, aggressive, or angry attitude in conveying the information is as damaging to your relationship and to your child's developing sexual attitudes as refusal to answer. The emotional content behind the answer is as important as the words themselves. The goal you are striving for is an answer and a way of answering that make you both feel comfortable.

Before you set your toddler loose in a nursery class or playground full of uninitiated kids, explain that this conversation is a private talk between the two of you. Otherwise, she'll want to announce her discovery to the world.

The same rule of using a simple sentence or two applies to other less sensitive, but equally complicated, scientific questions your child will ask. It helps to remember that not all answers can be simplified for a toddler's comprehension. "Why is the sky blue?" sounds simple enough, but try explaining to a toddler that the blue color is a result of the refractive effect of moisture and particles in the air upon light rays.

Encouraging Questions

Though you may doubt your sanity if you follow suggestions to increase the number of questions your child is already asking, this encouragement is important. You want your child to know that you value curiosity and that learning is enjoyable and exciting. If you give your child that attitude now, you will never have to worry about her being a reluctant student when she enters school.

Make your child feel that thoughtful questions please you, that you like to see her thinking. "That's a good question!" is a fine response to a child who wants knowledge. You might want to vary "good" with "interesting," "smart," or "clever." Of course, you won't use that exclamation every time she opens her mouth because then it is valueless, but when her question is grown-up, complicated, thoughtful, or creative, let her know it.

If the question lends itself to learning more about a subject, give a short answer of your own and suggest going to the library to find a book that elaborates. If you can include a trip to the library shortly after the question is asked, the trip is seen as a reward. A side effect of this response is the lesson you are teaching that learning through research is a pleasure, not a chore.

It's a nice idea to let your toddler overhear you praise her to the librarian: "Beth asked a very interesting question about spiders, so we're here to find a book about webs." If the librarian's on the ball, he'll ask your child to tell him her question and praise her cleverness too. If he misses his cue, you continue, "She wanted to know why spiders don't get stuck in their own webs." The librarian will probably respond at that point.

Some questions lend themselves to another question as a response. "What do you think the answer is?" can be a good way to find out how your child has solved the problem for herself. It also gets all her misconceptions out into the open. If you handle her hypotheses carefully—"That was very clever thinking!"—she will be encouraged to continue to reason out questions for herself and will take pride in herself for attempting to do so. (Never laugh at her attempt to reason for herself, no matter how primitive the results. Toddlers have sensitive feelings too.)

Research has shown that parent-child communication reveals much about their relationship. Parents of disturbed children make responses that are too brief and devoid of detail, more vague and digressive than responses of normal children's parents. Keeping your answers moderately detailed, to the point, and understandable keeps the questions coming.

Personality Development

Personality by Numbers

In the good old days social scientists studying child-rearing generally agreed that the style of upbringing a parent used could be guaranteed to produce a particular kind of child. Authoritarian parents, who brooked no nonsense from their offspring, were generally agreed to raise submissive children who displayed little creativity. At the other extreme, overly permissive parents were held to turn out aggressive types. Democratic couples were generally given the highest marks for producing children who displayed more moderate, appropriate behavior.

The parents who read the child-care books these scientists wrote came to believe that all they had to do was follow the instructions the researchers provided and they could raise a better child than otherwise possible. Like paint-by-number sets, the success of the finished product depended upon how carefully the amateur artist filled in the spaces that had been prenumbered: so much love, so much direction, a certain percentage of strictness, a certain amount of moral guidance, and so on.

Somewhere along the line, researchers noticed that while the rules may have been generally true, they weren't universally true. Not all children of permissive parents turned out to be aggressive or offspring of democratic parents well-rounded. At that point someone noticed the children. Maybe, just maybe, they surmised, children weren't really a totally blank canvas after all, for parents to color in as they wished. Perhaps inborn tendencies had something to do with the way a child reacted to different types of upbringing.

An interesting animal experiment illuminates the difficulty in determining whether nature or nurture is responsible for your child's developing personality, or how much influence heredity exerts over environment or vice versa. Beagles, basenjis, terriers, and Shetland sheep dogs were trained in either an indulgent manner or a strict one. After the training ended, all the dogs were shown bowls of food but instructed not to touch them. *None* of the sheep dogs, whether trained permissively or strictly, did. However, *all* of the basenjis ate the food. Only the terriers' and the beagles' behavior showed the influence of their upbringing; the animals trained without punishment obeyed the "don't eat" command for a much longer period of time than their more heavily disciplined counterparts. Heredity seems to hold the upper hand with half the group, type of training with the other half. The lesson seems to be that inborn personality traits can sometimes be moderated, not obliterated.

Further evidence of such moderating influence emerges from current studies of child-rearing. Cross-cultural comparisons demonstrate that societal attitudes affect a child's willingness to participate in new experiences. In societies that avoid blaming or shaming children for failure (but instead blame surrounding circumstances or the adult doing the teaching), children develop a healthy, positive attitude toward approaching new situations. This willingness to take on new challenges occurs when a child feels none of the pressures that failure and the ensuing blame and shame produce. When all a child can reap from effort is reward, he is naturally encouraged to make that effort. Conversely, upbringing which makes a child fear blame or shame for failure in any endeavor isn't likely to encourage participation, since the child strives instead to preserve his reputation.

Even with this kind of helpful information, parents must

abandon the idea that child-rearing can be simplified by adhering to a single set of precepts to accomplish the job successfully. Parents also need to examine the pronouncements even of contemporary experts with, if not a jaundiced eye, then certainly a pragmatic outlook and a large degree of simple common sense.

Consider, for example, the opposing views of two respected child-care authorities. One suggests that a child who dawdles uses this device to express his hostility toward his parents. From this point of view, dawdling is caused by some problem in the parent-child relationship and is correctible. The other expert states that dawdling simply reflects a child's inborn tempo; some children conduct their lives in a rush from the moment of birth on, while others plod along steadily. Which to believe?

The pragmatic parents' test of conflicting advice must lie with their child. If the dawdling seems to have occurred suddenly, then maybe there is some underlying difficulty which ought to be resolved. If your child has always been a tortoise type, he might be encouraged to speed up a little, but the chances that you'll turn him into a human dynamo seem remote. The point is to look at your child as he is and decide if the expert advice makes sense for your situation.

You should also be aware that expert advice has a habit of reflecting popular opinion of the period. Can you imagine a child-care expert in Victorian times suggesting that children's questions about sex ought to be answered frankly? Or an expert in the 1960's stating that discussions about sex with your child should be taboo? These "expert" opinions mirror the bias of their times, not hard, scientific research about what actually is best for the child. And that, of course, is the question every parent must test all advice against: What is best for my child?

What Is Best for Your Child?

Certain suggestions have emerged from research and child study which seem destined to remain as "givens" in child care and no longer subject to the whims of a particular period's overall philosophy.

The first is that love is essential. No matter how carefully parents follow all other advice, without love the results will be unsatisfactory. For the child to benefit, he must feel this warmth.

The second is that communication between parents and child aids emotional, social, and intellectual development.

The third is that rarely does a single event determine the success or failure of raising a child. This is very reassuring—you have to make mistakes consistently, rather than intermittently, for them to influence the outcome of your efforts. The overall pattern of interaction between parents and child is the important factor in successful upbringing.

Parents who accept and are happy with *themselves* and their accomplishments have the best success in raising happy, confident children. These parents can accept their children as they are, thus fostering a positive attitude in them about their abilities and competence. A parent's sound mental health could be his or her child's most important asset.

Having a relaxed attitude toward bringing up a child helps parents avoid extremes in their own behavior. Successful parents do not adhere to an all-or-nothing philosophy: rigid discipline or total absence of control, constant praise or constant criticism, over solicitude or total rejection. Moderation makes good sense. This middle-ground approach usually means the child will avoid extremes in his own behavior and reactions as well.

Tug of War

Becoming more knowledgeable about child-rearing does not mean banishing the headaches of the process. It may be possible to moderate some problems and perhaps eliminate others, but growing up is a difficult process under the best of circumstances. For some parents the most difficult part of all is the battle between parent and child for power. And the balance—or imbalance—of power you and your child achieve affects the harmony in your home now and in the future and has some implications for your child's safety as well.

Do you believe there is only one correct way for accomplishing a task—your way? If so, your child is going to have to fight harder than usual for his right to do things his way. He cannot practice making decisions, finding solutions to problems, or persevering when solutions don't work if you don't give him the opportunity to learn how. Lack of practice in using intellectual or emotional skills creates just as much dependency as lack of practice in getting dressed. If your child doesn't learn how to do these jobs for himself, he'll forever need to depend upon you to accomplish them for him. Don't teach your child to be incompetent by denying him the opportunities to help himself.

Do you always capitulate to your child's desires in order to keep the peace? A peace-at-any-price policy means your child can't learn compromise or cooperation. Your job is to decide when the tug of war goes to your side and when to your child's. The contest won't be a tie, but if all the rope lies on one side of the line, adjustments are needed in the balance of power.

An unseen safety factor exists in allowing some defiance of authority. In developing sound judgment, your child will not fall into the trap of obeying all adults mindlessly. When your child is older, you will need to instruct him in how to keep himself safe when you are not with him. If you have never permitted him to buck adult orders, you'll have an impossible task teaching him to resist an adult who might harm him. The father of a Florida child who was abducted and later found murdered said afterward that he wished he had taught his son not to accommodate adult orders so obligingly, not to be unfailingly polite to his elders. Perhaps if he had, he said, his son might still be alive.

"Yesterday upon the stair/I saw a man who wasn't there"

Between the ages of thirty and thirty-six months many children create imaginary companions. Though such fantasy often alarms parents, especially since it may extend over a period of weeks or months, under ordinary conditions it is just a passing phase that the child will outgrow shortly.

Like other security devices—favorite blanket or stuffed toy—imaginary companions make life easier for a toddler, who discards them when they have served their purpose. And these inventions indirectly make many positive statements about a toddler.

The phenomenon generally occurs about the same time the child learns to use the personal pronoun "I." Studies have shown that children who create fantasy friends are more cooperative, friendly, and less violent, watch less television, and use more sophisticated language than other children.

Imaginary companions are the product of a bright, creative mind, for a dull child would be unable to supply the kind and variety of detail that accompanies their creation. One child, for example, invented two entire families of people, called the Fahkis and the Vavas, and was able to describe their homes, cars, appearances, and relationships. He was friendly with both of these families, parents and children equally. He could recite the entire household schedule and routine, and he would chatter at length about what transpired during his visits to their homes.

These companions may either be animal or human and serve a number of functions for the creative toddler. Some imaginary friends or pets help allay a toddler's fears. A docile lion or elephant around the house helps a toddler cope with a fear of animals or a fear of the dark, since this fierce beast can be summoned for aid. An imaginary companion may help alleviate loneliness, or it may aid a child in accepting and handling the unacceptable or destructive impulses that he wishes to deny. In such an instance the fantasy friend is handy to have on tap to receive blame when the child has done something he shouldn't. Having the same preferences or dislikes as their creators, these alter egos can demand or refuse meals with impunity.

Only when a child continually excludes the real world in order to retreat into his fantasy land or when the fantasy persists beyond a few months is there any need for a parent to become concerned about the situation. If the motive for the invention of a fantasy friend is apparent, a parent might hasten the disappearance of this household guest by fulfilling the unmet need. A lonely child who finds real friends will probably abandon the fantasy abruptly.

Daily Routines

Eating

Sampling New Foods

If your toddler still resists an opportunity to sample new foods, try making some minor changes in the presentation or preparation. Often the toddler will relish foods she previously rejected when the setting in which they are presented

is changed. Having a guest for lunch or sharing a meal at a friend's house may overcome her resistance to a particular vegetable. This strategy works particularly well if the other child is older than your own, since toddlers readily model their behavior on that of older children if they have the opportunity to do so.

Dining in a new locale may induce a toddler to throw caution to the winds and sample a new food. Somehow shredded carrots taste better at a picnic lunch in your backyard or a nearby park than they do in your kitchen. Sometimes changing the shapes of certain foods increases their desirability. Leave the broccoli in little tree shapes rather than chopping it, or slice steamed carrots into circles rather than into skinny sticks.

Reluctant tasters may be induced to try a new food if it is mixed with one they already know and like. Vegetables lend themselves well to such combinations, so if your child is wild about cooked carrots, she may offer little resistance to carrots and peas or carrots and squash, etc. If you find her picking out just the carrots and leaving the other item, then serve the new vegetable a different way the next time, and she's unlikely to recognize it.

Remember that hunger is your best ally in convincing a toddler to try new dishes. If you schedule your toddler's snacks close to mealtime, she will be less inclined to sample something different from her usual fare.

Small, manageable portions can also stimulate a picky toddler's appetite. Tailor your serving size to your child; many parents heap overwhelming amounts on a child's plate. Let her know that seconds are available if she's still hungry.

Several techniques should never be used to encourage a reluctant child to taste unfamiliar food. Never beg your child to do so. This means never offering sweets or other rewards for tasting an item and never suggesting that the child's refusal to eat the item will make Mommy or Daddy suicidal or that agreeing to taste it will make their day. Avoid inducing guilt over her refusal to try a new dish; "I made this just for you, and you're not even going to taste it?" makes eating into a responsibility that ranks with "Honor thy father and mother."

Never demand that your child taste a food she adamantly refuses—as in: "You're not leaving this table until you try the zucchini, and I don't care if we sit here all night." You might say, "Maybe you'll want to try it when you're older." Then avoid giving the rejection any further attention.

When you do resubmit the same food for approval at a later date, don't remind your child of her previous response or you'll be asking for another rejection. Unless the food tasted truly unpalatable the first time, she's likely to have forgotten the earlier incident entirely (especially if you've prepared or presented it differently) and will approach this taste test unhampered by past reactions.

Do not attempt to introduce more than one new food at a time if your toddler isn't the type of child who is flexible and open to new experiences. Otherwise, she's liable to allow distaste for the first item to influence her opinion of the rest.

Says one mother of three hearty eaters, "My philosophy consisted of putting the food I prepared on the children's plates and letting them take over from there. If they didn't want a particular item, they didn't have to eat it, and they could always have seconds of what they did like.

"But I refused to fall into the trap of catering to their tastes for three reasons. First, their tastes were unstable; from day to day I could never predict with any certainty what items were acceptable and which were taboo. Second, if I tried to please three individual palates, I'd wind up spending my life in the kitchen preparing three different entrees for each meal. My kitchen is not a restaurant. And third, I often imagined my kids as grownups at a business dinner. If they still didn't eat string beans at thirty-five, at least they wouldn't have a tantrum if the waiter put some on their plate.

"Maturity means openness to new experiences, and I wanted to make sure that my kids developed that openness. I also didn't want them to miss out on millions of delicious dishes which might have strange names or look unusual but which taste delicious. Eating well is one of life's great pleasures; who'd want his child to miss out on that?"

Multivitamin Supplements

There is no universal agreement among pediatricians about prescribing vitamin supplements for toddlers. Some doctors do it routinely, while others feel that a child who eats a well-balanced diet gets all the vitamins she needs from her meals. You will want to discuss this issue with your pediatrician and decide whether or not your child is a candidate for a daily multivitamin.

Even if your child does take vitamins, you cannot ignore the quality of the foods she eats. A multivitamin supplement is meant to serve as an addition to a well-rounded diet; it is not a substitute for nutritious meals. A varied diet also supplies many trace elements required for healthy growth and development. Without proper nutrition your child will be deprived of these even if she takes her vitamins daily.

Although many people associate vitamins with robust health, it is dangerous to give your child more than the prescribed amount. While the body excretes excessive amounts of some vitamins, it stores others, so that an overdose of certain vitamins can be toxic.

In order to make vitamin supplements more palatable and attractive to children, drug manufacturers often flavor the supplements and design them to resemble popular cartoon characters. You must help your child understand that these supplements are medicine, not candy, and that taking more than what the doctor prescribes can be harmful. After you give your child her daily supplement, promptly replace the childproof cap, then put the container of vitamins out of your child's sight and reach.

Tooth Care

Extra Protection From Cavities

When your child is about three years of age, the dentist may want to help protect her baby teeth by giving them a fluoride treatment. The child bites down into a mold filled with a fruit-flavored, jellylike substance containing fluoride. The mold remains on the teeth for several minutes so that the fluoride can work its way into all the nooks and crevices. Eating and drinking are restricted for a short time afterward to prevent premature removal of the newly applied fluoride. Therefore, this treatment should be scheduled between meals so that you will not be faced with a starving child who isn't permitted to eat.

Sleeping

Timing the Transfer From Crib to Bed

Timing can make the difference between a successful, happy switch from the crib to a bed and a traumatic experience for your child. When is a good time to begin making the change? Avoid, if possible, scheduling the transfer during the months of your toddler's negative, obstinate stage, when she may refuse to cooperate just for the pleasure of being independent. The switch proceeds most smoothly when everyone's attitude is positive. Between thirty and thirty-six months many toddlers develop a sunny, flexible disposition that makes this age ideal for trying new experiences.

You may find that your child raises the issue herself. Often a request for a bed follows shortly after a child begins nursery school or play group. Once she visits the homes of school companions and sees that others have discarded the crib, she usually wants a bed too.

Because most children think of their crib as a cozy, protective refuge, switching them to a bed when home life is frenetic isn't a good idea. If tension exists due to recent job changes, a return to work, separation or divorce, etc., postpone making the change until things calm down. The last thing a toddler needs at such times is more upheaval. A child who feels insecure weathers changes poorly.

Arrange to make the switch when your toddler is healthy. She needs the comfort and security of a familiar mattress when ill. In addition, a toddler often sleeps more restlessly than usual when sick and she runs a greater risk of tumbling out of bed if she is tossing and turning.

If you will need the crib for a new baby, have your toddler make the change from crib to bed well in advance of her sibling's arrival. Few events can be as devastating as finding one's sleeping quarters usurped by an intruder. Think back to the three bears' famous refrain: "Someone's been sleeping in *my* bed," a line that never fails to grab a toddler's attention. The instinct to preserve one's own territory is strong, and your toddler will have a hard time learning to love a crib thief.

The Mechanics of the Move

If the crib you own is the type that converts to a youth bed, you need only reassemble the crib into bed form now. These convertible cribs help make a toddler feel secure during the transfer, since the bed feels, as well as looks, familiar.

If you don't already own a bed to use for the transfer, buy a twin-size mattress and box spring of the highest quality you can afford. Many parents make the mistake of purchasing an inexpensive set and frame only to find in a short time that cheap construction does not withstand the rigorous play and abuse to which a child and her friends subject them, even if you ban using the bed as a trampoline. A quality set of bedding should last ten or more years and will carry a guarantee for a three-to-five-year period; a cheap set may not hold up even for two.

Make the outing to purchase the bedding a special occasion and have your toddler accompany you. Bedding salesmen expect customers to test the mattresses, and your child will feel she has contributed to the selection process if she tries out one or two. Prepare her in advance by telling her how she is expected to behave and that jumping on the samples is not permitted. Have her show you her bed-testing technique on a bed in your home so that she understands that the showroom isn't a playground. If you are purchasing a headboard, let her help select it.

When you first make the switch, do not bother to assemble the bed frame. Position the mattress and box spring, or just the mattress alone, on the floor. This way your child can't fall very far or injure herself if she should roll out. When she has acclimated herself to this arrangement, you can install the frame.

Until you are certain that your child won't roll out, use an exercise mat or some sofa pillows to cushion any falls. Exercise mats are available inexpensively at many sporting goods stores and serve a double purpose, since toddlers enjoy using them for elementary gymnastic routines.

The ideal way to make the switch is to leave the crib right where it is and to set up a bed in your toddler's room at the same time. Then let her decide where to sleep. Some children will use the bed to rest during the day or will start the night off in the bed and then decide they want to go back to the crib. After several nights of such indecision they usually feel comfortable enough with the bed to sleep there. When the crib remains available, it seems to offer a child a feeling of security which enables her to transfer easily. Even if this arrangement means that your child's room will hold wall-to-wall bedding for a few nights, the inconvenience is worth the extra security your child gains from having her choice of sleeping quarters. Once your child uses the bed permanently, the crib can be dismantled.

If your nursery is so small that both the bed and the crib simply won't fit, then you need to prepare your child in advance for the change. Several days before you anticipate making the substitution, tell your child about the coming event. Make your announcement positive: She is being given a bed because she is growing bigger and needs more space to sleep comfortably at night.

She will get a thrill out of helping to disassemble the crib and assembling the bed. Having had a hand in creating the new arrangement, she will be proud to sleep in her handiwork. Do not arrange to have the switch made when she is not at home and then present this monumental change in her life as a surprise. Toddlers have difficulty adjusting to earth-shattering surprises, and yours may just decide that she'd rather have the old arrangement back. To avoid this headache, allow her participation. (If you must disassemble the crib, use the crib mattress next to the bed as roll-out protection.)

Superhero or cartoon character sheets can also ease the transition to a bed. Timid children especially gain confidence from association with strong, fantasy characters, so if you can purchase bedding of this sort, your child will probably be eager to use the bed at once.

Because parents view the switch to a bed as a milestone, many are tempted to suggest that the toddler take an additional step toward maturity and stop sucking her thumb or abandon her favorite stuffed animal or blanket at this time. Such suggestions only serve to upset the child, who cannot happily anticipate sleeping in a bed if it imposes such difficult restrictions on her behavior. In fact, she may depend upon these security devices even more heavily for a few nights until she adjusts to the transfer. One change at a time is a good rule for toddlerhood, whether at meals, bedtime, or learning any new activity.

Bathing and Dressing

Taking a Shower

A short shower can be a welcome substitute for a long bath on evenings when you are pressed for time. However, even toddlers who adore water play and bathtub fun are frequently reluctant to use a shower. Many find the sound of the running water scary, and those who have been subjected to the vagaries of a temperamental plumbing system become terrified of unpredictable water temperatures. If balky plumbing frightens your child, your plumber can install a device in your shower nozzle to maintain an even temperature. Showers are such time-savers that the expense of the installation is worth the investment.

If you have access to an outdoor shower at a beach or pool or to a lawn sprinkler system or garden hose, these are good ways of getting a reluctant child accustomed to the idea of using a shower. Because she can run under and out of the spray at will, your toddler finds these showers less frightening than the more confining one in your bathroom.

Allowing a child to rinse herself off after a bath with one of the spray attachments that connect to the shower nozzle is another good introduction to showering. These hand-held devices also offer a toddler enough control over the situation to calm her fears.

Before you attempt to shower your child, lay a large terry

bath mat outside the tub area to soak up the overflow and position a large rubber mat inside the tub for steady footing. If your home is equipped with a stall shower, use that shower to initiate your toddler. A stall shower makes entering and exiting easy, and toddlers find it less intimidating than the more restrictive tub variety.

Regulate the water temperature to a comfortable level, adjust the force of the spray to a gentle setting, and ask your child to stand outside the tub (or shower enclosure) and just wet her hands. If she is willing, ask her next to wash several of her toys while still standing outside the shower. Most toddlers find this activity so engrossing that they forget their fear of the spray.

When she seems relaxed, encourage her to get into the tub at the opposite end from the shower head and to hold one foot at a time under the spray. With a stall shower she can manage this maneuver by standing at the doorway to the shower. Then ask her to demonstrate how much of her legs she can wash and rinse. Can she do her ankles, her shins, her knees? Most toddlers like to surpass whatever level you set. Teach her to turn her back on the spray while she is soaping herself, since toddlers often dislike the sensation of water spray in the face.

If your child is reluctant, offer to get in with her. Some toddlers need this extra security to begin and will tolerate the shower with an adult there for protection. She may want you to hold her.

If she is willing to wash only her hands and her toys but refuses to enter the shower, accommodate her. Don't force her to go beyond the level at which she feels comfortable. End the shower on a positive note, and save the next step for another day. Reassure her that soon she will be able to overcome her fear and that she can try again another time.

Showering saves time once your child gets the hang of it. As you can see from these steps, initially it is a rather drawn-out process. If you attempt to rush the introduction by ignoring your child's very natural fears of a new experience, by forcing her under the spray without considering her feelings, or by rushing her through each of the steps without allowing sufficient time for her to overcome her fright, she is likely to be very uncooperative about showering. Calling her a baby or ridiculing her fear is a poor technique for building her confidence. Spend the extra time making her feel secure about the shower now to save both time and tantrums in the future.

If the introduction to the shower hasn't gone smoothly, you might try letting your toddler use a small watering can in the tub to give a doll a shower. Acting out the scene may give her the confidence she needs to become a participant in it.

Choosing One's Own Clothes

A toddler who is becoming self-sufficient should be able to choose her own clothes when getting dressed. However, if you simply turn your child loose in her closet without any instruction, she's likely to come out looking like a reject from "The Gong Show." She's going to need some educating before she can handle this task well enough so that you don't blush to be seen in public with her.

The first step in helping a toddler learn to select her apparel is to put it within her reach. Position a pole in her closet at her shoulder height so that she can remove and return hanging garments without assistance. Hang out-of-season garments on the upper rack. Next, put the current season's clothes in the bottommost drawers of her bureau.

Make a game of learning how to match items, and let your child know that the prize for learning the rules of your game is the right to pick out her own outfit each day. Then explain that the object is to match a polo shirt and pants whose colors look good together. This is the part that gets a little tricky, since to a toddler's eye puce and chartreuse blend beautifully.

One mother made a chart that she hung on the bulletin board in her toddler's room. On the left side she cut a large square of a color, and on the line to the right she cut smaller squares of the colors her daughter could choose to wear with it. She wisely stipulated that only one half of any outfit could be patterned; that way her daughter didn't go out to play resembling the test pattern on a TV screen.

You might also lay out three or four polo shirts and three or four pairs of pants in obvious color combinations, and let your toddler practice matching the red and white striped shirt to the red corduroy overalls and the blue jeans to the shirt with the blue balloons on it. Whenever you take your toddler shopping for clothes, ask her to select a shirt that matches the pants you've chosen, or give her a choice between two items and ask which better matches the clothing already selected.

If you will feel uncomfortable allowing your child to sport unsupervised combinations, state from the start that she must show you her choices before she gets dressed. It is unfair to expect her to change after she has struggled into an outfit, and this policy will avoid any altercation after she has dressed herself. Do not expect your child to pay any attention to the weather; she'll see nothing wrong in pairing summer shorts with a thick sweater. Keep out-of-season clothing out of sight or out of reach.

You should also designate certain clothes as everyday wear and others as party and special occasion outfits. This rule takes care of little girls who think organdy dresses and Mary Janes are suitable for play group or those who want to wear stained jeans to a birthday celebration.

Learning these skills makes your toddler more competent and independent and offers valuable practice in making choices. Selecting her attire and then donning the clothes herself also eliminates dressing time as a battleground. Keep in mind that making a selection will probably require extra minutes in the morning; plan for it—the benefits it offers are worth the extra time.

Playtime

Encouraging Sociability

The sociable child enjoys many advantages denied to the introvert. She is calmer and less fearful in group situations than a shy child, and she adjusts to them more easily because she wastes little time worrying about how to initiate or respond to social interaction. This inner tranquility often translates into both greater academic success and greater pleasure from social encounters than the shy child achieves.

You can give your child the advantages of sociability in three important ways: by helping her establish the right frame of mind to develop this trait, by helping her hone the necessary social skills, and by providing the supportive environment required for their continued growth.

To develop sociability, your child needs two specific building blocks: confidence and competence. Confidence depends upon a good self-image, so if your child seems excessively shy, you will want to work harder at making her feel good about herself. Praise her successes and ignore her failures. You are your child's mirror. If she sees in this mirror a positive reflection of herself, she will internalize that view as her self-image. If the mirror reveals instead that she repeatedly fails to meet her parents' standards and to win their unqualified approval, her self-confidence will be seriously damaged. It's difficult, if not impossible, to be sociable if your self-image is negative.

Confidence also grows from competence. A competent child finds it easy to believe in herself, and her positive self-image naturally attracts friendship. If your three-year-old is very introverted, you must question whether you are inhibiting her natural drive toward independence and thereby restricting opportunities for her to learn to believe in herself. Is your toddler feeding herself, washing herself, dressing herself, etc.? If not, the time is overdue for loosening some of the ties that bind.

Competence in other areas will help a reserved child initiate interaction with playmates. Can she catch a ball, do a somersault, play some simple games? If you help her learn such skills, she possesses built-in icebreakers for social gatherings with friends. Few children can resist the attraction of learning some new activity from a companion.

Just as you can teach your child the skill of matching clothes for dressing, you can teach her the skills necessary to sociability. Having these skills will reduce her anxiety in social situations. Together with your toddler, produce a little skit about making new friends. Three-year-olds love to pretend, so pretend that both of you are children in the playground and that you haven't met before. "Hello," you say, "my name is Jodi. What's your name?" If your child can't create a response, tell her, "Now you say, 'My name is Jessica. Want to go on the slide?'" Repeat this type of little play frequently over several days until your child can handle such introductions easily.

After your toddler learns to make introductions, vary the script so that she will enjoy the flexibility of being able to launch friendships in a variety of settings: Want to play house? Let's build with blocks, color with crayons, etc. Then switch roles and allow her to initiate the introduction. Try using hand puppets to dramatize some similar conversations, since introverts sometimes find learning to be sociable easier when they can do so from the security of another identity.

When your toddler handles these scenarios easily, continue the playacting so that she develops the ability to cement a blossoming friendship. Pretend to play with blocks, for example, and then say, "I'm tired of building." If your toddler makes no response, ask, "What can we do now?" Give her a chance to make a suggestion for a different activity. Encourage conversation during each activity so that your child learns to elicit others' feelings and to express her own.

With enough practice she will be able to transfer these techniques to relationships with other toddlers. As with any other skill, each of these steps takes time to learn, so don't throw them all at her at once; wait until one lesson is mastered before beginning the next.

A slightly older child provides an excellent role model for imparting social skills by example if you can arrange for such a meeting. Older children enjoy directing and coordinating play activities, relieving the shy child of the burden. Toddlers seem to assimilate lessons demonstrated by a child faster than they internalize the same information from an adult, perhaps because they identify more closely with another youngster. Playing with a somewhat younger child can also benefit a shy toddler, since the toddler usually relaxes when the playmate is less competent and aggressive than she.

Once your toddler plays easily with a single companion, enlarge her circle of friends so that she becomes accustomed to some variety in social situations. Otherwise, the pattern of play established with one particular friend becomes the standard for her social behavior, and you don't want her locked into one particular role before she's had an opportunity to find the social identity with which she's most comfortable. Playing with an assortment of friends, your child has a chance to assume a variety of roles—leader or follower, boisterous or subdued, etc. As she becomes more socially adept, you might also encourage her to invite several friends to play simultaneously so that she gradually acquires the skills involved in group play.

Like physical skills, social skills require practice for improvement. The more practice your toddler gets, the more confident she becomes in the art of sociability. This means that your child should frequently spend time with other toddlers in order for her social skills to mature. While attendance at play group or nursery school certainly offers opportunity for practice, your child also needs to play with peers in a less structured setting, such as her own backyard or local playground. The absence of teacher involvement and organization in such settings forces the shy child to rely upon her own resourcefulness in making friends. Even constant interaction with parents or other adults doesn't serve the same purpose as peer play, since the toddler isn't required to exert as much effort or inventiveness in initiating and sustaining conversation and play as she must with companions of her own age.

You should also consider whether your attitude toward your toddler's play might be hampering her efforts to become sociable. Many parents pay lip service to the benefits of social play but gripe so much about the mess and effort required in arranging and supervising such occasions (especially on a frequent basis) that the child is actually discouraged from real involvement.

If this is your problem, you can solve it to some extent by deciding in advance which activities you can tolerate and banning the ones you can't. It's better to declare finger paints off limits than to allow their use and make your child feel uncomfortable afterward. Before toddler guests arrive, remove the toys containing a thousand pieces whose cleanup becomes your responsibility at the end of the session. If pleasant playtimes culminate in unpleasant recriminations, sociability loses much of its allure.

Also avoid criticizing your child's social performance after her friends have gone home. If the first get-togethers do not fulfill your expectations, stress the skills your child used well and ignore the problems: "I liked the way you showed Carrie where the games were." Not: "Why did you keep your thumb in your mouth when Carrie came to play?" With enough practice and compliments from you your toddler's social behavior will improve.

Finally, do you personally provide a good social example for your toddler? A child will imitate her parents' social behavior in the same way she imitates their other habits. Visiting friends and having guests provide powerful examples for your toddler to emulate.

Sociability and Sickness

The more your child is exposed to other children, the greater the opportunity for her to catch whatever germs are circulating in your neighborhood. This is an unfortunate fact of life, and toddlers seem especially vulnerable, since they have not yet developed much immunity to contagious illnesses.

Keeping your toddler swaddled in the overprotective cocoon of her own room isn't the answer. One way to reduce this problem is to notify the parents of your toddler's friends that invitations depend upon the guests' health. Any considerate parent would not, of course, send a sick child to your home; however, not all parents are considerate. You can protect your child by announcing your rule concerning sneezes and sniffles when you extend the invitation.

The problem of contact with sick children increases when a toddler attends nursery school, for a parent who would hesitate to send a child with a cold to a friend's house often doesn't hesitate to send a toddler in that condition to school. This is especially true if the parent works and relies upon the school for day-care services.

If this problem arises at your child's school, pressure the administration to establish a policy concerning children who are sent to school feeling ill and to notify all students' families of the regulations. These should stipulate that parents will be required to remove any pupil judged contagious. You may need to organize a parent lobby to convince the school of the need for such a policy, since school personnel dislike dealing with disgruntled parents. This is another instance in which becoming an advocate for your child's welfare is difficult but necessary. Finding other parents who agree with your stand will make the confrontation easier to handle.

Elimination

Toileting Accidents

You might have thought toileting problems would become ancient history once your toddler abandoned diapers; instead, you have probably discovered by now that some toileting concerns continue to be current events. For "accidents" have a way of happening long after toilet teaching has been successful.

Actually, most toilet accidents of three-year-olds aren't mishaps at all. They occur when a child is either too engrossed in an activity to notice her body signaling the need for elimination or when a child receives the signals but ignores them in favor of continuing her play for a few minutes longer. A toddler doesn't tolerate interruptions patiently during any activity and especially not during play, and she gambles that she can hold out for a more convenient moment. Because the toddler cannot yet gauge the urgency of her signal well, this is a gamble she often loses.

The child who postpones a trip to the bathroom usually indicates by her actions or behavior that she needs to use the toilet. Holding the genitals, fidgeting or jiggling while at play, and sitting or standing with the legs tightly crossed are toddler attempts at inhibiting the urge to urinate.

Because these signals are so blatant, they alert the parent to the problem and offer some leeway for avoiding catastrophe. Most parents approach the problem in a self-defeating manner. Noticing one of the signals, the parent asks the toddler, "Do you need to use the toilet?" To an adult this question actually means, "I think you need to use the toilet." The toddler, however, lacks the sophistication to understand a rhetorical question, and no three-year-old in the entire history of the world has ever responded to that query by stating, "Yes, I do need a toilet. I'll be right back." Instead, the toddler takes the question at face value—her parent isn't sure of her need for a toilet. This interpretation allows her to deny its necessity. Two minutes later, of course, the toddler has lost her gamble and her entire outfit, including her shoes, is soaked.

There are some compelling reasons for allowing your toddler to wet her clothes this way a few times. The first is that she cannot learn how urgent a signal is unless she has some chance to test it. If you whisk her off to the bathroom the moment she begins to dance around, you deny her the opportunity to find the limits of her endurance. In addition, by age three most toddlers are usually both unhappy and uncomfortable in wet clothing. Experiencing the consequences of postponing toileting can provide a powerful incentive to reach the bathroom with greater haste the next time.

If your toddler continues to ignore her body's signals, let her handle the responsibility of remedying the results. Without making too big a commotion over the accident (so that it does not become an effective means for getting attention in a negative way), put your child in charge of taking her wet clothes off, disposing of them, and dressing herself again. You might point out that dressing and undressing interrupt her playtime longer than using the toilet would have. (If you say this angrily, however, your child will absorb the tone of your voice and not the lesson, so stay

calm.) Be sure to make complimentary comments about successful trips to the toilet. Successes should garner more feedback than failures.

If the habit continues despite this step, do not ask your child whether she needs to visit the toilet when you can clearly see she does. Instead, alert her to the signal: "When you hop around like that, you need to use the toilet." Then, to reduce her resistance to ceasing her play, allow her to take some item to the bathroom with her: "You can take your car with you." Parents often resist allowing this continuity because carrying a toy to the bathroom seems an unnecessary burden. To a toddler, however, it provides a guarantee that she can resume play afterward.

If she still resists leaving her play, insist that she go to the bathroom and accompany her if necessary. As you head her toward the bathroom, you can focus your remarks on some interesting way for her to use her toys when she resumes play: "Have you tried putting your farm animals in the wagon?" This usually guarantees cooperation in the bathroom in order to return quickly to her play. Most toddlers need only a few such reminders before they begin to heed the signals without being reminded to do so.

One aid to reducing accidents of this sort is to dress your child in clothing that allows easy removal for toileting. The more she must fuss with straps or hard-to-handle buttons, the longer the excursion to the bathroom takes and the more frustrating it becomes. Don't put unnecessary obstacles in the path of answering toileting signals.

Remember that such accidents can happen away from home as well as in it, so do yourself a favor by keeping a spare set of clothing in your car for emergencies. Such planning helps keep reactions to accidents calm and reasonable, while preventing both ruined outings and the resulting migraine headaches.

Toileting at Nursery School

Two common problems can interfere with successful toileting at nursery school. First, stress is often responsible for incontinence, and enrolling in nursery school can be a stressful situation for many toddlers. Second, some toddlers are reluctant to use any bathroom other than the familiar one in their home, and such children attempt to hold out until they can reach the toilet in their own house. This reluctance, combined with a toddler's natural antipathy to interrupting her play, increases the likelihood of toilet accidents at school.

The toddler who either ignores or is only mildly upset by an accident that happens at home can be devastated by the same event in a school setting. With a few simple steps you can reduce both the possibility of accidents and the trauma they can cause. The more familiar your child is with her school, her teacher, and her classmates, the less stressful attendance becomes. Visit the school before she enrolls, show her the route from her classroom to the bathroom, find where the supplies of toilet paper and towels are kept, and encourage her to use the bathroom while you are with her.

If she resists this step, you may at least be able to get her to "try out" the sink by washing her hands. Then when she attends school, the bathroom there will seem a little more familiar.

You should also prepare your toddler for possible toilet problems so that she does not worry about them once school begins. "Suppose you need to use the toilet, and you can't get the zipper open on your pants," you ask her, "what would you do?" This simple question will stump most toddler. If yours can't answer, the reply should be, "Whenever you have a problem at school, ask the teacher for help." Ask your toddler this question until she doesn't have to think to answer it. When she answers easily, ask her to pretend that you are the teacher and that she has a problem with her jeans. How will she ask for help? Knowing that she should ask the teacher and being able to phrase the question are two different skills. Learning one without the other won't help her resolve her difficulty. If she cannot state the question by herself, help her compose one. Then rehearse it a few times until she is comfortable with the knowledge that she can control any problems of this nature that occur during school hours.

Your toddler should store a box containing a spare set of clothing, along with a plastic bag for bringing wet clothing home, in school in case of accidents. Orientation day is a good time to locate a safe spot for her spare outfit because she will be too distracted on her first day to remember its location. Accidents during school hours become less traumatic when she has a means to remedy their effects promptly.

Make sure that your child's teacher permits students to visit the bathroom at will, and encourage your toddler to use the bathroom in your home before class in order to keep toilet accidents to a minimum.

"What! Still in diapers?"

Do not be concerned if your child is still not ready for toilet teaching, even though a majority of her friends may no longer need diapers. Many children who have supposedly learned to use the toilet have enough daily accidents to make anyone other than their parents question whether they are really ready to abandon their diapers. Frequently, toddlers simply need more physical maturation, and they will not be successful at using the toilet regularly until they are three and a half or four years old. Though such children may be labeled "late bloomers," this developmental rate is considered perfectly normal.

Tactless adults who make negative comments about the continued need for diapers can make a late bloomer's life miserable. On the theory that the recalcitrant sinner will shape up immediately upon hearing such criticism, the remarks are made within earshot of the offender. Such criticism, especially when directed at a child who wants desperately to graduate from diapers but lacks the physical control necessary to doing so, damages self-esteem.

The parents of a diaper-clad child also come under attack. Older relatives may suggest that the delay in toilet learning is a symptom of poor parenting skills or outright laziness. Their comments imply that if the parents cared enough, the child wouldn't experience this difficulty. Even though such attitudes have no basis in fact, they are difficult to tolerate, and it is a rare parent who doesn't feel a sense of failure when his or her child reaches the third birthday still in diapers.

Though you might feel better telling off a critic, consideration for your child's injured feelings should prompt you to keep your response low-key and positive: "I've checked with my pediatrician, and he says many children don't learn toileting until they're even older than Tabitha. She's doing fine." If you recognize and accept the fact that your child's lack of physical maturation is totally unrelated to your parenting skills, you'll find it hard to get angry at such misguided nonsense.

Enuresis

Nocturnal enuresis is the scientific name for bed-wetting. Because nighttime control requires more advanced physical maturation than daytime dryness, it is not unusual for this condition to continue into the early elementary school years. Most physicians do not consider enuresis to be a problem requiring investigation until the child is at least five years old. In fact, in some children the particular portion of the brain controlling nighttime dryness doesn't mature until adolescence. As you might expect with a skill depending upon physical maturity, prolonged enuresis affects twice as many males as females.

With a few exceptions you need not worry if your child is still wetting her bed at age three. Prolonged nocturnal enuresis stems from three basic causes: slow developmental rate, disease or congenital abnormality, and psychological factors. Time eventually cures the first cause.

A return to bed-wetting after having achieved periods of dryness, however, can indicate the presence of infection, and medication prescribed for the underlying infection usually solves the second problem. Other symptoms indicating a medical condition requiring treatment are pain during urination, frequent urination, and any change in the color of the urine or in the type of stream produced. The combination of bed-wetting and frequent urination may indicate the presence of diabetes. If your child complains about any of these symptoms, have her examined immediately. Urinary infections can have very harmful consequences and even result in kidney damage if left untreated. Congenital abnormalities of the excretory system which cause prolonged bed-wetting may require corrective surgery.

Many psychological causes of enuresis arise from stress-related situations. These include moving, enrolling in nursery school, the arrival of a sibling, divorce, etc. Bed-wetting resulting from these sources usually disappears once the toddler finds a means of coping with the disruption. In such cases bed-wetting signals a child's fragile mental state and a feeling of being overwhelmed by forces she cannot control. She reacts by regressing to babyish habits, and she needs much love, attention, and reassurance to help her through this difficult time. She acts babyish because she *needs* to be babied. There is no harm in catering to her needs and allowing her to take one step backward before progress toward mature behavior resumes.

Some experts feel that unnecessarily harsh parental attitudes during toilet teaching can cause or prolong nighttime difficulties. Others suggest that bed-wetting sometimes expresses a child's severe emotional distress in response to rigid parental control of daytime activities.

Some parents seem unconsciously to encourage bed-wetting because they wish to keep the child babyish and dependent; let your toddler know that you value maturity and independence, and she will have a motive to strive for them.

Toddlers may indicate a readiness to remain dry at night when they can manage to get through longer daytime periods without urinating and when the number of accidents begins to taper off. If your toddler is physically mature enough to remain dry at night, you can take several steps to help her do so. Some evidence suggests that enuresis is related to small bladder size; though you won't want to forbid a thirsty child from having a drink of water prior to bedtime, you might try to satisfy your child's thirst with the smallest amount of water that does so, rather than a huge glassful. Keep the hours prior to bedtime calm so that your child goes to bed relaxed; avoid scary stories or television shows, since fearful dreams may contribute to bed-wetting. Give your toddler plenty of attention throughout the day and at bedtime so that she goes to sleep feeling secure and loved.

Guide to Good Parenting

Appreciating Individuality

Kevin's and Paul's parents stand waiting at the door to the nursery school classroom for their children to be dismissed. Kevin, trailing a laughing line of children in his wake, climbs nimbly from rung to rung of an indoor jungle gym. Paul sits quietly at a table looking at a book about dinosaurs.

"I wish Paul were more outgoing like Kevin," says Paul's mother. "I'd be happier if he were a more aggressive child."

"Oh, no," protests Kevin's father. "I wish Kevin were more like Paul. He's so mature, and he's already starting to read. Kevin hardly knows the sounds of the letters."

If this conversation weren't so common, it might be comical. But it's repeated thousands of times a day, whenever two parents have an opportunity to compare their children's personalities and accomplishments. And the child is often greener on the other side of the fence. Parents of athletes prefer scholars; parents of scholars admire athletes. The shy child's folks laud gregariousness; the social butterfly's parents encourage introspection.

Most parents consider certain traits essential to the "perfect" child, and the parents' own experiences play a large role in determining which characteristics they admire. Parents who are reasonably content with their own lives may want to see duplicated in their offspring the traits that have contributed to their happiness and success. Parents who are dissatisfied with their achievements may be distressed when

they notice evidence of their own disliked traits in their children.

The important lesson to remember is that children are separate human beings from their parents; each child arrives with his own individual set of characteristics and quirks. Each is perfect in his own way.

"His own way" is an important phrase. Parents who allow for "his own way" without attempting to superimpose their vision of the ideal personality on their child, and who enjoy and admire their child's unique individuality, are the parents who come about as close to parenting perfection as heaven allows.

Raising a Superkid—Can You? Should You?

Perhaps the most common of all parental ambitions is the desire to raise a superkid—you know, a genius who reads at two, computes algebraic equations at three, and discovers a cure for the common cold at age four. Parents who strive for this goal are just as guilty of poor parenting as those who try to foster the "perfect personality" in their offspring, for superparents cannot tolerate the thought that their child might be average instead of outstanding.

Woe unto the child who shows precocity (or even just a mild interest!) in adding or subtracting, in kicking or catching a ball, or in picking out a tune on the family piano. Superparents seize upon their child's strengths and demand distinguished performance from the child in those areas. No ordinary child for them.

Why so many parents focus on this goal isn't completely clear. Some seem to believe that superior intelligence or ability guarantees happiness, though no study has ever in any way supported such an idea. Others hope that it will predict financial success. Yet, superkid instruction, with its emphasis on using every minute to advance learning or improve skills, leaves no breathing room in which creativity and flexibility can flourish, and these traits are often more predictive of future success than early academic progress. Perhaps the desire to hasten maturation simply results from living in a society which puts a premium on speed in all aspects of life. It's only a short jump from microwave cooking to microwave parenting.

Parents intent upon raising superkids devour books detailing techniques for teaching babies to read or pay hundreds of dollars for lectures or toys guaranteed to increase a child's intellectual potential. While there are many benefits associated with offering a child an enriched environment, even in child-rearing it is possible to provide a toddler with too much of a good thing. One study, for example, found that overstimulation can prove detrimental. Overstimulation depletes a child's personal initiative so that he eventually loses the desire to investigate and explore independently. The parents, instead of encouraging real learning, are fostering a kind of learned incompetence.

In this situation too much enrichment robs the child of the inquisitiveness that makes learning a joy. It might create a toddler who can read at three, but it also produces a child who is eternally dependent upon his parents for information, stimulation, and entertainment.

To their chagrin many parents fail to recognize the harm they have done until after this destructive pattern is well established. The problem commonly occurs when over-zealous parents attempt to benefit a first child. Says one, "Jamie throws a tantrum if I don't spend all day playing with him. If I leave him alone with his toys, he's lost. He doesn't know how to amuse himself." Jamie never learned this skill because he was never given the opportunity to draw on his own resources; his parents were too busy bombarding him with stories and games and flashcards. They didn't allow him to do any independent learning because he didn't progress rapidly enough to suit them.

Besides robbing a toddler of initiative, attempting to raise a superkid through superstimulation has other detrimental effects. As you have noticed in observing your toddler's growth and development, a child does not mature simultaneously in all spheres. Nature seems to have arrived at this balance to avoid overtaxing an organism by demanding growth in too many areas all at once. When the child takes an important maturational step, other advances slow for a while. The child who talks before he walks, for example, doesn't expand his vocabulary very much once he starts walking. Only when he has mastered this skill does word building resume at its previous pace.

Interrupting a child's natural timetable by overstressing academic achievement may create an early reader, but many experts also fear that such intellectual achievements are accomplished at the expense of social and emotional growth. Parents of superkids tend to devalue growth in these other spheres (perhaps because emotional maturity and social adeptness are not eminently braggable skills), yet the people we admire most, the ones we consider to have lived the most fulfilling lives, possess more than just superior intelligence. They are individuals who know how to interact with others; as the song insists, "People who need people are the luckiest people in the world." Parents who are truly concerned with their children's welfare recognize the importance of social and emotional, as well as intellectual, skills.

In addition, early proficiency in a skill does not guarantee later interest in the activity. A child who excels in musicality at age three will not necessarily become a virtuoso violinist when he grows older. If parents force instruction in any particular field, they should not be surprised to find that their child later avoids that entire discipline altogether. Education can have pleasurable feelings attached to it only if instruction results from a child's request, not from parental requirement, and progresses at a pace consistent with both the child's abilities and his interest.

Sometimes pushing a child into an activity too soon will destroy the chance for a more positive, productive introduction at a more suitable age. From the day Johanna wandered over to the piano and slammed her fingers down on the keys, her parents were convinced that she possessed musical genius. That pass at the keys was followed by lessons that began the next week. Within two weeks Johanna, whose attention span was entirely appropriate to her age, wanted nothing to do with the instrument. Her parents begged, pleaded, and cajoled. Then they yelled and screamed. Finally they gave up.

Johanna's musical talent never had a chance to flourish in that atmosphere, and it's unlikely that the child will ever again express any enthusiasm for learning to play. In addition, Johanna was so young at the time her lessons began that she would have needed six months to learn skills requiring practice of only a week or less when she was just a few years older. Had Johanna's parents harnessed their own enthusiasm, they might now have a daughter who enjoys music.

Premature emphasis on achievement can lead to other problems besides missed opportunities for later success.

Fulfilling the demands of parents who have set their hearts upon raising a superkid is an endless task. A pressured child easily comes to believe that satisfying his parents' ambitions is an impossibility, that no achievement will ever suffice. And indeed, for superparents no achievement ever will. The parents continually demand higher levels of accomplishment, and inability to meet them can lead a child to despair.

Certainly, such demands and the inability to fulfill them play havoc with the child's establishment of self-esteem. Superparents never stop to consider that if they teach a child equations, all he learns are equations. If they give him self-esteem, he can do *anything*!

The constant pressure to perform convinces a child that his parents love him not for himself but for his accomplishments. As the child grows, he will find himself putting ever greater emotional distance between himself and his parents, for the burden under which he labors is simply too great a load to support forever. How long can he continue to outdo himself before the strain tells? Being destroyed by the pressure or completely separating himself from his parents is his alternative; he must obliterate the relationship if he himself is to survive. Unfortunately, the instruction which some parents undertake with the intention of fostering a bond between their child and themselves can easily create a wedge between them instead.

When the break in family relationships finally occurs, parents often defend their behavior by suggesting that their efforts were exerted for the child's own good. This excuse will not suffice. It is evident that pushing toddlers to become superkids has much more to do with parents' unfulfilled desires than with the child's welfare.

Creating superkids affects not only family relationships but the child's peer relationships as well. Parental demands require that the child outshine his competition. Since the competition consists of the very children with whom the toddler most often comes into contact—classmates at school, local playmates, etc.—friendships suffer. How can a child establish close friendships with the very people who are his chief rivals?

When parents consider how much both they and their child forfeit in this pursuit and how uncertain and meager the rewards, they must conclude that the effort to raise a superkid simply isn't worth the price.

6. Away From Everyday Routines

Going Visiting—What to Expect

Probably the best advice for parents taking a toddler on an outing is the old saw: Expect the worst, hope for the best, and take what comes. Expectations play an important role in determining the success or failure of any family trip.

In many families the parents' unrealistic expectations doom an outing to failure before it even begins. Why? Because these parents view such occasions as a kind of mini-vacation or, at the very least, a brief respite from the burdens of parenting. They erroneously expect to enjoy a reduction of responsibility along with the change in scenery.

In reality any separation of a toddler from everyday routines and from the convenience of one's own home and equipment creates *more* work for parents, not less. Away from home parents must maintain extraordinary vigilance to insure their toddler's safety. They are saddled with an unwieldy amount of paraphernalia and must maintain a flexible, positive attitude despite all difficulties. Parents who

243

don't expect outings to be vacations won't be disappointed when their unrealistic dreams don't become reality.

What other kinds of expectations should you harbor when "expecting the worst"? Be reasonable; consider the probability that very few activities will interest toddler and parents equally. If the outing you've planned isn't likely to hold much appeal for your toddler, either make enough preparations to keep your child occupied and happy while you chat with friends or shop for wallpaper, or hire a baby sitter so that you can accomplish your goal in peace.

Even the success of a visit to friends with a child the same age as yours can't be guaranteed, since the toddlers may not socialize together as well as you and your friends do. If you are too inflexible to cope with your toddler's uncooperative attitude, you're likely to experience a most unpleasant outing.

While you're disposing of unrealistic expectations, eliminate the notion that your child will behave in her usual manner once you have departed from your daily schedule. Expect routines to go awry when you are away from home. Excitement-induced fatigue may make your toddler crankier than usual, yet she'll refuse to sleep at her usual naptime; she may eat twice as much as usual for a meal or nothing at all. The excitement or unfamiliar food may produce an unexpected upset stomach or even diarrhea.

Expect activity and energy levels to change too. Away from home your placid toddler may suddenly become a hyperactive show-off, or your usually energetic youngster may turn catatonic. A toddler out of her normal environment is an exceedingly unpredictable creature. A good rule is simply to expect the unexpected.

If your toddler is one of those children who become supercharged and overwound from the excitement of visiting, plan a few activities in advance which will allow her to expend some of her excess energy *immediately upon arrival* at your destination. Relying upon repeated threats or punishment to calm an overactive toddler is likely to leave you frustrated and exhausted; such discipline is usually unsuccessful anyway.

Here are better ways to handle the problem: When visiting friends, try taking your toddler for a walk around the neighborhood or for a short outing at a local playground before settling down inside. If the weather or location precludes such activities, assign your toddler some helpful, indoor task that will occupy her attention. Sometimes the closeness of being held in your lap for a few minutes and joining the conversation will offer sufficient attention and warmth to calm her.

If your hosts are unfamiliar with the behavior of toddlers, prepare them in advance for your visit. Their unrealistic expectations can also ruin a visit. Without such preparation you will be caught between attempting to accommodate your hosts' fantasy of a perfectly behaved child and the reality of dealing with a rambunctious, inquisitive, or uncooperative toddler. This is especially true if you are visiting people who are elderly, childless, overly fussy, or just plain nervous.

Try to maintain realistic expectations concerning your toddler's attention span. Even the most engrossing of activities or intriguing of toys can't hold a toddler's interest forever. Your toddler's behavior will be most satisfactory to you on outings if you can arrange to alternate high-energy activities with quiet times just as you do daily. Then she can easily resume her usual routine when you return home. Without any freedom to run, she'll have a storehouse of unused energy when you get her home. If she does little but run all afternoon, she's likely to be excessively cranky at night. And an overwound child often doesn't fall asleep easily.

It is just common courtesy to be considerate of your toddler's feelings. Many parents, however, ignore their child's needs in favor of their own desires when on an outing. If the outing is not a pleasurable one for her—shopping or a visit with friends of yours—set a time limit on your stay. The child who is an angel for an hour may become a devil when you tarry fifteen minutes beyond that. Don't expect her to have patience beyond her years, and you won't be disappointed by her behavior.

Finally, discard the belief that a well-planned outing will proceed as planned. As one mother notes, "I always know in advance when my two-year-old will get sick; it happens whenever I make plans to go somewhere special." Toddlers don't plan their illnesses, though sometimes their timing seems to be part of a diabolical plot to keep their parents chained to the house until the child is ready for college. And another mother notes, "If my toddler doesn't get sick just before I'm scheduled to be somewhere, it's a certainty that the baby sitter will cancel." That's life with a toddler, and there's little to prevent this problem. About the best you can do is to accept what comes.

What to Bring

It is nearly impossible to travel light with a toddler in tow. Though you and your spouse may resemble immigrants on their way to the New World, carrying extra baggage is worth the inconvenience if your supplies keep parents or child happy during an outing. You need a large, sturdy bag (preferably plastic-lined) with lots of pockets and compartments to hold all the necessary equipment. The bigger your satchel the better, since it eliminates the need for carrying auxiliary packages which make travel that much more burdensome.

Toddlers need frequent snacks and drinks to keep them happy, so pack a supply of nonperishable, nutritious items. Avoid taking any food that becomes sticky or drippy when eaten. Even with this precaution you might want to keep some extra bibs in your bag for snack time and a package of premoistened disposable towelettes to clean hands and to make diaper changes easier.

Napping proceeds more smoothly during your outing when you plan ahead. Does your toddler acquiesce to a nap in her stroller with a pillow for her head? Bring it along, as well as the stuffed animal or quilt which helps quiet her quickly. Despite their bulk, packing these items is worth the effort, for a tired toddler is a horrible traveling companion.

Your toddler may raise less fuss about napping in an unfamiliar setting if she's been prepared in advance: "We're going to visit Grandma, and you're going to take your nap in the crib that she keeps especially for you." Whenever possible, arrange your schedule so that your toddler's nap coincides with your travel time, since a ride in the car lulls most toddlers to sleep easily.

You won't have much success getting your toddler to nap immediately after arrival, especially if your destination involves a new, unexplored site. To avoid this hassle, arrive early enough for your toddler to do some investigating before you schedule her nap.

After you've packed supplies for meal or snack times and for naps, be sure to include some items to entertain your toddler, particularly if you'll be visiting a toyless environment.

Visiting the Nonchildproofed Home

A visit to a nonchildproofed home tests parents' mettle. Can you grab your toddler before she smashes a priceless collection of crystal figurines? Will you reach the poisons stored in the kitchen and bathroom in time to prevent tragedy? How often will you shout "No, don't touch!" during your visit? Passing the test means you win the grand prize: a headache of truly awesome proportions for your trip home.

There is a way to avoid this problem, but don't expect your hosts to take the initiative. If you are aware of problem areas in your hosts' home, such as that priceless collection of crystal, ask your hosts to safeguard their possessions by putting fragile items safely out of your toddler's reach before you arrive. Most will happily oblige.

In the rare instance where the hosts cannot or will not fulfill your request, you have two choices: Either be prepared to spend the entire visit shadowing your toddler to keep her out of trouble and protect her from danger, or leave her home with a sitter. The second alternative is the smarter, since the first is neither fair nor comfortable for parents or toddler.

When your inquisitive toddler must accompany you, take your play yard along with you. A younger toddler can be induced to remain cooped up for a while if you supply an interesting assortment of toys for her entertainment. With an older toddler the best solution to this uncomfortable situation is to spend as little time in the glass menagerie as possible. Remove both your toddler and your hosts from the problem environment; go for a walk. Bring your toddler's tricycle along with you and you can stretch your visit a little longer. Toting along a portable safety gate is another solution; then you, your hosts, and your toddler can gather in one room. This strategy allows you to confine your surveillance to a limited area instead of patrolling the entire house. Combine these maneuvers with a very brief stay, and you'll eliminate much of the frustration of this most unpleasant of visits.

Visiting Grandparents

Visiting with loving grandparents ought to be one of the most enjoyable outings to take with a toddler. All too often, however, such visits culminate in less-than-loving relationships. "I can't stand visiting my parents," says one young mother. "My mother stuffs Cory with junk food from the minute we arrive; she spoils him with too many toys and generally allows him to destroy her house. When I object, she says that spoiling a child is a grandparent's prerogative. Then my father sits around and grumbles under his breath about how poorly behaved Cory is."

This situation is a common one, and unfortunately the toddler finds herself torn between the two sides in a family tug of war. Sometimes such battles represent continuing skirmishes in a long-standing war for independence and control. Grandmother refuses to relinquish the control she has exercised over her own children. Ignoring their adult status, she attempts to wield the same influence over her grandchild that she had over her children. And there's no denying her pleasure in playing Lady Bountiful, a role that parents who live with the child daily cannot assume if they wish to remain sane and financially solvent.

As adults, the parents are fighting the very same battles for independence they waged throughout their youth. Their child merely provides them with new ammunition. The more uncertain the parents of their abilities, the worse this tug of war will be. Confident parents don't interpret a grandparent's every action as a challenge to their competence and authority. Disagreements or criticisms between the two generations may also reflect their competitiveness as each battles to prove its superiority in the art of parenthood.

If you confront this problem in your family, the best solution is to sit down with your parents and discuss your concerns. If the problem of too many sweets troubles you, try putting your objections on a more neutral ground than personal disapproval: "The dentist told me to limit the amount of sweets Jenny eats. He thinks Jenny's cavity-prone." This approach reduces intergenerational conflict.

You might satisfy Grandma's urge to nurture by scheduling your toddler's lunch at her house during visits and offering some suggestions about her favorite menus. Perhaps you can agree on one sweet treat per visit as a compromise, and keep a toothbrush for your toddler in Grandma's bathroom as well. You might also try suggesting that hugs and kisses express loving feelings without contributing to tooth decay; grandparents as well as toddlers sometimes have difficulty thinking of alternatives to unacceptable behavior.

Too many gifts pose a similar problem and encourage the "what did you get me" syndrome in young children. Encourage the use of odds and ends as gifts, since toddlers often appreciate these items more than expensive toys: different-size boxes, for example, or old hats and pocketbooks for dress-up. Another fine substitute for too many gifts is to encourage grandparents to lavish their time rather than expensive presents on their grandchild. This might mean providing a few books from your toddler's library especially for Grandpa or Grandma to read, or storing a game at the grandparents' home for them to play with their grandchild.

In fact, every child enjoys some activity (reading a very long, favorite story? collecting interesting rocks or leaves?) in which her parents rarely have the time or patience to participate. These activities can be ideal experiences for grandparents and grandchild to share. Starting some kind of collection—a scrapbook of leaves for older toddlers, for example—to keep at the grandparents' house is an especially good choice, since it can be enlarged with each visit. Then the grandparents can visit the children's section of their local library to find appropriate, related reading material to share with their grandchild. These kinds of experiences strengthen the grandparent-grandchild bond far more than simply handing over a gift at every opportunity.

If you find stemming the flow of gifts an impossibility, you can restrict the number of toys available for play when you get them home. There's no need to make them all available simultaneously. This policy counteracts at least part of the detrimental effect of grandparent largesse. Some grandparents can be persuaded to decrease their gift-giving if you store some playthings in their home for future get-togethers. This alleviates the worry that the toddler will be bored when she visits, one motive prompting the purchase of so many toys.

Avoiding Restaurant Roulette

"Would I take Bobby to a restaurant? Not unless I'd gone completely crazy!" Does this situation sound familiar? Being the parent of a toddler doesn't mean never eating out again or always leaving your toddler home. Nor does it mean that you must gamble every time you enter a restaurant on whether or not your meal will be pleasant. Dining out with a toddler does require some careful advance planning, though, if you want the experience to be a success.

First, choose the restaurant with some thought to how

welcome your toddler will be there. Fine dining and rambunctious toddlers generally don't mix well, and your child does not need cordon bleu cooking to learn restaurant manners. Let her learn first and graduate to haute cuisine later when her behavior, manners, palate, and patience warrant the expense. Initially, stick to restaurants that are billed as "family type," to diners, or to fast-food shops for service that is understanding and generally toddler-tolerant.

Second, plan to arrive at the restaurant early, well before the lunch or dinner rush begins and well before your toddler lapses into obnoxiousness from hunger. Waiting on line for an available table with a famished toddler in tow is not one of life's better experiences.

Third, bring some diversion, such as a small toy, to occupy your child until the food is served; otherwise, you have only yourself to blame when she grabs the salt shakers, sugar packets, or napkin dispenser for amusement.

Many restaurants make a practice of serving the beverage you order long before your meal arrives. With a toddler this practice guarantees she will be too full of liquid by the time her food appears to take even one bite. If you're wise, you'll instruct your waitress to hold all drinks until the food is ready.

Older toddlers can learn to place their own order with a waitress. If your child speaks clearly and is not unusually shy, let her learn to order her own food. This is another step in her independence, and she will enjoy feeling grown-up enough to complete this task.

After she has decided on her entree from the two or three choices you offer, tell her that she may give the waitress her order. Ask her to practice ordering her meal from you before the waitress appears. If your child should suddenly turn speechless when the time comes to order, or if you are the only person who can understand her speech, don't pressure her to perform. Simply assure her that soon she'll be able to order her own lunch, and give the waitress her order yourself.

Exposing your toddler to a variety of foods is another positive aspect of restaurant dining. If your child is not an adventurous eater, order her old standbys but encourage her to taste your selection. Don't abandon your habits of not forcing food on her when she is full. You want her to learn that, in a restaurant just as at home, a meal ends when hunger is sated; don't make her stuff herself simply because you are paying for her plate anyway. Have the waiter wrap the remainder and take the leftovers home instead.

Finally, a child belongs in only one place in a restaurant—her seat. If your toddler cannot remain seated throughout an entire meal, she isn't old enough to be eating out. The single exception to this rule are the fast-food restaurants that reserve a special area of the floor for child-size furniture and perhaps some play equipment; these spots are designed for fidgety diners. In any other circumstance allowing a toddler to roam the aisles is a dangerous practice. Waiters carrying heavy trays or pots of scalding coffee can trip over a wandering child, severely injuring her with their load. In the event of an emergency (such as a fire), you would be unable to locate your child quickly and evacuate safely. In addition, an unsupervised toddler often annoys other patrons, who are entitled to an undisturbed meal. Don't jeopardize your child's welfare and others' enjoyment by permitting your toddler to wander.

Happy Birthday

A whole year's growth and achievement deserve a celebration. One- and two-year-olds don't understand the concept of a birthday and don't tolerate much hoopla very well

anyway, so the best birthday party for them is a family get-together with just a few relatives attending. They won't miss either toddler guests or even presents at this age. A happy birthday song and a decorated cake with candles to blow out is all the celebration they need.

Three-year-olds, however, relish the idea of claiming the

spotlight on their own special day. A birthday party for a three-year-old offers an opportunity for an education in social planning and party manners as well.

Have your toddler help select the invitations and paper goods. Let her choose her guests while you write the guest list. (Try to limit the list to guests of approximately the same age so that the activities you plan will appeal to all.) Your toddler can also help set the party table, participate in the baking if you are making the cake at home, or choose the special decoration if it is store-bought. Solicit her suggestions for party games, since she may want some of her nursery school favorites on the list.

Toddlers also love to deliver the invitations; if your guests don't live within hand-delivery range, your toddler can mail them. Unless you are planning to invite her entire nursery school class, distributing the invitations in school is a poor lesson in social etiquette, as the children who do not receive them are bound to feel miserable at being excluded. (Well-run nursery schools do not permit school distribution of invitations.)

Before the big day arrives, help your toddler practice greeting guests and responding with a "thank you" to happy birthday wishes from adults and gifts from guests. She can also learn to say "Thank you for coming" as a guest departs.

This is also a good time to decide where she will store the gifts as the guests arrive. Inform her that the gifts will remain wrapped until the party is over and the guests have gone home. Setting the gifts aside makes good sense for several reasons. First, new toys and games that appear during the party have great appeal for your little guests and may not survive the party itself. Setting them aside insures that your child will have the pleasure of playing with her presents before they disintegrate.

Second, a three-year-old's intense anticipation of a party sometimes culminates in a disappointing letdown when the celebration ends. If you postpone opening the gifts until after the guests depart, you create a perfect segue into a quiet, enormously attractive, postparty activity for your child.

Reduce party anticipation to a manageable level by

grouping all party-related planning and shopping as close to the party date as possible. Too much advance preparation can create an overexcited toddler who has worked herself into an emotional frenzy by the time her birthday finally arrives. By then she is literally sick with excitement and prone to tantrums. Often the birthday child is the toddler who enjoys her own party least of all. An abundance of advance planning intensifies a toddler's postparty blues as well, for the event which aroused all the anticipation ends all too quickly. "Low-key" is the magic word in preparing for a three-year-old's birthday, and remember that this is your child's special day. Pleasing her should be your main goal.

Veteran party-givers agree on a few basic guidelines for celebrating a child's birthday successfully. The accepted rule of thumb advises inviting one guest for each year of a child's age (or a guest for each year plus one), keeping parties brief (no more than an hour and a half long), and scheduling them early in the day, when a three-year-old is generally at her sunniest. Parents who ignore these suggestions when planning a party generally pay the price on party day in the form of either a toddler tantrum or their own exhaustion from coping with too many youngsters for too long a time.

You can make party time easier by arranging to hold either part or all of the party outdoors, assuming fair weather and an available backyard. Spills and clean-ups are less catastrophic when they occur on a lawn or patio rather than inside your home. Outdoor settings also allow for more unrestricted movement and activity, a good choice for threes. When planning an outdoor celebration, be sure to schedule some indoor alternative in case of inclement weather.

If you choose to have your party at home, provide your early arrivals with planned activities to keep them busy until everyone arrives. This prevents unsafe, unsupervised horsing around, which can be difficult to quell once all the guests have gathered and you are ready to begin the party. Distribute paper and crayons at the door and have early guests draw pictures of a birthday cake while waiting for the other children to arrive. Or blow up a few balloons for throwing into the air and playing "Keep It Up" in your yard. Lay a two-by-four on its wide side on the ground, and your early guests can attempt to walk the length of it without falling off.

Plan as many activities for the party itself as you can devise, even though you will probably not have time to use them all. Extra activities prevent parent panic when the children don't participate well in a game. Simply select another choice from your list.

Group games, rather than elimination contests, are good activity choices to entertain toddlers. While there are no winners, there are no losers (and no tears) either, and everyone plays happily. Avoid Musical Chairs, Wonder Ball, and the like. Try Duck, Duck, Goose, in which toddlers sit in a circle and one player is "it." She taps the head of each seated child, saying, "Duck, duck, duck..." until she taps one and says "goose." The goose must chase the child who is "it" around the circle and try to tag her before "it" can claim the goose's seat. The goose becomes "it" next.

Put a record on the phonograph and play "Follow the Leader." Pick a leader and the group must imitate her activity—jumping, hopping on one foot, clapping hands, etc. Then the leader chooses a new leader, who must demonstrate an activity that is different from the previous one. The song "Did You Ever See a Lassie" suits this game perfectly. The "Hokey Pokey" and "Farmer in the Dell" are also popular among this age group. Simple songs like "B-i-n-g-o" and "This Old Man" are especially enjoyable if you can scare up an amateur guitarist for accompaniment.

If you own a video camera and a VCR, record the party and show the film to your guests as part of the entertainment. Three-year-olds find seeing themselves on film positively fascinating. You can also use your VCR to screen a cartoon for the children. To calm the children, use this quiet activity as a follow-up to a more energetic game. Attempting to show more than one cartoon is not a good idea, since you will have a very restless group on your hands at the end.

An arts and crafts project that is not too messy is a good addition to your activity list, especially since the guests can take the finished product home with them. Stringing large beads for necklaces, for example, is a project that older toddlers enjoy. You will not be able to organize the activities, serve refreshments, and take photographs without assistance, so either enlist adult aid or hire some local teenagers to help you supervise, serve, and clean up afterward.

An attractive alternative to a party at home is reserving time at some establishment that caters to toddlers—a ceramics studio that organizes children's parties around an hour of molding and painting clay and provides space for a few refreshments, or a local gymnastics academy that will keep your guests rolling, tumbling, and jumping safely for the duration of the party.

Avoid choosing activities beyond the age, abilities, interests, or comprehension of your guests. For example, video game parlors which cater children's parties are too advanced for this age group. You may be tempted to hire a clown, magician, or puppet show to keep your guests occupied. This entertainment appeals more to four- and five-year-olds than to three-year-olds, who may be frightened by the makeup or the story. Toddlers find the entire world magical, so a magic show presented to this age group is a waste of time; your guests will be singularly unimpressed.

No matter how well planned your party and how enticing the activities, there is usually at least one child who will refuse to participate. Less of this reluctance to participate occurs when elimination games are avoided, so the toddlers needn't worry about losing the game or being the first one out. Encourage a reluctant child gently, then leave the child alone if you are unsuccessful and try again in a few minutes. Because some children take a while to warm up to unfamiliar surroundings and new activities, it's wise to allow these children a few minutes to acclimate themselves. The smaller the party, the easier their adjustment.

If you are serving a meal along with the cake, keep the portions very small, since excitement often dulls a toddler's appetite. Stick to familiar, popular foods like hamburgers or even peanut butter and jelly sandwiches cut into fanciful shapes. Instead of soda, offer your guests fruit juice spiked with seltzer for zip.

For a toddler no party is complete without a loot or booty

bag. Traditionally, these bags contain all sorts of junk food that are terrible for children's teeth. You might try substituting some small toys, stickers, or crayons and pad instead of sugary foods. Include one treat to keep your guests from disappointment. These bags should be taped shut. If your guests are not permitted to open them until they depart, you will overcome their reluctance to leaving the party.

Often nursery schools celebrate a toddler's birthday with a song and cupcakes during a class session. To a child who has already enjoyed a party at home, this second party can be confusing. "Does this mean I'm four?" one child asked her mother after her second party for turning three. To avoid such confusion, explain to your toddler in advance of the second celebration that this is another party in honor of the same birthday.

Taking a Trip

Regardless of your mode of transportation, the length of your journey, or your destination, certain rules hold true of all successful trips. The first rule is perhaps the Golden Rule of child-rearing, as well as of traveling: Be positive, be flexible, be realistic. With the right mental attitude you prevent all the little inconveniences and slip-ups that invariably occur during travel from ruining your enjoyment.

Being realistic means not overestimating your toddler's attention span, energy level, and patience—or your own either. Continuing to sightsee after exhausting any of these three elements guarantees turning a nice time into a disaster. When your child becomes fidgety, whether en route or at your destination, make a concerted effort to remedy the situation *immediately*. Don't ignore the early-warning signals (crankiness and whining, lethargy, hyperactivity, etc.) that demand attention, and don't attempt to postpone the inevitable. Instead, take action well before the warning metamorphoses into a full-blown tantrum: Change the activity; take a lunch break; take time for a nap. Take whatever steps you must to avert disaster early. Rule #2 for wise travelers is: Don't push your luck.

Being realistic also means scheduling your most tedious or most strenuous activities for the early-morning hours, when your toddler can best tolerate them. Ignoring your toddler's internal timetable sabotages your chances for an enjoyable trip.

Rule #3 requires planning, planning, and more planning. Impromptu travel with a toddler may or may not work; the odds don't favor success. Advance planning smooths your path. If you have never previously visited your destination, take time to contact the local chamber of commerce in advance to learn about places of interest for you and your toddler. Are the schedules for these attractions convenient for you? Can you use a stroller to tour them? Are tickets for them difficult to secure on short notice? If so, you may want to purchase them by mail in advance. Can the chamber supply you with a phone number for a bonded baby-sitting service if you want to go out without your toddler at night? Advance preparation forestalls disappointments.

Inquire about the equipment your hotel might provide: a crib, a booster seat or high chair, etc. Scrounging for necessary supplies at the last minute or sharing your bed with your toddler because no crib is available won't enhance your vacation. Preparing for a trip resembles planning a successful birthday party. Scheduling more activities than seem necessary and being flexible enough to eliminate the ones that turn out to be impractical or unappealing will make your stay more pleasant.

Traveling by Car

Some toddlers enjoy the variety of changes in their daily routines while traveling; most, however, adapt poorly. If your child is one who functions best within the confines of a specific schedule, try to transfer as many elements of your daily routine as possible to your automobile trip.

One mother who has traveled extensively with her three children suggests that you rouse your child very early (she prefers four A.M.) to begin a lengthy car trip. Let the child travel in her pajamas; the combination of the early hour and her apparel will prompt her to resume sleeping in her car seat. Then, dress her in the car when you stop for breakfast at her usual time.

"We do our best traveling between the hours of four and eight A.M.," she says, "because we can ride without stopping and without needing to keep the children entertained. This system has worked very well for us." Travel time should coincide with your child's normal sleep schedule whenever possible, since the motion of the car induces sleep and relieves you of the burden of entertaining your child en route.

Once your child has eaten breakfast and is fully awake, you can't expect the passing scenery to keep her entertained indefinitely. She will require your attention; ignoring her won't improve her traveling behavior. So point out the sights along the way and include her in your conversation. A selection of interesting toys suitable for car play—such as dolls, stuffed animals, and picture books—also helps to pass the time.

Older toddlers will enjoy some traveling games such as "Guess Who I Am." (You give simple clues: I am an animal. I say "Moo." I give milk. Can you guess who I am?) Choose animals, household or playground equipment, relatives, etc., for identification. In another game challenge your toddler to spot as many red cars as she can or to count whether she sees more red cars or blue ones in a two-minute time span. Yelling "Beaver!" whenever a station wagon is sighted is a game toddlers love, but don't teach it to your child unless the person who is driving your car can tolerate hearing "Beaver!" every other second. A car trip is also a fine time for a family sing-along; sing some familiar nursery school songs and teach your child some new ones too. Look for a book in your local library on finger play (you're probably familiar with the one that begins "Here is the church; here is the steeple"), and you will keep your toddler amused for quite a while with the combination of rhyme and accompanying hand movements. Toddlers love learning to do these themselves.

Health, Safety, and Sanitary Preparations for a Car Trip

Before you leave for a trip of any duration, have your pediatrician give your child a thorough checkup, paying particular attention to ear inflammations or infections. If your child is prone to motion sickness, ask the doctor what he or she recommends. Children who get carsick may find some relief from having a window next to their seat left open, and books should be omitted from the assortment of travel toys, since concentrating on small pictures may aggravate the problem.

On all automobile trips—indeed, every time you ride in the car—enforce two unbreakable safety rules for your family's well-being: Parents should always wear seat belts, and infants and toddlers should always be secured in their auto restraints. Children who have outgrown their safety seats must also be properly secured.

Pay attention to the items that lie loose on the car floor or on the back window ledge. Short stops or accidents could propel them at top speed, injuring the occupants of your car. For safety's sake, any heavy or sharp objects belong in the trunk.

You should plan to make fairly frequent stops along your route for both your toddler's comfort and your own. Adults who want to reach their destination quickly may not tolerate these interruptions gracefully, but they are necessary for a child, to whom a car seat may resemble a prison. Everyone feels better after having had a chance to stretch, even though these exercise breaks will slow your progress.

Try to schedule your stops so that your toddler will have some time to run around and play a bit. A toddler doesn't comprehend (or cooperate with) short stops very well, and you'll have a difficult time getting her to return to her car seat just a few minutes after she's been set free. To help keep rest-room stops to a minimum if your child is out of diapers, have her use the bathroom before you leave each of your exercise breaks.

You'll need to take some sanitary supplies with you—a large plastic trash bag for all your discards, a container of premoistened disposable towelettes for cleanups, a box of tissues, a roll of paper towels, and disposable toilet seat covers for rest-room stops. An extra pillowcase can be used for a laundry bag, since your toddler may require clothing changes along the way. You should also carry a small, but well-stocked, first-aid kit containing bandages, some ointment or spray for cuts and burns, and some calamine lotion.

Travel Outfits

Forethought in dressing, as well as in planning your itinerary, simplifies traveling with a toddler. Avoid using one-piece coveralls when traveling; they are more difficult to change than two-piece outfits. If your toddler's diaper soaks through or if she spills a drink on her shirt, you'll have to change her entire outfit, even though only half of it actually needs replacing. Take along a plentiful supply of bibs to keep such changes to a minimum.

Dressing your child in layers of clothing, rather than in her heaviest clothes in the winter and her coolest outfits in summer, also makes good sense. In the course of a day you are likely to experience a wide range of temperatures— from the frigidity of restaurant air conditioning to sweltering heat during your stretch stops while on the road, for example. A child wearing layers of clothing is prepared for many different situations. This is a simple way to insure your child's comfort.

On days when you will tour attractions that draw large crowds, dress your child in the most colorful outfit she owns. Doing so makes spotting her easier if you should somehow become separated.

Packing Your Luggage

The standard advice to travelers is to "travel light." Such advice to a toddler's parents is likely to draw gales of laughter. If you are equipped to meet most situations with equanimity, carrying a minimum of luggage is usually a near impossibility.

However, even if you can't eliminate many items, you

can at least consolidate your luggage. Fewer large suitcases are preferable to many littler ones. Use suitcases with wheels attached or treat yourself to a lightweight luggage trolley to which you can strap your bags for easy maneuverability.

Pack one small bag with items you will use frequently while on the road. Doing so eliminates frustrating searches through gigantic suitcases for a toothbrush or for a change of clothing for a wet toddler. It also minimizes the repacking of overstuffed suitcases that invariably occurs en route.

Consider using a backpack to store supplies for daily outings away from your hotel; it holds many items and frees your hands for other tasks. It is also kind to your back, since the weight it holds is distributed evenly across your shoulders. A hand-held tote bag becomes more tiresome to carry and strains each arm alternately.

International Travel

Young children are far better tolerated and supplies for them more easily located in some foreign countries than in others. If you have a choice of destination, choose Holland, Italy, Spain, or Greece, for example, where both the citizens and all but the poshest restaurants enthusiastically welcome children. In countries where children are appreciated, traveling with a toddler adds a marvelous dimension to your trip, since young children seem to facilitate social contact with others.

You will also make your trip easier if you forgo choosing the more primitive spots in the world and select highly civilized areas. Disposable diapers rank right behind the invention of the wheel in importance—especially when they are not available. In addition, you will need be less concerned with the purity of the water and food in these places. Fast food is widely available in westernized countries, a helpful situation if your child is a picky eater and reluctant to taste exotic, unfamiliar dishes. When you need to restock child-care supplies or baby food abroad, buy them in markets and shops whenever possible, rather than at your hotel, where they will be considerably more expensive. Your travel agent can guide you in making appropriate choices of destination for travel and sightseeing with a toddler.

The advance planning rule holds doubly true of international trips. Then make use of the concierge at your hotel and the resources of the American Embassy to smooth any of the details that were overlooked at home. Both are also helpful in locating an English-speaking doctor should you require one.

Somehow foreign locales often make travelers relax the vigilance they would apply to safety precautions and procedures at home. Always check any toys purchased abroad to be sure that there are no sharp points or edges, no small parts or parts that can be easily detached, and no toxic finishes or materials. Toys sold in the United States are supposed to meet certain safety standards, but such regulations are not universal, and you must become your own Office of Safety and Health. Driver etiquette also varies widely, and speed limits may be nonexistent or totally ignored, so watch your child very carefully when you are pedestrians.

7. Health Care

Fear of Examinations

As children enter toddlerhood, many become fearful of physical examinations. Such fear coincides with the fear of strangers that emerges around the time of the first birthday. Fearful reactions to both strangers and the pediatrician are related, for the healthy toddler doesn't visit the doctor's office frequently enough to recognize his physician as a familiar face. This unfamiliar adult seems even more threatening to a toddler than the ordinary stranger because the doctor doesn't keep her distance; she touches and handles the child during the checkup.

By the time the toddler's expanding memory skill enables him to recall the pediatrician's face from one visit to the next, he also vividly remembers that the doctor dispenses the painful injections and unwelcome pokes and prods that accompany an exam. As a result of these memories, the toddler re-identifies the doctor—from a stranger to an enemy. So you shouldn't be surprised if your toddler doesn't relish a trip to the doctor's office, even if your pediatrician is the most pleasant sort.

In some ways you or your pediatrician and her staff may unconsciously increase your toddler's fear and discomfort during examinations. Do you threaten your child with visits to the doctor, with injections, or with possible illness as retribution for his misbehavior? "If you don't finish your milk, you'll get sick and Dr. Smith will have to give you a shot" doesn't inspire great willingness to undergo a physical. Ultimately, such threats make a child reluctant to enter a doctor's office at all.

Your own attitude about health care may also contribute to this problem. Studies demonstrate that a child's anxiety in a health-care situation is affected by the level of parental anxiety. Parents accompanying a sick child to the pediatrician's office may be annoyed at the extra burden the sickness is likely to impose upon their schedule, or they may worry that the illness results from inadequate parenting and blame themselves for their child's discomfort. They may even subconsciously blame the child for getting sick: "If Jeff had gone to sleep when he was told to, this wouldn't have happened." The irrationality of these emotions doesn't reduce their potency. Whatever the cause of parental anxiety, its presence is likely to affect the child's view of doctors adversely.

Pay careful attention to the kind of treatment your child receives from your pediatrician's staff. Handling uncooperative, screaming children all day is a difficult job, and sometimes the strain begins to show in the form of insensitive treatment. Are the nurses kind and concerned, or are patients handled like so many cars on an assembly line?

On one visit to an allergist a toddler undergoing an uncomfortable series of scratch tests to determine allergic reactions told the nurse, "I'm going to throw up." The nurse responded sternly, "No you're not!" The child's mother, appalled at the nurse's cold manner, still relishes the moment when her child vomited in the nurse's lap. Learn to protest if your child receives less than optimum treatment—verbal as well as physical.

The doctor, too, may aggravate the problem by failing to make personal contact with her young patient. If your pediatrician talks only to you and ignores your youngster, she is not doing her job well; she has a responsibility to *both* of you—not only to safeguard the child's health, but also to make both of you as comfortable and confident as possible while doing so.

When the pediatrician makes inappropriate contact with her patient, she's setting the stage for future problems. One doctor, for example, made no comment when three-year-old Joanne screamed through an entire examination and a booster shot. As she and her mother were about to leave the office, the doctor leaned over and whispered to the child, "Joanne's a big baby!" Such callous response to a child's fright and pain leaves lasting psychological scars.

Many children have found themselves feeling betrayed by their parents' assurances during a checkup that "this shot won't hurt." Most experts suggest that children be told the truth about impending pain in a manner they can handle: "This shot may hurt for a moment, and then it will stop hurting."

If you give your child some control over his response to the pain, he has an acceptable way to handle his discomfort and a helpful distraction from his troubles as well: "If the shot hurts, you squeeze my hand as hard as you can and let out a yell." Wielding such control protects the child from feeling like a helpless victim and removes some of the reluctance to return to the doctor's office in the future.

If your toddler does cry from the pain of an injection, comfort him, but do not deny his feelings. "That didn't really hurt, did it?" offers little solace to a child in pain, even if the pain is fleeting. Avoid ridicule as well: "Only a scaredy-cat cries over a little shot" merely adds insult to injury.

Many parents who make such responses aren't insensitive; rather, witnessing their child's misery is painful to them. By denying the existence of the pain, they calm themselves. Others feel inadequate to comfort a frantic child. A more helpful response is simply to hold the child, and then try to distract him from his pain with a toy you've brought along, a song, or a nursery rhyme.

Scheduling some attractive activity immediately following the checkup is another way to divert your child's attention from the unwanted examination. If you discuss these plans while your child is waiting to be examined and mention them again during the exam, your toddler may be less affected by the unpleasant present.

Many of the procedures the doctor must perform in the course of an ordinary checkup can be done while the child remains in the comforting arms of his parent. Separation from his parent, even though she or he remains in sight, is usually viewed with alarm. Being held, at least at the beginning of the exam, tends to soothe the nervous, year-old toddler and may calm him enough to release his parent from his grip for the duration of the physical. If your doctor doesn't suggest this approach, mention it to her yourself.

For some toddlers even the wait in the doctor's office before the exam signals impending doom. The hubbub of patients arriving and departing, the boredom of a confining play space, the wails of other patients, all combine to alert him to danger. You can eliminate much of this unpleasantness by calling your pediatrician's office fifteen minutes or so before your appointment to inquire if the doctor is keeping to her schedule. If she is, you can go to the office assured that your child will be seen promptly. If the doctor's schedule is running late, ask how delayed she is, and let the receptionist know that you will call again soon to check her progress. In this way you can avoid the waste of time, exposure to illness, and the unpleasantness of sitting in the crowded waiting room. Continue to call at twenty-minute intervals until you get the okay to proceed to your appointment. This is an imperfect solution at best, but it beats being cooped up in the stuffy waiting room with other howling, contagious children.

If your pediatrician's office always resembles rush hour in a crowded railroad station, you should make your objections known to the doctor and her staff. Consider switching to another physician if the situation remains intolerable. Every doctor treats emergencies, which can play havoc with an office schedule, but emergencies aren't constant and shouldn't be used to excuse overbooking of appointments.

Well-Child Checkups

Once your child enters toddlerhood, well-child checkups are scheduled less frequently than in infancy, usually every three to four months. For several reasons these physicals should be scheduled when your child is healthy, not combined with office visits for illnesses that may occur between checkups. If your pediatrician examines your child only

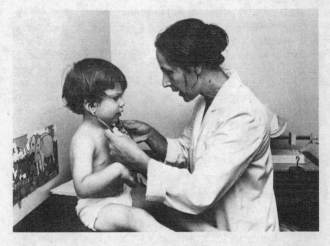

when he is sick, the doctor has no basis for comparison of behavior and appearance with the child's healthy state. In addition, a sick child is already suffering and certainly doesn't need the additional misery of enduring a thorough physical. Being examined while feeling ill won't increase the level of cooperation offered, making the exam more difficult to complete. Also, illness may complicate reactions to inoculation. Many vaccinations cause fever or rash, and determining whether these symptoms occurred as a result of the injections or unrelated sickness would be difficult. Necessary treatment might be delayed while the physician waits to pinpoint their cause.

Whenever possible, schedule your toddler's well-child checkups early in the morning, when he is usually most alert and cooperative. The second-best choice is after nap and snack time. If your child usually wakes from his nap in a cranky mood, postpone the physical for a half hour or so after waking to allow time for his sunny disposition to reassert itself. The worst time for a toddler to undergo an exam is in the late afternoon, when many youngsters are either wild with exhaustion or too tired and cranky to tolerate the procedure.

Well-child checkups should include examination of growth and weight gain, blood pressure, a check of the eyes, ears, nose, throat, glands, reflexes, and the spine to detect scoliosis (curvature of the spine). Heart and lung function should also be checked. When your child is approximately one year old, a blood sample will be taken to detect anemia, and when he is about three, a urinanalysis will be done mainly to detect signs of diabetes. During toddler checkups many preventive and booster immunizations must also be scheduled.

Immunizations

Previously, immunizations were hailed as miracles that prevented many crippling or fatal childhood diseases. Lately, though, they have received some adverse publicity regarding the possibility of brain damage as a side effect of the pertussis (whooping cough) vaccination. However, serious side effects from immunizations occur very rarely, and damaging or fatal complications are far more likely to result from contracting these preventable diseases than from having a child inoculated against them. All major medical groups concerned with child health recommend immunization, but extra precaution is necessary for children who have immune system deficiencies, neurological problems, or who are prone to seizures.

A DTP series protects against diphtheria, tetanus, and

pertussis, or whooping cough. It begins with three injections in infancy and requires a booster at eighteen months and another sometime between the ages of four and six. Common reactions to the injection include low-grade fever, some soreness and swelling at the injection site, and irritable behavior. If your child displays any of the following reactions, you should contact your pediatrician promptly: convulsions, excessive sleepiness, limpness or paleness, high-pitched persistent crying, and temperature of 103° F. or higher.

The MMR series safeguards a child against measles, mumps, and rubella (German measles). This vaccine is usually given at fifteen months of age and requires no boosters. Possible side effects include fever and rash.

Two or three doses of the polio vaccine are taken orally in infancy, and boosters are required at approximately eighteen months and between four and six years of age.

In 1985 the Food and Drug Administration approved a vaccine for bacterial meningitis, and it is recommended that children receive the vaccine when they are two years old. It is of special benefit to children in day-care centers who run higher-than-average risk of exposure to this disease, which kills a thousand children yearly. The vaccine is not recommended for children under eighteen months, and it is uncertain if it is effective for children between the ages of eighteen and twenty-three months.

A vaccine for chicken pox is being developed, but as of mid-1986 it was still in the experimental stage. If your child contracts this disease, you should be aware that there is evidence which links the use of aspirin to treat chicken pox and flu with a rare but serious disease called Reye's syndrome. Because of the suspected link, the American Academy of Pediatrics recommends that aspirin not be used to treat children with such viral infections as chicken pox and flu.

When to Call the Doctor

Few situations make parents as anxious as deciding whether a physical complaint or symptom warrants a phone call to the pediatrician. A toddler's symptoms may be vague or inconsistent; the parents worry about appearing stupid or incompetent, and the thought usually occurs that they may be needlessly disturbing the doctor's busy schedule.

Spend little time worrying about bothering the doctor; in fact, you would do well to ignore this thought entirely. Your main concern should focus on whether or not your child needs medical care. If your doctor makes you feel uncomfortable about calling when you are in doubt, you should discuss this problem with her or find another pediatrician with whom your relationship is more relaxed. Answering questions and calming parental fears are as much a part of a pediatrician's job as giving injections.

Your judgment alerts you if your child's behavior or appearance changes from the ordinary. If he seems unusually listless and lethargic or if he becomes extraordinarily cranky and remains so despite naps, meals, etc., you should suspect illness of some sort and alert your doctor. Changes in sleep patterns, persistent coughing, a rash, constipation or diarrhea, vomiting, high color or pallor, a dullness or glassiness to the eyes, and, of course, fever also merit a phone discussion.

Have all pertinent information about the problem collected and arranged in front of you before you phone the doctor. Prior to calling, jot down both the information you have gathered and any questions you want answered. Such organization guarantees that you won't forget to give the doctor any necessary piece of information, and after hanging up the phone, you will not suddenly discover a hundred questions you neglected to ask.

On a piece of paper list all symptoms and describe the ways in which your child's appearance or behavior is unusual for him. Note when you first observed the problem, and take your child's temperature so that you can give your pediatrician exact information. Telling your doctor that "Jason's head feels warm" isn't very helpful; she needs to know how warm and how long it's been so. Also mention any steps you may have taken to help remedy the problem. Have the telephone number of your local pharmacy on hand in case your doctor wants to phone in a prescription on the spot.

When you are able to reach only your doctor's answering service and must wait for your pediatrician to call you back, ask how long you will have to wait for a return call. If your call is urgent, say so. The answering service may make an effort to reach the doctor more quickly than it would under less pressing circumstances. Be sure to state your name, your child's name, and his age as a preface to your description when your physician finally returns your phone call. Messages from answering services are often incomplete or garbled by the time they reach the doctor.

Medicine

When your doctor prescribes medicine, you should make use of the opportunity to ask a few important questions. First, inquire about any side effects common to the prescribed drug. The potency of some drugs is affected by their combination with food. Find out if the medication must be taken well before or long after a meal or snack, and if any food in particular doesn't combine well with the drug.

Your pediatrician has a range of medicine available for treating most common illnesses, so you will save yourself some difficulty by requesting a medicine that must be administered as infrequently as possible. If your toddler makes medicine time a wrestling match, you'll appreciate addressing the problem only three times a day rather than four.

Mary Poppins managed to get medicine into her charges with a spoonful of sugar. You don't have this option, but you can reduce the hassle of administering medicine to toddlers by combining it (if food doesn't affect its efficiency) with the smallest possible quantity of applesauce or mashed banana to disguise its taste. Many pharmacies stock special, hollow-handled medicine spoons that resemble different animals. Some toddlers can be induced to swallow the medicine with a minimum of fuss using one of these spoons. Try the trick of focusing on an attractive event scheduled immediately after the child has downed the medicine: "We're going to watch "Sesame Street" (or listen to a record) as soon as you take your medicine."

If you have tried all the pleasant diversions and none works, you have no choice but to restrain the child and spoon the medication in. This is easier to do if one adult holds the child and another maneuvers the medicine; otherwise, much of the medicine winds up everywhere but in the child's stomach.

Never discontinue the medicine before you have finished the full dosage the doctor prescribed. Some medicines effect a very rapid recovery, but symptoms return in greater strength if allowed to regroup before they've been completely eradicated.

One final word about medications: Over-the-counter remedies are so commonly used in our society that we tend to forget that they are drugs and should be used judiciously. As with prescription medicines, you should follow your pediatrician's recommendations on the use of over-the-counter drugs when your child is ill.

Epilogue: Looking Ahead

Age three—the sunniest of times—has arrived. Descriptions of three-year-olds are so positive they sound almost too good to be true: cooperative, cheerful, friendly, well-coordinated, and communicative. Believe it or not, this marvelous creature is the new, improved version of your toddler. Emotionally, the three-year-old is a child who is content with herself and her world, and her serenity makes life lovely. The next few months promise a wonderfully calm and happy time.

Magic didn't produce this sunny disposition, though a magic spell may seem responsible when the transition from the cantankerous two's to the placid three's is especially abrupt. This is nature's handiwork. Age three is a developmental period when mental and physical desires and abilities mesh. Both time and practice have resolved many of the problems which frustrated your toddler earlier. Her coordination has improved, and she meets success, rather than exasperation, at the tasks she tries.

Now she can express herself well, too, and words substitute for tantrums, fists, and tears. In fact, being verbal means she can avert difficulties even before they become major emotional upsets: She can announce fatigue, hunger, thirst, or a desire to play.

The encouragement you have offered in language development bears full bloom now. In contrast to early toddlerhood, when your child jabbered to herself, she now wants a conversational partner for her chatter. The three-year-old loves to talk, loves words and sounds, loves to listen to stories.

Because your child now participates in so many activities, and possibly attends nursery school or play group as well, you may not feel as pressing a need to read to her now as you once did. Try not to abandon the habit of reading aloud, however, as few other activities foster such closeness between parent and child. In addition, story time will continue to expand your child's vocabulary, feed her curiosity and imagination, and give her practice in using the comprehension and inference skills she'll need when she herself learns to read.

Perhaps the most striking characteristic of age three is your child's drive to socialize. Your responsibility now is to meet this need by providing a variety of social situations in which she can practice and improve her social skills.

This increased sociability signals growing independence, and wise parents will continue to foster their child's self-reliance. Choosing clothes, dressing and undressing, feeding, and cleaning up after playtime should increasingly become the child's province. Give your child the makings of a sandwich and let her assemble her own; let her pour her drinks too.

In the same vein, avoid jumping too precipitously into your child's disputes with her new-found friends. Give her a chance to learn to settle arguments without adult interference. Of course, if a disagreement escalates into a full-blown battle, you'll have to intercede. But even then, try to leave the resolution to the children. "How can we settle this fight over the truck?" teaches a better lesson than "Rachel, give Kevin the truck RIGHT NOW!"

New maturity also makes daily routines move along smoothly. Most three's display a heartier appetite and far less picky tastes than just a few months ago. This could be the time to reintroduce foods your child spurned in her more negative days. Minus the compulsive list of evening activities your child may have previously demanded, bedtime routines can now be kept to a minimum. Toileting is less certain an accomplishment than the other routines, and normal behavior ranges from those who possess round-the-clock mastery to those who are rank beginners.

As your child approaches the half-year mark, you may begin to see behavior that reminds you of the more difficult period of toddlerhood. Rebelliousness, stuttering, and lack of coordination often characterize the three-and-a-half-year-old. Be prepared to muster extra reserves of patience as the smooth road turns bumpy.

Remember that the road to maturity doesn't progress steadily upward in an unbroken incline. Rather, it is an alternating series of progressions and regressions. If you think of these difficult times as being necessary to developing maturity and independence, they will be easier to bear. Keep in mind the thought that the difficult times are stages your child will outgrow; they don't last forever.

Remember, too, that continuing to read about your child's growth and development is the best way to keep your expectations reasonable. Knowledgeable, understanding parents are the best friends a child of any age or stage can have.

Bibliography:
The Toddler Bookshelf

Twelve to Eighteen Months

Many of the following books for the youngest group of toddlers contain elements that twelve-to-eighteen-month-olds particularly enjoy: animal sounds, repetition of key words, simple, identifiable illustrations bright with color, and textures to touch or moveable pieces. A child this age often has little tolerance for reading as a spectator sport; he wants to be a participant in the process. Books which prompt him to repeat words, to touch textures, or to lift a flap to find a surprise picture underneath are irresistible.

Asch, Frank. *Just Like Daddy*. New Jersey: Prentice-Hall, 1981.

Alexander, Martha. *Pigs Say Oink*. New York: Random House, 1978.

Carle, Eric. *The Very Hungry Caterpillar*. New York: Philomel Books, 1983.

Chwast, Seymour. *Tall City, Wide Country*. New York: Viking Press, 1983.

Komori, Atsushi. *Animal Mothers*. New York: Philomel Books New York, 1983.

Kunhardt, Dorothy. *Pat the Bunny*. New York: Golden Book, Western Publishing, 1940.

Kunhardt, Dorothy. *The Telephone Book*. New York: Western Publishing, 1984.

Kunhardt, Edith. *Pat the Cat*. New York: Golden Book, Western Publishing, 1984.

Over in the Meadow. New York: Scholastic, Inc., 1971.

Pearson, Tracey Campbell. *Old MacDonald*. New York: Dial Press, 1984.

Richter, Mischa. *Quack*. New York: Harper and Row, 1978.

Eighteen to Twenty-four Months

Toddlers in this second stage enjoy following a simple story, counting along with the reader, and reciting the parts of the alphabet they know. Before you bring any book home from the bookstore or library, make sure you like it enough to read and reread it aloud repeatedly, since toddler preferences can be unpredictable. You'll be reciting his favorites constantly.

Encourage observation skills by asking him to find objects in the illustrations. Expand your child's vocabulary by having him answer "What's this?" when you point to a detail in the picture.

Brown, Margaret Wise. *Goodnight, Moon*. New York: Harper and Row, 1947.

Hutchins, Pat. *Rosie's Walk*. New York: Macmillan, 1968.

Kessler, Ethel and Leonard. *Do Baby Bears Sit in Chairs?* Doubleday, Garden City, New York, 1961.

Kruss, James. *Three by Three*. New York: Macmillan, 1965.

Rice, Eve. *Goodnight, Goodnight*. New York: Greenwillow, 1980.

Schwerin, Doris. *The Tomorrow Book*. New York: Pantheon, 1984.

Twenty-four to Thirty Months

Goody-goody characters won't interest a two-year-old. To capture his imagination, select stories containing lots of action and characters who get themselves into trouble and back out again. In the midst of battling for his own independence, your toddler will identify with strong-willed characters, while his developing sense of humor will appreciate silly rhymes and broad, slapstick humor.

Heller, Ruth. *Chickens Aren't the Only Ones*. New York: Grosset and Dunlap, 1981.

Hoban, Russell. *Bedtime for Francis*. New York: Harper and Row, 1960.

Is It Rough? Is It Smooth? Is It Shiny? New York: Greenwillow, 1984.

Keats, Jack Ezra. *The Snowy Day*. New York: Viking, 1962.

Krauss, Ruth. *The Carrot Seed*. New York: Harper and Row, 1945.

McCloskey, Robert. *Blueberries for Sal*. New York: Viking, 1948.

Piper, Watty. *The Little Engine That Could*. New York: Platt and Monk, 1961.

Rey, H. A. *Curious George*. Boston: Houghton Mifflin, Company, 1969. (This is the first of a whole series of adventures of the irrepressible monkey George, who creates mayhem wherever he goes. Toddlers will love all his disasters.)

Thomson, Pat. *Rhymes Around the Day*. New York: Lothrop, Lee and Shepard Books, 1983.

Zolotow, Charlotte. *Summer Is*. New York: Thomas Crowell, 1967.

Thirty to Thirty-six Months

At this age your toddler demonstrates his growing maturity in a longer attention span and the ability to understand a story with a plot. Because the child himself is no longer as frenetic in his activity as he was a few months ago, the stories that appeal to him now can be less action-packed than before. Begin to look for stories with expanded emphasis on characterization and understanding emotions. In addition, simple science books that answer questions about animals' habits, about the changing seasons, and about the world around him often become great favorites.

Daugherty, James. *Andy and the Lion*. New York: Viking Press, 1938.

Flack, Marjorie. *The Story About Ping*. New York: Viking Press, 1933.

Freeman, Don. *Corderoy*. New York: Viking Press, 1968.

Geisel, Theodor Seuss. *Dr. Seuss's Sleep Book*. New York: Random House, 1962.

Gelman, Rita Golden. *The Biggest Sandwich Ever*. New York: Scholastic Book Services, 1980.

Leaf, Munro. *The Story of Ferdinand*. New York: Viking Press, 1936.

McCloskey, Robert. *Make Way for Ducklings*. New York, Viking Press, 1941.

Noble, Trinka Hakes. *The Day Jimmy's Boa Ate the Wash*. New York: Pied Piper/Dial, 1984.

Patz, Nancy. *Moses Supposes His Toeses Are Roses*. New York: Harcourt Brace Jovanovich, 1983.

Petersham, Maud and Miska, editors. *The Rooster Crows: A Book of American Rhymes and Jingles*. New York: Macmillan Company, 1945.

Sendak, Maurice. *Where the Wild Things Are*. New York: Harper and Row, 1963.

Slobodkina, Esphyr. *Caps for Sale*. Reading, Massachusetts: Addison-Wesley, 1947.

Zion, Gene. *Harry the Dirty Dog*. New York: Harper and Row, 1956.

Index

About the Author

Adrienne Popper is a writer whose articles have appeared in many national publications, including *Parents*, *Woman's Day*, and *The New York Times*. She is also the author of *SUMMER CAMPS AND TEEN TOURS: Everything Parents and Kids Should Know*. She is a former teacher, and she and her husband are the parents of two sons.

Parents® MAGAZINE
READ ALOUD
BOOK CLUB

READING ALOUD—the loving, personal gift for you and your child to share.

Children's reading experts agree . . . reading aloud offers the easiest, most effective way to turn your child into a lifelong reader. And, it's as much fun for you as it is for your child.

Easy access to a variety of such important "first" books (read-aloud books) has presented a major problem for busy parents. And a challenge that *Parents* Magazine was well suited to undertake.

The result—a book club that can be your child's *first club*. A club for sharing and reading aloud. An early reading habit to last a lifetime, with books designed, created and published solely for this purpose. *Parents* Magazine Read Aloud Book Club.

If you're a concerned parent, and would like more information about our club and your free gift, just fill in the coupon below, and mail it in.

Parents® MAGAZINE
READ ALOUD BOOK CLUB

1 PARENTS CIRCLE
P.O. BOX 10264
DES MOINES, IA 50380-0264

Yes, I would like to receive free information on *Parents* Magazine Read Aloud Book Club.

To find out how to receive free gifts along with membership, simply fill out this coupon and mail it today. There's no risk or obligation.

YOUR NAME   (PLEASE PRINT)

ADDRESS   APT. NO.

CITY   STATE   ZIP

BRINGING UP
BABY

A series of practical baby care and family living guides developed with the staff of *PARENTS*™ *MAGAZINE*. Explains both the whys and how-to's of infant care.

TA-66